THE 1979 - 1983 TESTING AT LOS MORTEROS (AZ AA:12:57 ASM), A LARGE HOHOKAM VILLAGE SITE IN THE TUCSON BASIN

by

Richard C. Lange

and

William L. Deaver

Contributions by

Susan L. Brantley
Laverne Conway
T. Michael Fink
Paul R. Fish
Richard J. Harrington

James P. Holmlund
Felipe C. Jacome
Susan J. Wells
Sharon F. Urban

Compiled by Richard C. Lange

Archaeology Section
Research Division
Arizona State Museum
University of Arizona

1989

Archaeological Series 177

CONTENTS

[iii]

FIGURES

TABLES

PREFACE

Since 1980 archaeological research within the Tucson Basin has reached an intensity matched by few other locations in the country (see Doelle and Fish 1988). Disturbance of archaeological remains through rapid urban growth has been counterbalanced by a preservation-minded community and concerned public officials and developers. Research supported by this interest has been combined with an increased use of local resources by students and faculties at the University of Arizona and Pima College. Investigations at Los Morteros typify both the chronology and circumstances of this renaissance in regional archaeology.

Although acknowledged as one of the most significant archaeological localities in the region, no large-scale mapping or excavation program was undertaken at the site until development planning was well underway. At the urging of the historic preservation community and the Pima County Board of Supervisors, Lew McGinnis of the Pepper Tree Ranch Development began discussions with University of Arizona archaeologists in 1979 to seek ways of minimizing damage to this important property while proceeding with construction. The resulting plan involved donation by McGinnis of the central core of the site to the University of Arizona and a relatively restricted testing program to determine site extent and the kinds of resource to be lost to development. This testing program was initially funded by Pepper Tree Ranch, and later was extended through excavations and controlled surface collections conducted by a University of Arizona archaeological field methods class for undergraduates. These investigations are the subject of this report.

Like the Tucson Basin as a whole, much has been learned about Los Morteros since this initial research was conducted. Changes in development plans have created opportunities not included in the original preservation plans; excavation programs by the Institute for American Research (IAR) have provided insights into the configuration of several residential precincts. A report by Henry Wallace detailing the results of the IAR excavations is currently in preparation and will be forthcoming in their technical report series. In addition, large-scale survey in the northern Tucson Basin has shown dramatically that Los Morteros is not a unique and isolated site with public architecture (Doyel 1977), but rather part of larger community involving many smaller sites as well as a network of ballcourt and platform mound communities within the Basin (Fish and others 1989). Nonetheless, Los Morteros represents an important core of riverine settlement that continued to be occupied by relatively dense populations throughout the Hohokam sequence in the northern Tucson Basin.

The prospect for lasting preservation and public enjoyment of a significant portion of Los Morteros finally seems to be at hand. At present, Pima County is consolidating a variety of land parcels adjacent to the original McGinnis gift to the University, more than doubling the size of the original donation and including the trincheras features in the foothills above the site (Downum 1986; Fish and others 1984). As residential development proceeds, it is anticipated that these combined properties will be managed and interpreted by Pima County Parks and Recreation.

The Los Morteros Testing Project was made possible through the generosity of numerous individuals, but rests upon the farsighted donation of a substantial portion of the site to the University of Arizona Foundation. Lew S. McGinnis, S. L. Schorr, Raymond H. Thompson, R. Gwinn Vivian, and Richard F. Imwalle were all instrumental in this remarkable undertaking. Jerry Reeves of the Development Office of the University of Arizona Foundation continued to provide valuable assistance long after the project was out of the field.

Over the years, many have given their time and expertise to the project. These include students from the University of Arizona Undergraduate and Continuing Education field schools, Central Arizona College Field School, and St. Gregory High School. In addition, volunteers from the community and the Arizona Archaeological and Historical Society assisted in both excavation and laboratory processing of artifactual materials. Museum and Anthropology Department personnel contributed their special knowledge, including Christian Downum, Suzanne Fish, Bruce Huckell, John Madsen, and Charles Miksicek. A special thanks goes to Rose Slavin and Annette Cvitkovich for wrestling with the text, tables, and references to get the report into shape on the computer. Many, many thanks also to Linda Gregonis for editing, Ron Beckwith for drafting and paste-up, and Carol Heathington for the initial assistance in putting it all together. William Deaver oversaw the final stages of producing the report, and Sue Ruiz expertly arranged the text, tables, and figures into the final format.

Mr. and Mrs. O'Daniels, Mssrs. Waddell and Haskins, and Mr. and Mrs. Welter allowed free access to the portions of the site they controlled and to their knowledge of archaeological remains at the site. The new owners of the property, American Continental Corporation, have followed in the same line of the trend first established by Mr. McGinnis. They have made an additional donation of acreage in the core area of the site, and have contributed the major resources required to bring this report to publication.

Two volunteers, Frank Kenny and Russell Wilde, deserve special mention for the long hours spent proofreading, editing, and organizing ceramic tallies and collections.

Thank you all for you contributions.

Paul R. Fish
Richard C. Lange

Chapter 1

INTRODUCTION

Richard C. Lange

Los Morteros (AZ AA:12:57 [ASM]) is a large Hohokam village site
located at the northern end of the Tucson Mountains along the Santa Cruz
River. Named for the bedrock mortars located near the center of the
site, Los Morteros has a rich and varied history. Several phases of
prehistoric occupation are suggested by ceramics representing the
Colonial, Sedentary, and Classic periods (A.D. 500 to 1450). The range
of features present is considerable, including cremation pits, pit
houses, roasting pits, mounds, canals, petroglyphs, hill-side terraces
(trincheras), a ballcourt, and the bedrock mortars. Spatially, the site
covers a large area, but most features are clustered in a limited core
area (Fig. 1.1).

The area around Los Morteros has also been used during
historical times (see Stein 1982). In this report reference to the
historical period is limited to those events that bear directly on the
site of Los Morteros, in particular the history of archaeological
interest in the site. Our major concern is with the prehistoric
components at Los Morteros.

Background

Archaeological interests in Los Morteros were first recorded in
the early twentieth century. The site was then known as "Chakayuma" or
"Charco Yuma." Early notes on the site have been provided by Fewkes
(1909), Blake (1910), and particularly by Huntington (1912). These
writers noted the petroglyphs, mortars, trincheras, and mounds. Houses
seemed to be evident on the surface--marked by stones set on edge.

Emil W. Haury of the University of Arizona examined the caves in
the slope above the core site area in 1938. The caves were recorded as
AZ AA:12:27 in the Arizona State Museum Site Survey Files. The
trincheras and ballcourt were also noted, but were not recorded

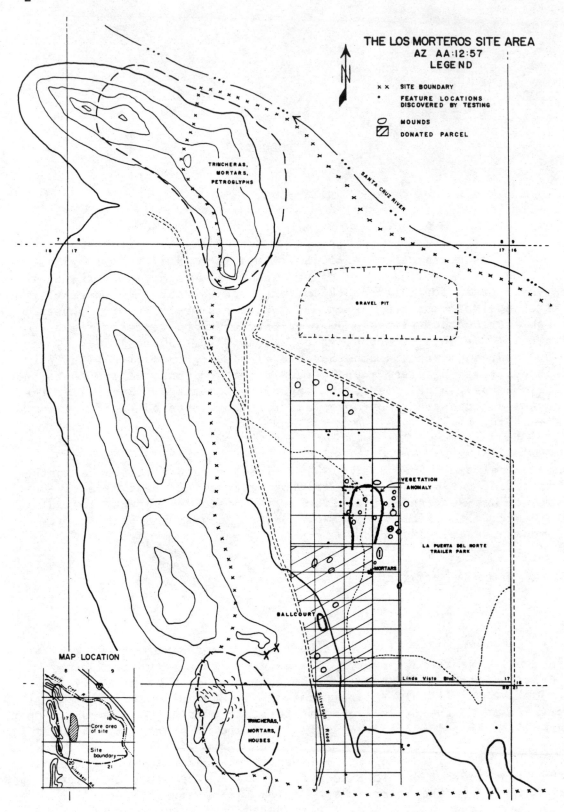

Figure 1.1. The Los Morteros site area.

separately. The main site area was first officially recorded as AZ AA:12:57 by R. E. Kelly and L.C.W. Landberg in 1962. This also marked the first formal use of the site name, Los Morteros.

In 1974, two undergraduate students at the University of Arizona, Henry Wallace and James Holmlund, were shown the site. Their interest in the site grew steadily over the years and helped provide data for several articles (Wallace and Holmlund 1983, 1984). As potential development at the site was rumored, they again brought the site to the attention of the Arizona State Museum. They also prepared a draft National Register nomination form as possibilities for protecting the site were explored. Concerns for the protection of Los Morteros were concentrated at this time because of planned industrial and residential development on and around the site, first by DOW Chemical Company, and later by Lew McGinnis's Peppertree Ranch development.

During the summer of 1979, Cella, Barr & Associates solicited a background statement from the Museum on the general history of the Los Morteros area. The significance of Los Morteros was stressed at this time. Despite some impact and development on the site (mainly due to agricultural use in the first three decades of the twentieth century), Los Morteros is unequalled in the urban Tucson area for the range and good state of preservation of the archaeological features present. A testing program to further determine the extent, quality, and nature of subsurface remains was further solicited by the developer, Mr. Lew S. McGinnis. Arrangements were made for the Arizona State Museum to do the testing through a donation of funds to the University of Arizona Foundation by Mr. McGinnis. He also donated a 32.185 acre parcel in the core area of the site to the Foundation to ensure its preservation. The donated parcel includes the bedrock mortars, the ballcourt, and several mounds.

Special mention should be made of the cooperation of the developer and planners. Mr. McGinnis's donations permitted the preservation and evaluation of this large, important Hohokam site. At the time, the donation was a gesture unique to the history of development in Arizona that an effort was made to conscientiously manage the cultural heritage and resources of this region. This laudable example is becoming more common as time goes on.

Overall direction for the project was provided by Paul R. Fish of the Arizona State Museum. Since the initial testing program with a small crew and two backhoes in December 1979 and the early months of 1980, the testing continued during the academic terms in the fall and spring of 1980-1981, fall and spring of 1981-1982, and the fall and spring of 1982-1983. At that time, threatened urban growth north and east of the Los Morteros area prompted the beginnings of the Northern Tucson Basin Survey, shifting research emphasis away from Los Morteros. This intensive survey of a large area along the Tortolita Mountains has greatly altered our perception of the settlement and agricultural adaptations of the early occupants of the Tucson Basin. Los Morteros is but one of several large sites that were supported by vast agricultural fields on the bajada slopes. Placing Los Morteros into the proper regional setting will be accomplished by this larger project.

The archaeological work done during the academic year sessions can only be considered testing. Intensive investigation was largely precluded by a number of factors. Work was done by way of training students in a field school situation. Only 8 to 12 field days could be planned each semester because of days "lost" to the field due to related trips or training, vacations and holidays, and bad weather. Machine assistance was available for excavation only on a very limited basis. Partially, the limitation was budgetary; mostly, machine work was undesirable. Deep excavations (trenches) posed unacceptable safety hazards between field days. Open areal exposures, now considered necessary to discovering and understanding Hohokam village structure, invited vandalism to visible features and destruction of features by nature between field days--due either to rain or extreme drying.

Only limited funds were available for the desired special analyses that resulted from the recovery of certain samples or data by excavation. Much of the analyses were completed by volunteers well after the conclusion of the field portion of the project. A tremendous amount of information was recovered about Los Morteros and many tantalizing evaluations and interpretations can be made. However, the full potential of the site has by no means been exhausted or even tapped, due to the circumstances creating less than ideal conditions under which to conduct an archaeological project.

What follows in this report is largely a descriptive summary of the procedures used, the artifacts recovered, and the features recorded and excavated. Special studies and investigations conducted by the project are also described and, where appropriate, included as part of the discussion of the site. The others are included as appendixes to the main body of this report.

Research Goals

During the Los Morteros Testing Project we sought to obtain a wide variety of archaeological data oriented toward evaluating the impact of past and proposed development at the site. The research strove to acquire basic archaeological data about Los Morteros, principally the length and nature of occupation, community structure and dynamics, and subsistence practices.

Emphasis was put on an extensive, systematic surface collection of the site. Heavy reliance was placed on diagnostic ceramics to indicate when the site was occupied and if horizontal stratification of the occupation could be discerned. Coupled with subsurface testing, further information was sought on whether the density of surface remains could be correlated with the presence of subsurface features and if the occupation span evident from the surface remains could be verified in subsurface deposits.

Some areas of the site had been impacted by plowing and bulldozing (Fig. 1.2). During testing we sought to determine if additional types of features were present that might not be visible on the surface. From both the planning and research perspectives it was important to determine if there were subsurface features and deposits, how deep these may be, and whether there was vertical stratification of the cultural deposits.

Further evaluation of the research potential of Los Morteros could be made if certain samples and materials could be recovered from the deposits. Chronometric techniques, such as radiocarbon and archaeomagnetic dating, could be used if appropriate samples could be recovered. Micro- and macro-botanical and osteological remains would provide valuable data on subsistence, environment, treatment of the dead, and general health of the population.

The work at Los Morteros is part of the long-term regional investigations being conducted by the Archaeology Section of the Arizona State Museum. The research orientation is to seek information on Hohokam institutions and social organization in the Tucson area. The regional survey permits examination of the evolution of institutions on a regional level, while Los Morteros would allow such research at the community level.

6

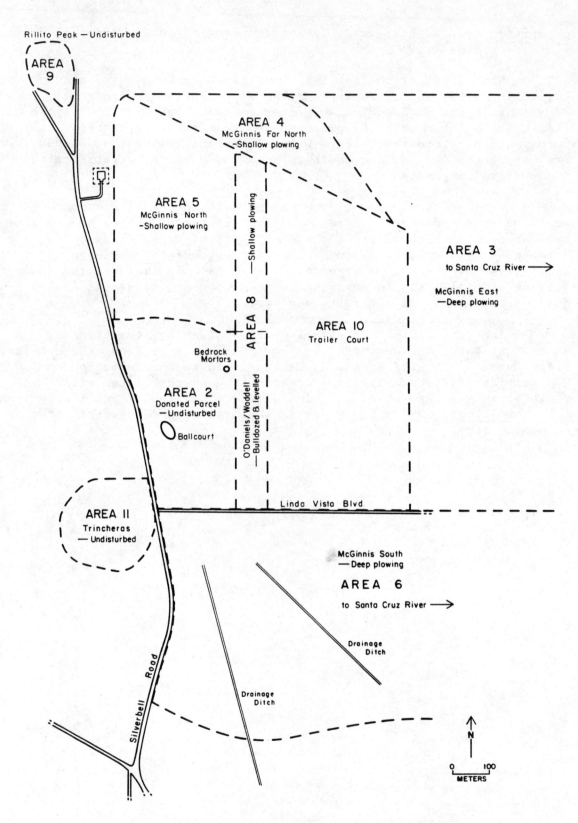

Rillito Peak — Undisturbed

AREA 9

AREA 4
McGinnis Far North
—Shallow plowing

AREA 5
McGinnis North
—Shallow plowing

AREA 8 — Shallow plowing

AREA 3
to Santa Cruz River →

McGinnis East
—Deep plowing

AREA 10
Trailer Court

Bedrock
Mortars

AREA 2
Donated Parcel
—Undisturbed

Ballcourt

O'Daniels/Waddell —Bulldozed & levelled

Linda Vista Blvd.

AREA 11
Trincheras
— Undisturbed

McGinnis South
—Deep plowing

AREA 6

to Santa Cruz River →

Drainage
Ditch

Silverbell Road

Drainage
Ditch

N

0   100
METERS

Figure 1.2.   Site areas and previous impacts.

Chapter 2

METHODS

Richard C. Lange

Techniques used to recover information at Los Morteros can best be described in reference to specific attempts to investigate particular problems or features. Investigations addressed the surface distribution of artifacts, distribution of subsurface features, and the nature of specific features such as houses, crematories, or the trincheras.

Distribution of Surface Artifacts

Investigation of the density and distribution of cultural remains required establishing a basic grid framework for the site. A north-south-oriented baseline was located near the center of the site and was aligned to the property boundary (approximately true north). A transit was used to establish the baseline, which was marked off in 50-m intervals by rebar or wooden stakes. The basic site grid, consisting of 50-m by 50-m units, was set out from this baseline by transit or tape triangulation. Grid units at Los Morteros are designated by the north and east coordinates of the northwest corner of the unit, followed by the unit size in parentheses. For example, N1600 E1000 (50) is a 50-m by 50-m unit occupying the area N1550 to N1600, E1000 to E1050.

The surface collection was done in two ways. One 5-m by 5-m unit located in the northwest corner of each 50-m by 50-m unit was completely collected. Data from this collection were used primarily to characterize artifact densities across the site. The remainder of the 50-m by 50-m unit was then searched for diagnostic artifacts and certain classes of artifacts: painted and rim sherds, shell, bone, chipped stone tools, and ground stone. These collections provided additional information about horizontal stratification of the site. The area of the site collected in this manner is shown in Figure 2.1. The results are discussed in detail by William L. Deaver in Chapter 3.

8

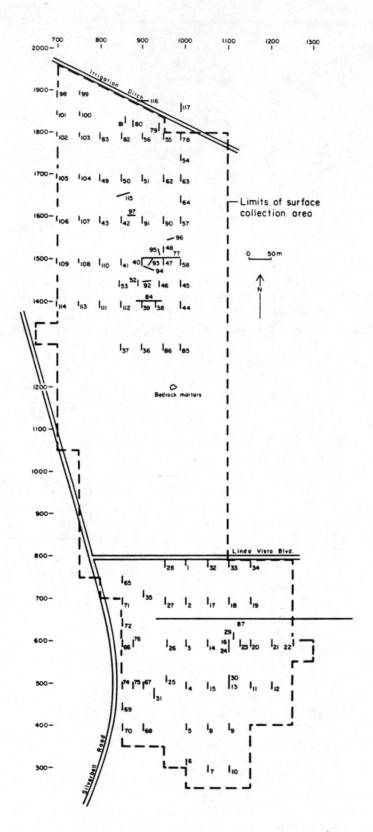

Figure 2.1. Surface collection areas and trenches excavated.

An evaluation of the ability of this type of collection strategy to locate artifact concentrations (and therefore features) was made by collecting additional 5-m by 5-m units within several 50-m by 50-m squares. This test, conducted by Diane Yakowitz, was inconclusive as to whether additional units provided greater resolution of the presence and extent of artifact concentrations (see Los Morteros Project files, Arizona State Museum).

The surface collections form the basis for discussions of density and period of occupation across the site. Subsurface tests were made in order to confirm and enhance the interpretations possible from the surface remains.

Subsurface Testing

Subsurface testing was done explicitly to investigate several of the research goals. Establishing the presence of preserved subsurface features (despite recent disturbance such as plowing), vertical stratification, and presence of certain classes of remains could only be confirmed through subsurface testing. This testing was accomplished in several ways. It involved systematically and intuitively placed, machine-excavated trenches across the general site area and in mounds. It also involved hand excavation of specific features discovered during the machine trenching.

Machine Trenching

In the early phase of the testing at Los Morteros, two backhoes were used to excavate a large number of trenches. The trenches were place systematically 50 m apart from east to west, and 100 m apart from north to south. Some backhoe trenches were then placed judgmentally to test particular areas, especially vegetation anomalies visible on the surface. The trenches covered most of the central area of the site, except the Donated Parcel (see Fig. 2.1). Depths of the backhoe trenches ranged from 1.2 m to 1.9 m on the average, with the deepest excavation being over 3 m. The length averaged between 10 m and 15 m. Three much longer trenches were excavated, oriented east-west, with lengths of 50 m, 90 m, and 460 m. Numbers of trenches and their orientations are summarized in Table 2.1. More detailed tabulations of trench number, location, and features recorded are provided in Appendix A.

Trenches were inspected immediately after excavation. Walls were trowelled by hand to define deposits and features, and notes and sketches were made for all trenches. Sherds and other diagnostic artifacts were collected from the trench backdirt. In two instances the

Table 2.1

NUMBERS AND ORIENTATIONS OF MACHINE-EXCAVATED TRENCHES

	Orientation		
Location	North-south	East-west	Total
North of Linda Vista Site Areas 4 & 5	56	8	64
South of Linda Vista Site Area 6	47	1	48
Totals	103	9	112

backdirt was screened (Trench 38, Feature 5; and Trench 62, Feature 20).
The backhoe trenches in the agricultural field south of Linda Vista
Boulevard were backfilled soon after opening. Those north of Linda
Vista were left open longer, a definite benefit because features became
more evident as the profiles dried. Detailed profile maps of the soil
zones, features, and cultural deposits were made. Artifacts embedded in
the trench walls were provenienced, plotted, and collected. Generalized
profiles were made of trenches with no cultural features, usually
extrapolating a profile for the trench from the northern 2 m. A
discussion of the typical soil zones is presented in Appendix E.
Profiles of trenches with cultural features are included in Chapter 5.

Some vandalism occurred after work hours and over weekends.
Grid stakes were removed and artifacts were dug out of the trench walls.
Most of the damage was minimal, however. Residents of the La Puerta del
Norte Trailer Park are to be commended for their interest in the site
and for policing themselves and others to limit vandalism and the loss
of important data.

A front-end loader was used on one occasion to open two large
trenches in the northeastern portion of a vegetation anomaly. This was
done in order to try to determine the cause of the denser vegetation and
large trees seen on the surface. Results of this testing are discussed
in the section labelled "Vegetation Anomaly" in Chapter 6.

Hand Excavation

As a result of the machine trenching across the site and in several mounds, specific features were excavated by hand. These included two large hornos, a smaller roasting pit, several crematory pits, and several houses. Excavation of these features permitted the recovery and analysis of several types of samples and remains including radiocarbon and archaeomagnetic dating samples, pollen and macrobotanical (flotation) samples, and human and animal osteological remains. These hand excavations are described in more detail, in the feature descriptions and in sections of the report devoted to particular testing activities.

The surface collections, ceramics, features, and other aspects of the archaeological work at Los Morteros are considered in the chapters that follow. These are largely descriptive discussions of the how and what of particular activities. The significance and possible roles of Los Morteros in the regional system will be interpreted in the context of the regionally focused Northern Tucson Basin Survey.

Analyses

In line with the heavy emphasis on learning about the nature of the occupations at Los Morteros, the greatest analytical effort was placed on the ceramics recovered. In addition to providing clues about the intensity of occupation in various areas of the site, ceramics supply information about the period of occupation and directions of prehistoric exchange. The results of the ceramic collection studies are presented in Chapters 3 and 4.

Lithic and ground stone materials have received only cursory analysis. Some of this information is presented in the appendixes of this report. Macrobotanical, faunal, and human remains and the shell have been studied in greater detail. Analyses of these materials are also reported in the appendixes. Two experiments are also reported, one involving a test of soil phosphate levels, the other determining the minerals involved in the paints used on Tanque Verde phase pottery.

Due to the fragmentary nature of the overall analysis of the materials recovered, complete inventories of materials from particular features cannot be discussed. The features are described and, when possible, have been assigned a tentative date based on the ceramics recovered from them (Chapter 5). Relatively little full excavation of features occurred; most were exposed and mapped in the walls of the backhoe trenches. Thus, what is presented in this report is a basic description of the materials recovered and the features recorded during activities conducted at Los Morteros between 1979 and 1983. There is much more that can be learned from the collections obtained, through additional analyses of the materials themselves, or through comparisons to new information collected recently at Los Morteros by the Institute for American Research.

Chapter 3

SURFACE DISTRIBUTION OF CERAMIC ARTIFACTS

William L. Deaver

A fundamental principle of archaeological fieldwork is that the location of past human activities can be identified through the discovery of physical evidence at or near the place where the activities occurred. This evidence is a byproduct of these past activities and can be in the form of discarded debris or permanent marks on the landscape. In southern Arizona, archaeological sites, particularly Hohokam sites, are largely represented by surface scatters of artifacts with varying densities, depending on the intensity, longevity, or kinds of past human activities. Occasionally, these artifact scatters are associated with visible features such as trash mounds, house mounds or depressions, ballcourts, canals, or roasting pits, but more typically these types of archaeological features remain buried beneath accumulated sediments. At Los Morteros, although there are visible archaeological features (such as the bedrock mortars, the ballcourt, trash mounds, and trincheras), the remains of the houses, storage and cooking pits, and burials, which are presumed to exist at this site, remain buried. The most common evidence of past human activities at Los Morteros is the scatter of sherds, chipped stone debris, stone tools, shell, and bone artifacts across the surface of the site area. One of the goals of the testing program at Los Morteros (see Chapter 2) was to identify the location of buried archaeological deposits and features for future resource management. This chapter presents a detailed investigation of the distribution of the surficial artifact scatter as an additional tool for predicting the location of buried archaeological remains.

Most archaeological surveys are done under severe time constraints. Under these conditions it is necessary to identify, define, and describe archaeological sites as rapidly as possible. The limits of archaeological sites are in most cases quickly and grossly defined to contain all the significant archaeological remains. The determination of what are significant versus what are insignificant archaeological remains is an issue that is beyond this discussion. It is enough that known archaeological sites are expected to represent the physical limits of significant past human activities. For those sites

13

that may represent a single, or at least a few activities, the site boundaries, even though quickly discerned, may be coterminous with the boundaries of the various activities that occurred. In most Hohokam sites typically classified as habitations, however, the site boundaries encompass the limits of many smaller activity areas, and in large habitation sites such as Los Morteros these limits may encompass several smaller discrete residential areas, or even discrete residential and ceremonial areas. In fact, the site boundaries may encompass a large amount of space where human activities never occurred. Regardless of why site boundaries are drawn the way they are, it is usually possible, when given more time, to apply more finely resolved techniques that can define, within the larger site boundaries, identifiably distinct loci of activities based on the differential distribution of artifacts.

The spatial limits defined for Los Morteros cover a rather large area and the type of archaeological evidence found leads to the classification of Los Morteros as a ballcourt village (see Chapter 1). Occupation of the site appears to span a period from the late Pioneer to the early Classic period (see Chapter 4). The site limits thus encompass an area where many different types of activities occurred over a long period of time. Because of the large size of Los Morteros it was anticipated that the site would not represent a spatially continuous record of past activities, but rather a broadly defined area that encompasses numerous activity loci. This presumption was in part based on and in part confirmed by the observation that artifacts were differentially distributed across the surface. The trenching program was designed to determine the distribution and integrity of subsurface deposits at the site (see Chapter 2).

Subsurface trenching with a backhoe is a costly and destructive technique, even if the information it yields is invaluable for accurately accessing the existence and condition of subsurface archaeological deposits at sites such as Los Morteros. The detailed study of the surface distribution of artifacts presented here was an attempt to determine the possibility of defining specific loci that had a high probability of having buried archaeological deposits, as well as areas that had a low probability of having buried archaeological remains. Only the distribution of ceramic artifacts was studied. This class of artifact was selected simply because it was the most numerous. Also, the concern of the testing was to identify residential areas. Past experience has shown that pottery is one of the primary artifacts associated with the range of activities that occurred in residential areas. Therefore, patterns in the distribution of ceramic artifacts may provide clues for identifying the limits of residential areas, and consequently, the location of the broadest range of buried archaeological features and deposits. Ceramics may also have been used in activities that occurred away from the residential area, and these activities also might be discerned in the distribution of ceramics.

The study of the pottery collected from the surface of Los Morteros also offered the opportunity to study the growth and development of the site over time. The distribution of ceramic

artifacts may indicate not only distinct loci of activities, but it may
be possible to discern the change in residential loci through time.
This aspect of the study is a combination of the ideas presented above
and the traditional application of ceramic typology in the Tucson Basin
as exemplified in Chapter 4. Thus, the relative chronological age of
the ceramic styles documents the length of occupation at Los Morteros,
and can also indicate that the occupation was differentially distributed
across the site.

To summarize, the study of the distribution of ceramic artifacts
was directed at two specific research goals. The first part of the
program was to identify intrasite patterns of activities by identifying
loci with greater density of ceramic remains. Presumably if there were
specific locales within the site that were occupied for a greater length
of time or more intensively than other areas, it should be expected that
these locations would be indicated by relatively greater densities of
ceramics. The second part of this program was to identify shifts in the
residence pattern over time. If the location of residence did shift, it
may be possible to document those shifts by tracing the surface
distribution of temporally sensitive ceramics.

Methods

Two sets of information were necessary to conduct the study:
(1) the quantitative distribution of ceramics from across the site and
(2) some knowledge of the distribution of subsurface features and
deposits. Prior to exploratory trenching, a systematic surface survey
and collection was undertaken. This provided a systematic, quantified
record of the distribution of ceramics across the area under
investigation. Information on the distribution of subsurface deposits
was obtained through the systematic backhoe trenching program. The
distribution of artifacts (particularly ceramics) across the surface of
the site was compared with the results of the backhoe exploration. The
expectation was that the surface remains should indicate the location of
subsurface deposits. If such a correlation could be demonstrated, then
it might be possible in future studies to develop an archaeological site
management plan based on intensive surface surveys without subsurface
explorations. If this proved possible, then at the outset of testing or
a large-scale data recovery project it would be possible to define the
distribution of surface artifacts and make informed decisions about
where and how to excavate.

The method employed in collecting the sample of surface
artifacts is described in more detail in Chapter 2. In short, artifacts
were obtained by first gridding the site into 50-m by 50-m grid units
and collecting all artifacts within a 5-m by 5-m unit situated at the
extreme northwest corner of each 50-m grid unit. The 5-m by 5-m
collection units would provide a systematic sample of ceramic artifacts
from 1 percent of the surface area within the total project area. I

have included in this investigation surface collection units that were
collected during the initial testing phase in 1980 as well as those
subsequently collected during the field school work up to 1983. For the
most part the time of collection is unimportant, except in the area
designated Linda Vista South where some of the collections during the
field school work were made at locations where backhoe trenches had been
excavated during the initial testing phase in 1980. Figure 2.1 shows
the extent of coverage of the surface collection. The 50-m spacing
between the 5-m by 5-m collection units was considered sufficiently
finely resolved for identifying residential areas. After each 5-m by
5-m square had been collected, all decorated sherds and plain ware rims
within the remainder of the 50-m by 50-m grid square were collected.
This was done in order to provide as large a sample as possible of
temporally diagnostic ceramics for interpreting changes in settlement
locations within the site. As it turns out, collecting all decorated
sherds in each 50-m by 50-m grid did not produce large quantities of
identifiable decorated pottery.

The variability in the number of ceramics from one collection
unit to another across the surface of the study area is depicted in
Figure 3.1. A technique analogous to drafting topographic contours was
used, wherein the total sherds collected in each 5-m by 5-m square is
considered to be the density "elevation" of the northwest grid corner
which designates each collection unit. Between these observed values
isograms were interpolated at arbitrarily selected values. This
technique produced a sherd density contour map of the study area
surface. In the area north of Linda Vista Boulevard (Fig. 1.2), which
includes McGinnis North, the Donated Parcel, and the O'Daniels/Waddell
property, when no sherds were found in a collection unit it was
interpreted as a zero value. In Linda Vista South, however, because
some of the field school collections were done after the original test
trenches were excavated, a zero observation in a collection unit may not
indicate a zero value prior to backhoe disturbance. Therefore, in this
area zero observations in the areas collected after the testing phase
were treated as missing values, and a hypothesized value for each unit
was determined by interpolation from surrounding units.

Information about the subsurface was obtained from the results
of the systematic trenching program (Fig. 2.1). The surface collection
program and trenching program were employed independently of each other
so that the results of one could be used to corroborate the results of
the other. The only relationship between these two techniques was that
backhoe trenches were excavated along the same grid lines as the 5-m by
5-m grids so there was a direct correspondence between the surface
collection data and subsurface data in backhoe trenches.

A critical point to consider is whether the surface nature of a
site should be taken as truly representative of the prehistoric
activities that took place. Initially, it is presumed that two factors
are responsible for the differential density of ceramic artifacts: (1)
the duration of the activity over time, and (2) the intensity of the
activity. Since the point in time when artifacts were discarded any

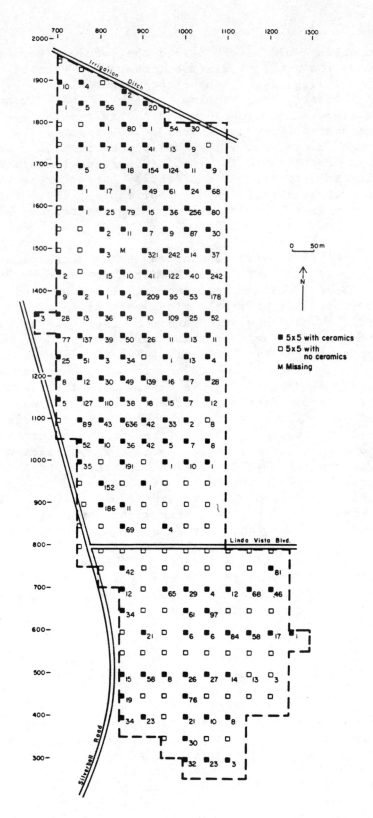

Figure 3.1. Surface collections: locations and sherd counts from 5-m by 5-m collection units.

number of processes could have occurred that would alter or even destroy
the integrity of the artifact distributions. For example, during the
occupation of a village later inhabitants might disturb earlier deposits
of refuse and relocate these remains. Although there is ample evidence
that this occurred, it is expected that the relocation would take place
within the residential area and therefore not destroy the information
that some type of human activities took place within the area. Also, we
did not presume to specifically pinpoint individual features associated
with particular activities, but to identify larger areas that should
have a higher probability of yielding buried deposits, however, there
are types of processes that can skew the representativeness of the
surface artifact record.

Since the prehistoric occupation at Los Morteros ended, the site
has been subject to a variety of disturbance processes, both geological
and man-made. We can presume that the site was subjected to geological
processes, but it is not presently clear what kinds of processes
occurred after the last occupation and what impact these may have on the
archaeological record. There is information as to the nature of man-
made disturbances to the site. Figure 1.2 depicts the study area and
the different parts of the site subject to various types of
disturbances. Not indicated in this figure are other disturbances. Los
Morteros has been a favorite spot for many years for individuals to hunt
arrowheads and pottery. It is likely that the surface distribution of
these items will be skewed. It is further possible that some areas,
given access or ground cover, may be more heavily impacted than others,
thus skewing the relative relationships between one part of the site and
another. Motorbike trails across the site and numerous "forts" dug into
the site by children also present interpretive difficulties because they
may have exposed buried deposits, which might abnormally accentuate the
surface artifact distribution. The site has also been subject to
vandalism, even in the areas indicated in Figure 1.2 as "undisturbed."
These disturbances had definite impacts on the reliability of the
surface artifact scatters to reflect the subsurface distribution of
archaeological remains, but did not prove to be an insurmountable
obstacle given the intent of this study.

The Ceramic Distribution

The investigation of the distribution of the ceramic artifacts
entailed two parts. The first was to determine if there was a
correlation between areas with notably high densities of ceramics and
the location of subsurface features. The second was to use the temporal
information possible from the decorated ceramics to determine if there
were changes in the location of residences at Los Morteros over time.
Figure 3.2 portrays the overall distribution of ceramic artifacts within
the study area. The contour intervals in Figure 3.2 represent an
increase of one sherd per square meter or 5 sherds per collection unit.
There was a definite clustering of ceramic artifacts; the site is not

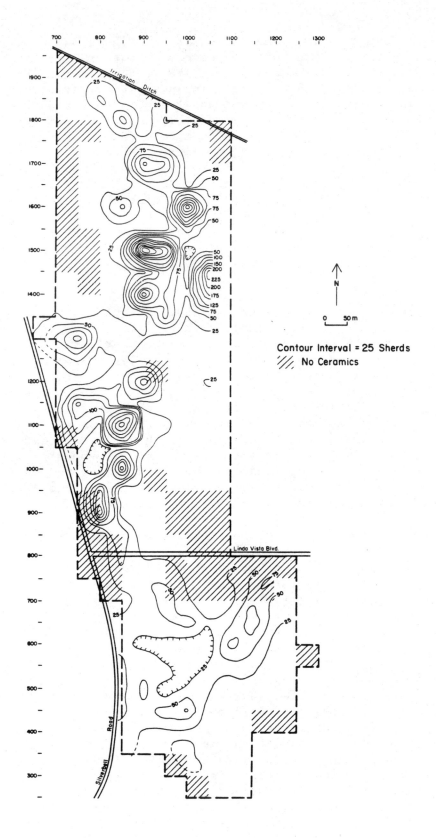

Figure 3.2. Sherd density based on 5-m by 5-m collection units.

characterized by a uniform surface scatter. Figure 3.3 shows an overlay of archaeological features discovered during the 1980 testing and subsequent field school excavations. The features shown indicate all archaeological features discovered, including those evident from surface indications (such as the ballcourt and trash mounds) and those discovered through subsurface testing. The distribution shows a good correlation between the location of features and those areas of the site that have high concentrations of ceramics. The only apparent anomalies are four trash mounds between N1150 to N1300 and E1050 to E1100. The lack of high sherd densities in this area is inexplicable. The overall correlation is enhanced by the failure to discover large numbers of subsurface features in areas characterized by low-density artifact scatters. Thus the distribution of ceramics would seem to be a good indicator of the location of subsurface features, even in areas of the site known to be heavily disturbed by plowing or bulldozing.

This distribution of ceramics shows two other notable patterns. First is the long, linear nature of the distribution, which seems to follow a slight rise in the landform (Fig. 3.4) and may somewhat correlate with a "high water mark" above the Santa Cruz River floodplain. The second notable feature is a large area of low ceramic density to the east and southeast of the ballcourt (Fig. 3.3). This is suggestive of a possible plaza or open communal area (see Wilcox and others 1981; Doelle 1985). The arc in the ceramic densities to the south and southeast of this area (Fig. 3.3) suggests a possibility that the distribution of ceramics (and hence archaeological features) may have encircled this area. This is a speculative proposition. Archaeological remains and features have been discovered in the trailer court to the east that may suggest a closure around this area, but the locations of these remains have not been plotted.

Despite the known disturbances to the site, the surface distribution of sherds correlates well with the known distribution of subsurface features. Thus it would seem that the sherd distribution can be used as a tool for isolating areas that have a higher probability of containing subsurface archaeological features. The results of correlating the surface sherd distribution with known subsurface features also supports the idea that it may be possible to trace the location of residential areas at the site over time. Unfortunately the number of decorated sherds identifiable to specific chronological phases were too few to permit a phase-by-phase reconstruction of the site development. It was noticed, however, that there was a major difference in the distribution of Preclassic and Classic period sherds. Figure 3.5 shows the distribution of Preclassic sherds and Figure 3.6 shows the distribution of Classic period sherds. Figure 3.5 indicates that the overall layout of Los Morteros was established during the Preclassic period. Figure 3.6 indicates that during the Classic period there was an abandonment of the area south of Linda Vista Boulevard and that the greatest amount of activity was limited to the site area north of the ballcourt.

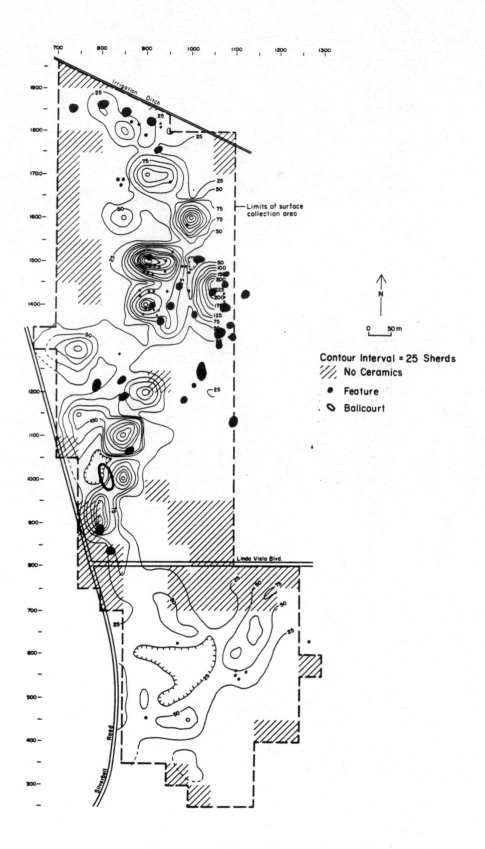

Figure 3.3.   Feature location compared to sherd concentrations.

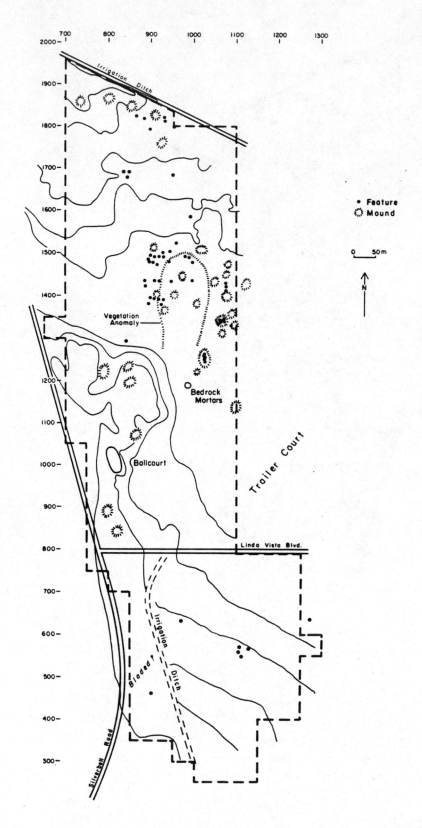

Figure 3.4. Feature locations and natural topography.

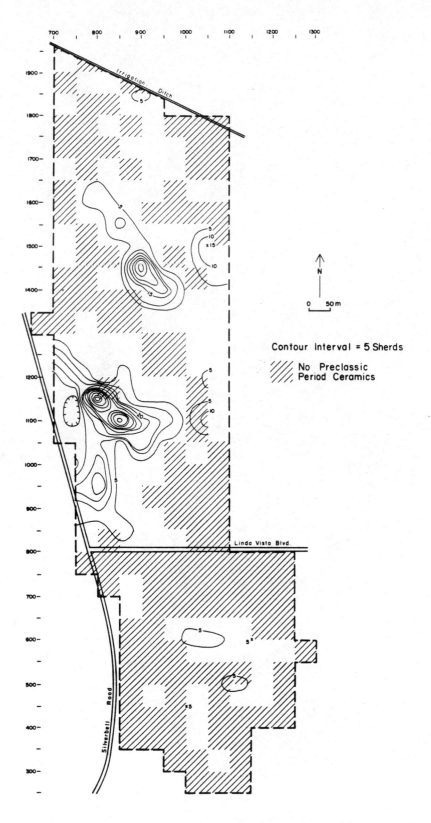

Figure 3.5.   Distribution of Preclassic period sherds.

24

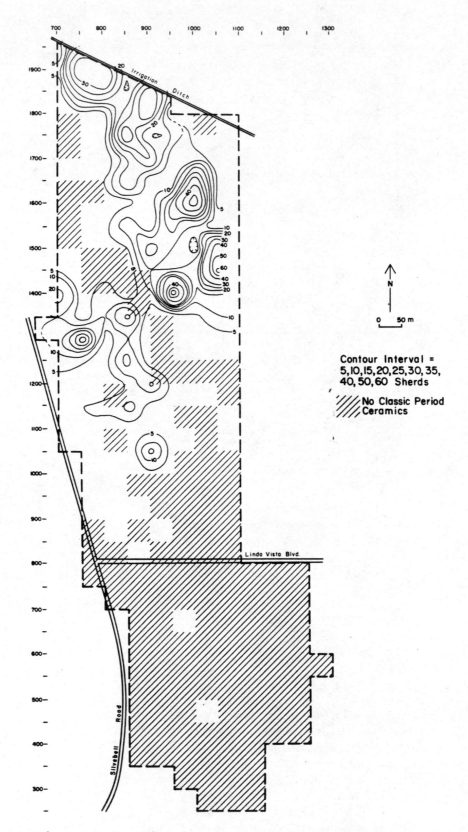

Figure 3.6.   Distribution of Classic period sherds.

The relative density of Classic period sherds is higher overall
than Preclassic sherds. If for the moment we accept the number of
sherds as a relative indicator of population (Hassan 1978) then this
information might indicate an increase in population at Los Morteros in
the Classic period. This proposition was not borne out by the
subsurface testing, in which Preclassic remains were discovered in
quantities rivaling the Classic period remains. Rather, it seems that
the increased visibility of the Classic period materials may be due to
the extensive plowing at the site. It seems likely to me that the
Classic period remains were stratigraphically higher than the Preclassic
remains and thus proportionately more Classic period materials were
brought to the surface by plowing. This still does not negate the
observation that by the Classic period the residential areas at Los
Morteros seem to have shifted to the north.

Conclusions

The investigation of the surface distribution of sherds at Los
Morteros correlates well with the distribution of archaeological
features discovered during the backhoe trenching operation. From this
it seems that there is value in conducting detailed investigations of
the surface distribution of artifacts to identify areas that would seem
to have a higher probability of subsurface remains. Rather than
deploying backhoe trenches uniformly over an extensive site area with
low resolution between trenches as was done at Los Morteros, the results
of investigations of surface artifact distributions could be used to
differentially deploy backhoe trenches, thus increasing the resolution
of subsurface testing in archaeologically sensitive areas. This
conclusion presumes that the surface distribution of sherds is
representative of the subsurface distribution of archaeological
features, which would be the case if the relationship between the
artifacts and features remains approximately the same as at the time the
site was abandoned. The use of surface artifact distributions to
determine the distribution of subsurface remains should also consider
the geologic processes and human activities that might have affected the
site since its abandonment. The known disturbances at Los Morteros are
rather extensive in nature, yet these did not obscure the correlation
between the distribution of sherds and the location of residential
features. Still, the technique could be made more sophisticated and
presumably a more powerful interpretive tool if the geomorphology of the
land form is known. Surface deposits of artifacts at sites
characterized by extensive depositional or erosional processes may not
be accurate records of the distribution of subsurface deposits, although
they may still be informative of the probable location of any subsurface
deposits. Finally, the temporal information inherent in decorated
sherds indicates that there was a major relocation of activities at Los
Morteros during the Preclassic and Classic periods. During the
Preclassic period, the residential units were spread throughout the
study area, but in the Classic period the remains were concentrated in

26

the northern part of the site area. There seems to have been a shift in residence (and related activities) to the north of the ballcourt.

Chapter 4

POTTERY AND OTHER CERAMIC ARTIFACTS

William L. Deaver

The initial archaeological testing and subsequent field school
excavations conducted by the Arizona State Museum at Los Morteros
unearthed over 100,000 ceramic artifacts. This chapter presents the
research orientation, structure, and results of the ceramic analysis,
which occurred on an intermittent basis over a four-year period. The
first ceramics were analyzed in 1980, the last in 1984. The same
research orientation established in 1980 was maintained throughout the
ceramic analysis. This point is important because beginning in 1980
Tucson Basin pottery was intensively studied, previous ideas concerning
the ceramic development were closely scrutinized and reevaluated, and
new perspectives emerged. These new perspectives were a logical
consequence of increased archaeological work in the Tucson Basin by the
Institute for American Research (IAR) and the Arizona State Museum
(ASM). The new insights have been published in various reports and
articles (see Deaver 1984; Wallace 1985a, 1986a, 1986c; Doelle and
Wallace 1986; Heidke 1986a, 1986b, 1988; Wallace and Heidke 1986;
Whittlesey 1986, 1987a, 1987b, 1988; Deaver 1988, 1989a, 1989b).

This brief history is critical toward understanding the
information and ideas presented in this chapter. The Los Morteros
analysis was my first attempt at formulating perceptions of the Tucson
Basin pottery tradition into a workable analytical system. During the
years between the initial and last analysis sessions of the Los Morteros
pottery, many of the typological categories defined in 1980 had become
outdated; some became even somewhat controversial. By 1984 my
perceptions had evolved into the form presented in the ANAMAX study
(Deaver 1984). Throughout the Los Morteros analysis I attempted to
apply the same typological constructs that I had developed in 1980 even
though my own confidence in the validity and usefulness of some had
diminished, while my confidence and conviction as to the validity and
usefulness of others had increased. My perceptions have continued to
change since the last Los Morteros ceramics were analyzed and the
publication of my views on the ceramic developments in the Tucson Basin
in 1984. In this chapter I have tried to bridge the gap between the
intent of initial analysis and the subsequent research and changes in my
perceptions. I also seek to bring the content of the Los Morteros
ceramic analysis into the current research on Tucson Basin pottery.

Research Objectives and Structure of Analysis

Three primary objectives determined the structure of the ceramic analysis. The first research objective was to determine the chronological age of the archaeological remains discovered. This was achieved by using a typological classification of the decorated pottery. Painted pottery provides a chronologically sensitive record; plain ware and red ware pottery may also provide some chronological information but usually not with the same resolution as painted pottery. Most pottery types in the Southwest represent expressions of pottery traditions at particular places and periods in time; therefore, identifying a sherd or pot to a known pottery type based on aspects of design style and technology yields the general age of that piece of pottery, which we can then associate with the site occupation. Both the Tucson Basin and Gila Basin Hohokam pottery sequences consist of phase-specific pottery types; these are the dominant pottery types present and are the primary records on the age of the prehistoric occupation at Los Morteros. Pottery types from other areas of the Southwest are infrequent but provide useful cross-correlation with the Hohokam pottery sequence.

In addition to the accepted phase-specific Tucson Basin pottery types of Cañada del Oro, Rillito, Rincon, and Tanque Verde red-on-brown wares, I attempted to identify the controversial and enigmatic type Cortaro Red-on-brown, which should occupy the chronological position between the Rincon and Tanque Verde phases. Recently completed analysis of ceramics from a small part of the Hardy Site (AZ BB:9:14 [ASM]) had renewed interest in evaluating the validity of Cortaro Red-on-brown and the Cortaro phase (Gregonis 1977, 1982; Reinhard 1982). As a student I had worked with Gregonis and Reinhard during the analysis of the Hardy Site ceramics and felt reasonably certain that Cortaro-like ceramics were present at Los Morteros. However, Reinhard and Gregonis had not yet provided a detailed description of Cortaro Red-on-brown, so I relied strongly on Gladwin's theoretical definition for this type (Kelly 1978: 47). As will be pointed out in the discussion that follows, the existence of the Cortaro phase is still not accepted and Gladwin's definition of the type is not practicable.

The second research objective was to identify patterns of exchange as depicted by the occurrence of nonindigenous pottery. This goal could also be satisfied using a typological classification. Concomittant with identifying a pot sherd to a typological category is associating that sherd with the localities where that type was known to have been manufactured. Again the painted pottery was the primary record.

The third primary research issue arose during the analysis. In the early stages I had observed several sherds that were stylistically identifiable as Tanque Verde Red-on-brown, but which appeared to have a blackish pigment rather than the more typical red. I was aware that an iron pigment could vary in color depending on the degree of oxidation or reduction during firing, or in the thickness of the applied paint, but these factors could not consistently explain this phenomenon. My interest was further focused when Bruce Huckell, a colleague at the Arizona State Museum, informed me that these sherds were similar to several found at Whiptail Ruin (AZ BB:10:3 [ASM]) that had come to be informally called "Tanque Verde Black Paint." It seemed that the Classic period Tucson Basin potters may have been using two different pigments in decorating pottery: one that fired to a reddish color, the other that fired out to a blackish color, both in an oxidizing atmosphere. This seemed the most likely explanation of the phenomenon observed among the Los Morteros pottery. The idea that Tanque Verde decorated pottery could be executed in a black-on-brown color scheme as well as a red-on-brown color scheme intrigued me.

The existence of Tanque Verde Black Paint was not documented in the literature, but knowledge of it existed among Tucson Basin archaeological folk lore. I then began to explore the extant literature in more detail and discovered published accounts of other kinds of similar variations. Thus the third primary research topic was to document the variety of technological variations of the Tucson Basin decorated pottery that seemed to be purposeful alterations of the decorative color scheme by Prehistoric potters. It soon became clear that the Tucson Basin pottery tradition was more varied and complex than I had originally expected. Many of these technological variations are unparalleled in the broader Hohokam pottery tradition; therefore, a full enumeration of these technological variations may help us to understand the cultural dynamics in the Tucson Basin during the Sedentary and Classic periods.

Other minor research objectives also affected the final structure of the ceramic analysis. As an aid to the interpretation of individual features, functional information in terms of the general formal class (bowl or jar) represented by a particular sherd was recorded. Also, although decorated pottery is the most useful for dating, a plain ware typology based on Kelly's (1978: 69-76) discussion of temporal changes in the Hodges site plain ware was attempted. This plain ware typology was intended to provide some chronological control, although it is not as precise as the decorated pottery typology. As will be discussed in detail later in this chapter, the typology is defined in such a manner that it is ambiguous and inconsistent and therefore cannot be used for the purpose for which it was designed, even though there are temporally sensitive shifts in plain ware technology. The final research interest that emerged during the analysis (one that is closely related to my interest in documenting the technological variation in the decorated pottery) is the technological variation observed in the red ware pottery.

The analysis was strictly typological. Each piece of pottery was classified according to two variables: pottery type or technological variety and vessel form. A composite list of all pottery

types known to occur at Tucson Basin sites was compiled from the
available literature. The primary sources of this information were
Kelly's (1978) work at the Hodges Ruin, Danson's (1957) description of
the University Indian Ruin pottery, Greenleaf's (1975) work at the Punta
de Agua Sites, and Doyel's (1977) work in the middle Santa Cruz River
Valley. These references provided the basic typological descriptions of
the Tucson Basin pottery types as well as a list of potentially
occurring intrusive pottery types. Type descriptions for the Gila Basin
Hohokam Buff Ware pottery were derived from the work at Snaketown
(Gladwin and others 1965; Haury 1976). Other intrusive pottery was
cross-checked against a variety of sources. Additional typological
categories accommodating technological variants were included as
different variants were observed. The list was left open-ended so that
any previously unanticipated pottery type or variety could be added to
the list. Of course, not all pieces of pottery could be definitively
identified to type categories, so indeterminate categories also were
added. These categories have chronological, geographical, and
technological information at some level of generalization less specific
than the pottery type.

I made the typological identification of all decorated pottery
from Los Morteros. Ms. Laverne Conway assisted in the analysis of plain
ware pottery recovered during the testing phase, and the plain ware
pottery recovered from the subsequent field school work was analyzed by
several students under the direction of Richard C. Lange. All
typological data were numerically encoded into the Arizona State Museum
computer system. Inventories of the Los Morteros pottery collection are
presented in Appendix B.

Chronological Age of the Los Morteros Occupation

The primary objective of the pottery analysis was to determine
the age of the archaeological occupation. The pottery types represented
in the Los Morteros ceramic collection (Appendix B, Table B.1) indicate
an overall occupation at the site spanning from the late Pioneer period
(Snaketown phase) to at least the early Classic period (Tanque Verde
phase). The possibility of a late, Tucson phase, occupation can also be
postulated based on the occurrence of Gila Polychrome pottery. This
time range includes the transition between the Sedentary and Classic
Periods, variously referred to as the Cortaro phase (Gregonis 1982;
Kelly 1978: 47-48; Reinhard 1982) or the Late Rincon phase (Bradley
1980; Ervin 1982; Greenleaf 1975, Fig. B; Huckell 1978; Wallace 1985b).
The attempt to document the occurrence of this transitional period using
the controversial and theoretical phase-diagnostic pottery type Cortaro
Red-on-brown produced problematical results.

At the time the Los Morteros ceramic analysis was initiated the
Cortaro phase concept had been recently resurrected based on the work at
the Hardy Site (Gregonis 1982; Reinhard 1982). Excavations there had

unearthed a large collection of sherds and several reconstructible
vessels that exhibited the attributes Harold S. Gladwin had postulated
for Cortaro Red-on-brown (Kelly 1978). My experience assisting with the
Hardy site ceramic analysis lead me in 1980 to include Cortaro Red-on-
brown in the Los Morteros ceramic analysis. This type was the hardest
of any to positively identify. This difficulty arose due to the
definition of Cortaro Red-on-brown used during the analysis. The
Cortaro type was not well defined in the contemporary literature. The
early 1980s was a time when the ceramic development during the Sedentary
period was being intensively investigated and new more detailed
descriptions of the ceramic development were emerging, but none of these
were in a form to be applied during the Los Morteros ceramic analysis.
A formal type description of the Hardy Site material was not available,
and although Greenleaf (1975: 60-66) had documented and described Late
Rincon Red-on-brown, which should have been synonomous with Cortaro Red-
on-brown from the Hardy Site, these descriptions were general and vague.
The typological definition of Cortaro Red-on-brown used during the Los
Morteros analysis was based on common conceptualization of this type
among researchers during the early 1980s, which essentially is the same
as Harold Gladwin's theoretical definition of Cortaro Red-on-brown as
presented by Isabel Kelly (1978). Essentially, Cortaro Red-on-brown
would be intermediate between the interior curvilinear designs of Rincon
Red-on-brown and the exterior angular designs of Tanque Verde Red-on-
brown. This would include interior decorated bowls with angular designs
resembling Tanque Verde Red-on-brown (Kelly 1978: 48). This definition
may reflect the early stages of the Hodges ceramic analysis when only
sherds painted on the concave surface were used to define the Tucson
Basin pottery types.

As would be expected, given the above definition, Cortaro Red-
on-brown pottery is represented at Los Morteros overwhelmingly by bowl
sherds (Appendix B, Table B.1). This situation certainly does not
result from temporary cessation of decorated jar production during the
the proposed Cortaro phase, but simply from an inadequacy of the
definition. Based on Gladwin's definition it was possible to identify
bowl sherds that exhibited the definitive attributes; however, jar
sherds were probably more often identified as Tanque Verde Red-on-brown.
Therefore, as defined by Gladwin, the typological category Cortaro Red-
on-brown is problematical, and it is not possible to subsume this
category at Los Morteros into either Rincon Red-on-brown or Tanque Verde
Red-on-brown ceramics. Subsequent studies of Rincon phase ceramics have
better defined the ceramic developments and stylistic trends during the
later part of the Rincon phase so the problems associated with Gladwin's
definition no longer occur (Deaver 1984: 262-265; Wallace 1985a: 109-
125, 1986c: 109-125; Doelle and Wallace 1986: 28-29).

The issue of revising the Tucson Basin Hohokam cultural
development to include a Cortaro phase (with the phase-diagnostic
pottery type, Cortaro Red-on-brown) immediately preceding the Tanque
Verde phase of the Classic period has oscillated wildly. The Cortaro
phase has been proposed (Kelly 1978: 48; Gregonis 1982; Reinhard 1982),
and rejected (Greenleaf 1975: 109; Wallace and Holmlund 1984; 172;

Wallace 1985b) twice. The classification of sherds from Los Morteros as
Cortaro Red-on-brown provides no significant contribution to the issue
of dividing the Sedentary period into more than one phase. Over the
past decade archaeological research has yielded new information that
clearly indicates that the Sedentary period could be divided into two
phases. Two cultural patterns characterize the Sedentary period: one
represents the finale of the late Colonial period cultural pattern, the
other heralds the beginnings of the Classic period cultural pattern.
Thus the legitimacy of the Cortaro phase seems to have been
substantiated by this recent archaeological work. As Wallace (1986c:
20) has pointed out, however, any revision of the Sedentary period
chronology would likely be along different lines than those proposed for
the Cortaro phase. The major shifts in the cultural pattern seem to
occur around A.D. 1000, earlier than the range from A.D. 1075 to 1150
postulated for the beginning of the Cortaro phase (Greenleaf 1975, Fig.
B; Reinhard 1982; Wallace and Holmlund 1984; Wallace 1985b: 532). Also,
the ceramic attributes traditionally assigned to the Cortaro or Late
Rincon phenomenon have their roots anchored firmly among changes in the
ceramic tradition that appear in the middle of the Sedentary period,
around A.D. 1000 (Deaver 1984; Wallace 1985a: 121, 1986c: 55). The
following discussion is not intended to provide a revision of the Tucson
Basin chronological sequence, but instead to present an overview of the
available information, which indicates the need to reconsider revising
the Tucson Basin cultural sequence.

Few Tucson Basin archaeologists would disagree that during the
later part of the Sedentary period there were demonstrable shifts in the
ceramic tradition away from the curvilinear designs of the Colonial and
early Sedentary periods to the more angular stylistic developments that
led to Tanque Verde Red-on-brown ceramics. This late Sedentary period
ceramic style is recognizable, definable, and temporally diagnostic
(Bradley 1980; Deaver 1984; Doelle and Wallace 1986; Ervin 1982;
Greenleaf 1975; Gregonis 1982; Huckell 1978; Huntington 1982; Reinhard
1982; Wallace 1985a, 1985b, 1986c). The stylistic developments of the
Sedentary period are currently used to distinguish early, middle, and
late chronological sub-divisions of the Rincon phase (Deaver 1984;
Wallace 1986c; Doelle and Wallace 1986: 18-29; Huckell 1987). My
current opinion, is that Sedentary period pottery can be divided into
only two distinct pottery styles: an "early" style that was a
continuation of the late Colonial stylistic tradition, and a "late"
style characterized by a preference for plaited and paneled designs,
which represents the beginnings of the Classic period stylistic
tradition (Deaver 1984: 381). It is the occurrence of one style at the
virtual exclusion of the other or the occurrence of both stlyes together
that seems to characterize the three chronological subdivisions of the
Sedentary period. During the early part of the Sedentary period,
decorated pottery was essentially a continuation of the late Colonial
stylistic pattern. In the middle Sedentary period there appeared a
rectilinear style emphasizing plaited and other related sectioned
designs (Deaver 1984: 262; Wallace 1985a: 103-109, 1986c: 38-40) which
occurred with, but subsequently replaced, the previously dominant
Colonial-derived style. Some of the ceramic collections originally

identified as Late Rincon, such as those from the Observatory Site (Ervin 1982) and BB:13:74 (Bradley 1980), have been reevaluated in light of more recent information and are now considered as either middle Rincon in age (Deaver and Tagg 1984) or as transitional between the middle Rincon and Late Rincon subphases (Wallace 1985a: 111). Finally, the decorated tradition of the late Sedentary period was marked by an increasing simplification of the rectilinear style verging on the Classic period stylistic pattern (Greenleaf 1975: 109; Deaver 1984: 262-265; Wallace 1985a: 109-125, 1986c: 53-62). The early appearances of the rectilinear decorative tradition during the middle Sedentary does not fall within the extant definitions of Cortaro Red-on-brown or Late Rincon Red-on-brown types.

Wallace (1985b: 540), in his appraisal of the Cortaro phase concept, correctly follows Gladwin's (1937: 249) admonition that a phase of human development must not be based on a single component. Specifically, in the case of the Cortaro phase, this is to avoid "ceramic determinism" (Greenleaf 1975: 109) by defining the phase solely on the existence of a recognizable style of pottery. New evidence indicates that associated with the appearance of the rectilinear style during the middle Sedentary are other changes in the ceramic complex, as well as other aspects of culture. These changes include the addition of red ware and polychrome wares to the ceramic tradition, as well as extensive variation in the decorative color scheme (Deaver 1982, 1984: 386-392; Doelle and Wallace 1986: 34; Greenleaf 1975: 109; Wallace 1986a: 172-176, 1986c: 90); changes in architectural style (Ervin 1982; Greenleaf 1975; Wallace 1985b: 534); changes in settlement pattern evidenced by the abandonment of earlier villages, appearance of new communities, and restructuring of village organization (Doelle 1988; Doelle and Wallace 1986: 77; Ferg 1984: 816-817; Wallace 1985b: 537-538); and changes in patterns of regional exchange evidenced by the decline in frequency of Gila Basin buff wares and an increase in pottery from the east and northeast (Doelle and Wallace 1986: 37; Greenleaf 1975: 75; Wallace 1985a: 131, 1985b: 538, 1986a: 176, 1986c: 102, 1988). During the middle and late Rincon subphases, there may also have been a rejection of the ideological system associated with ballcourts (Wallace 1985b: 539).

The appearance of the rectilinear late Sedentary design style is a recognizable horizon marker for these changes in the Tucson Basin cultural pattern. The postulated Cortaro phase has been dated to the temporal interval of A.D. 1075 to 1215 (Greenleaf 1975: 109; Reinhard 1982; Wallace 1985b: 532; Wallace and Holmlund 1984) based primarily on archaeomagnetic dates from the Punta de Agua Sites (Greenleaf 1975; Wallace 1985b: 533, Table 1), AZ BB:13:74 (Bradley 1980; Wallace 1985b: 533, Table 1), and the Valencia Site (Doelle 1985; Wallace 1985b: 533, Table 1). A single archaeomagnetic date from a late Rincon structure at the Hardy Site of A.D. 1175-1215 (Gregonis 1982: 30) supports the latter part of this range. However, the Sternberg date options for the archaeomagnetic samples from AZ BB:13:74 and the Valencia Site indicate the possibility for an early eleventh-century appearance of the rectilinear Sedentary pottery style (Wallace 1985b: 533, Table 1).

Archaeomagnetic dates derived from samples from the Observatory Site (Ervin 1982; Deaver and Tagg 1984: 30) and AZ EE:1:158 (Huckell 1987: 75) provide further support for an early eleventh century emergence. The archaeomagnetic sample from the Observatory Site yielded a dual-option date of A.D. 1000-1080 or A.D. 1200-1350; the A.D. 1000-1080 date seems the more plausible option (Deaver and Tagg 1984: 30). The decorated ceramics from AZ EE:1:158 have been stylistically defined as Rincon-red-on-brown Style A and Style B (Huckell 1987: 75). The co-occurrence of these two styles is interpreted as indicative of the middle Sedentary period. An associated archaeomagnetic sample yielded a dual option date of A.D. 890-1070 or A.D. 1280-1450 (Huckell 1987: 75). The older option is consistent with the body of archaeological evidence (Huckell 1987: 75). These two dates indicate that the rectilinear pottery style may appear earlier than A.D. 1075. A recent evaluation of the Tucson Basin chronology (Wallace and Craig 1988) places the beginning of the Middle Rincon subphase, hence the beginning of the rectilinear style of pottery, at A.D. 1000.

Clearly, there are important changes that occur during the Sedentary period that result in a new cultural pattern. This new pattern is not based simply on a developmental shift in ceramic decoration, but by a constellation of traits that correlate with a radical shift in the decorative tradition. These traits indicate a division of the Sedentary period into two distinct developments: the early Sedentary appears to be the final episode in a Colonial period cultural pattern, whereas the latter part of the Sedentary period represents an emergence of what leads to the Classic period cultural pattern. It seems more than just coincidence that the emergence of a new rectilinear style of pottery is correlated, along with unprecedented and unparalleled experimentation and variation in the ceramic tradition (see below), with changes in settlement location and organization, with changes in architectural style, with changes in the pattern of interregional exchange of pottery, and with the possible abandonment in the Tucson Basin of the ballcourt system. We should not be reticent about questioning and revising the existing chronology. The Tucson Basin chronology developed by Kelly (1978) should be seen as a starting point, not as a final solution.

Logically the later cultural developments would seem to fulfill the requirements of the Cortaro phase. As has been pointed out, however, the rectilinear ceramic style associated with the later cultural pattern is different from that defined for either Cortaro or Late Rincon Red-on-brown. These latter two concepts define only a particular temporal interval in the developmental history of the rectilinear style that immediately precedes the Classic period. Also, the other changes in the cultural pattern correlated with the appearance of the rectilinear ceramic style appear before A.D. 1100, earlier than the defined beginning of the Cortaro or Late Rincon phase. The question now does not seem to be whether a revision of the Tucson Basin chronology is warranted, but rather what to label this new phase. Applying the Cortaro or Late Rincon labels would require expanding and redefining these concepts. An ultimately less confusing perspective

would be to approach the revision of the Sedentary period retaining the
Rincon label for the early Sedentary cultural pattern, but using a new
label free of preconceived connotations for the late Sedentary cultural
pattern.

Regional Exchange: Intrusive Pottery

Nonindigenous pottery found at Los Morteros provides indications
of contacts with other regions. The tabulation of intrusive pottery is
presented in Appendix B, Table B.1, and is summarized by culture area in
Table 4.1. Plain wares, red wares, and decorated wares are represented
in the intrusive pottery. As expected, Gila Basin Hohokam pottery is

Table 4.1

SUMMARY OF INTRUSIVE POTTERY

Culture Area	Frequency	Percentage
Gila Basin Hohokam Buff Wares	2813	93.4
Mogollon	107	3.5
Papaguería	60	2.0
Salado	18	0.6
Anasazi/Western Pueblo	14	0.5
Total	3012	100.0

the dominant intrusive recovered with both decorated and plain ware
pottery types identified. Decorated pottery amounts to approximately 99
percent of the Gila Basin intrusives, the remaining 1 percent are 32
sherds which were identified as Gila Plain. The majority of the
decorated buff wares (81.1 percent) were too small or eroded to be
identified to type. Of the remaining decorated sherds, Sacaton Red-on-
buff (16.5 percent of the decorated buff wares) is clearly the dominant
type recovered, followed by Santa Cruz Red-on-buff (1.8 percent), and
finally by Casa Grande Red-on-buff (0.4 percent).

The next most frequent group of intrusive pottery is that which
I have grouped together as Mogollon (Table 4.1). Mogollon pottery is

represented by decorated, plain, and red-slipped types. The dominant
type of pottery is an indeterminate plain brown ware (59.8 percent of
Mogollon types). These sherds are characterized by a fine-textured,
brown to gray paste. Many also exhibit a burnished and smudged surface.
In paste characteristics they resemble plain brown wares from the
Forestdale and Reserve areas. The remaining Mogollon types are San
Carlos Red (26.2 percent) and San Carlos Red-on-brown (14.0 percent).

The third most frequent group of intrusives came from the
Papaguería and is represented by a single type, Sells Red, which is the
dominant intrusive red ware at Los Morteros. The incidence of Sells
phase intrusives may be higher than is indicated, as Sells Red is
associated with the production of Tanque Verde Red-on-brown in the
Papaguería. Some of this Papaguerían Tanque Verde Red-on-brown pottery
could have been imported into Los Morteros; there is no information
presently available to distinguish Tanque Verde Red-on-brown produced in
the Papaguería from that produced in the Tucson Basin.

The remaining intrusive sherds represent contacts with the
Salado culture and the Anasazi/Western Pueblo culture of east-central
Arizona. The Salado pottery is represented by 17 sherds of Gila Red and
1 sherd of Gila Polychrome. Although these sherds indicate contacts
with areas where these types were produced, it is not possible to
specify the particular region where these sherds derived, only that it
could be from the north, northeast, or east. Fourteen Anasazi/Western
Pueblo sherds that could not be identified to type were recovered. One-
half are undecorated white ware fragments. These white ware and
unidentified black-on-white sherds all seem to be of the Cibola White
Ware tradition.

Overall the intrusive pottery from Los Morteros supports the
pattern of intrusive pottery previously documented for the Tucson Basin.
The greatest diversity of intrusive pottery seems to correspond to the
Classic period occupation at Los Morteros. The only intrusives that can
be confidently associated with Preclassic phases are the Gila Basin Buff
Wares.

Plain Ware Pottery

The analysis of plain ware pottery at Los Morteros was directed
at determining if this class of pottery could be used to provide some
type of temporal information in the absence of decorated pottery. The
premise of this study was the idea commonly accepted in 1980 that early
plain wares were micaceous whereas later plain wares were not. This
premise clearly reflects Kelly's (1978: 69-76) discussion of Tucson
Basin plain wares where she notes that the Pioneer plain wares were nonmicaceous, the Colonial period pottery is noticeably more micaceous, and
finally the Sedentary and Classic period plain wares are again
nonmicaceous. Thus at Los Morteros two plain ware categories were

established: "micaceous" and "nonmicaceous." It was anticipated that the relative percentage of "micaceous" plain ware would indicate Colonial age deposits.

As the classification of plain ware pottery progressed it became clear that these categories were difficult to use. Very little pottery was nonmicaceous. The distinction was not in the presence or absence of mica, but in the relative proportion. A sample of the plain ware pottery from one provenience was arranged according to the relative quantity of mica visible on the surface. What emerged from this exercise was a more-or-less continuous distribution from those that had no visible surface mica to those that had a definite micaceous sheen. It was quite easy to distinguish between sherds representing each end of the continuum, but the difficulty was in determining a recognizable break point in the middle between micaceous and nonmicaceous pottery. My conclusion is that the distinction between micaceous and nonmicaceous pottery is highly arbitrary and inconsistent from day-to-day by the same analyst, and especially from one analyst to another. Therefore, it is probably best to ignore the counts of micaceous and nonmicaceous plain ware and treat the body of plain ware pottery as one typological category.

Since this unsuccessful attempt at studying the variability in the Tucson Basin plain ware pottery, more sophisticated studies have been made (Deaver 1984; Doelle 1985; Heidke 1986a, 1986b). These studies have begun to confirm the observations made by Kelly (1978) on which the Los Morteros classification was attempted. But rather than relying on the quantity of surface mica, the important attribute appears to be the addition of crushed micaceous rock as a temper.

Red-Slipped Pottery

A total of 627 red-slipped sherds were recovered from the work at Los Morteros. Of these, 105 were intrusives and were discussed previously. The remaining sherds are apparently all locally produced products. Just under one-half of the locally produced red-slipped sherds (233 sherds) were identified as Rincon Red. Bowl sherds dominated this type; many having both interior and exterior slips. The majority of the local red-slipped wares was classified as "Unidentified Red." This group of red-slipped wares seems to have been comprised of two subgroups. The first was characterized by a dark gray to black paste with often dull and fugitive slips. The second group also exhibited a fugitive red slip, but the paste was brick-red, sometimes with a dark core. The latter group may represent the same kind of red ware as the first except that the paste was more fully oxidized during firing.

Color Scheme Variations on Decorated Pottery

Throughout the prehistoric period in the Tucson Basin the dominant decorative color scheme on ceramics was a red design applied to a brown background field, hence the red-on-brown label appended to the Tucson Basin ceramic sequence. The actual color of the paint and background vary considerably, depending on the nature and uniformity of the firing atmosphere, the thickness and homogeneity of the paint, and the iron content of the clay. Thus it seems that the prehistoric Tucson Basin potters strove to achieve a red-on-brown decoration with varying degrees of success. From this analysis, it is apparent that the Tucson Basin potters deliberately manipulated the background and paint colors to produce different decorative effects. The earliest archaeologically recognized example of this was the presence of smudging to produce, a red-on-black or red-on-gray color scheme (Hawley 1930; Gabel 1931; Fraps 1935; Kelly 1978). Since the recognition that the Tucson Basin potters smudged to alter the decorative color scheme and prior to the work at Los Morteros in 1980, other researchers have noted other decorative color combinations achieved by the Tucson Basin potters (Frick 1954; DiPeso 1956; Danson 1957; Greenleaf 1975; Doyel 1977; Zahniser 1965, 1966, 1970; Grebinger and Adams 1974). The full range of variation or the significance of this variation was not pursued until the work at Los Morteros. Since the first public presentation of my interest in specifically documenting the range of decorative color combinations at the Tucson Basin conference in 1982 (Deaver 1982), other researchers have become conscious of this aspect of the Tucson Basin pottery tradition and have documented numerous examples where the potters had diverged in some manner from the more standard red-on-brown decorative scheme (Huntington 1982; Ervin 1982; Simpson and Wells 1983, 1984; Deaver 1984; Wallace 1985a, 1986a, 1986c; Doelle and Wallace 1986; Whittlesey 1986, 1987a; Beckwith 1987; Slawson 1988). Consequently, knowledge of both the range of variation and the geographic occurrences of various types of variation have expanded. In this section I explore the possible and observed departures from the red-on-brown color scheme, discuss the overall significance of this variation, and synthesize this variability into a coherent picture of ceramic development in the Tucson Basin.

Documenting the Range of Variation

The variety of decorative color schemes created by the prehistoric Tucson Basin potters is explored from two avenues. First is a more or less theoretical perspective based on our present knowledge of the Tucson Basin decorated ceramic tradition. The use of red, black, and white paint pigments have been documented (Kelly 1978; Frick 1954; DiPeso 1956; Danson 1957; Hayden 1957; Zahniser 1970; Greenleaf 1975; Doyel 1977) as well as the use of brown, red-slipped, white-slipped, and smudged-black background colors (Hawley 1930; Gabel 1931; Fraps 1935; Kelly 1978; Scantling 1940; DiPeso 1956; Danson 1957; Zahniser 1965,

1966; Grebinger and Adams 1974; Greenleaf 1975; Doyel 1977). From this list of known resources, possible bichromatic and polychromatic decorative combinations are generated. The second avenue is to document which of the possible color combinations occur in the archaeological record.

Bichromatic Color Schemes

Three paint colors and four background colors were available to the Tucson Basin potters at various times during the course of prehistory. A simple permutation of these elements yields 12 possible bichrome color schemes: (1) red-on-brown, (2) black-on-brown, (3) white-on-brown, (4) red-on-white, (5) black-on-white, (6) white-on-white, (7) red-on-black, (8) black-on-black, (9) white-on-black, (10) red-on-red, (11) black-on-red, and (12) white-on-red. Not all of these are considered to be viable alternatives. Because the black background is produced by smudging, black-on-black and white-on-black are not possible. White-on-white is also not a viable color scheme. Similarly, red-on-red would appear to be nonviable because of a lack of contrast between the paint and background; however, the color of the red paints and slips are sufficiently different that a red-on-red pottery is considered possible. Thus a total of nine possible bichrome color schemes can be considered.

Polychromatic Color Schemes

At this time polychrome color schemes are only considered with respect to a single decorative field. When more than one design field occurs on a vessel, the use of multiple color schemes is possible and results in a sort of polychromatic vessel. Delineating polychromatic schemes is not as simple as bichromatic schemes. Based on existing knowledge of Tucson Basin pottery, potters occasionally used two paint colors on a single background color such as in Rio Rico Polychrome (Doyel 1977, 1988). There are three two-paint combinations possible: red-and-black, red-and-white, and black-and-white. Each of these could be associated with any one of the four background colors, thus there are 12 possible two-paint polychrome combinations. Seven of these combinations are considered viable: (1) red-and-black-on-brown, (2) red-and-black-on-white, (3) red-and-black-on-red, (4) red-and-white-on-brown, (5) red-and-white-on-red, (6) black-and-white-on-brown, and (7) black-and-white-on-red. None of the two-paint polychrome color schemes involving a smudged-black background would be viable; the smudging process would most likely obliterate one or both paint colors. Also, the two combinations that would involve a white paint on a white background are nonviable.

It is also possible that the potters could use three paints in a polychrome scheme. There is only one paint combination that can be used in conjunction with the four background field colors. Thus, although four combinations are possible, only two are considered viable: red-and-black-and-white-on-brown, and red-and-black-and-white-on-red.

Until now, each of the color schemes defined has been based on a painted design using one, two, or three paints on a single background color. Rincon Polychrome presents another possible way Tucson Basin potters created polychrome color schemes, that is, by using more than one background color. For example, Rincon Polychrome typically is characterized by a black-painted design applied to white-slipped area; this area can be a panel or a band (Greenleaf 1975: 67-73; Wallace 1986a: 172-176, 1986c: 81-96). The remaining area surrounding the white-slipped panel or band is typically red-slipped. The visual effect is black-on-white-on-red. Thus each of the viable bichrome and polychrome color schemes identified above (N = 18) could occur on any one of the four background colors. Thus, there are 72 theoretical combinations employing two background field colors; however, only 20 are considered viable. These are not presented here; as will be shown below, the color scheme associated with Rincon Polychrome is the only one of this category that is known to occur. The process of permutating possible color schemes could continue up to three background colors or even four, but the range presented here encompasses all observed variation.

Observed Color Scheme Variation

The theoretical exercise above has suggested that the Tucson Basin potters had the resources to produce no less than 9 bichromatic color schemes and 29 polychromatic color schemes. The following list presents the range of color schemes actually produced, as gleaned from the existing literature: (1) red-on-brown, (2) red-on-white, (3) red-on-black, (4) black-on-brown, (5) black-on-white, (6) black-on-red, (7) white-on-brown, (8) red-and-black-on-brown, (9) red-and-black-on-white, (10) red-and-white-on-brown, (11) black-and-white-on-red, and (12) black-on-white-on-red. A complete inventory of occurrences of these variations and references is presented in Appendix B.

From this list it is clear that the Tucson Basin potters explored many, but not all, of the possible color scheme combinations. Seven of the possible bichrome color schemes and four of the seven two-paint polychrome schemes are identified. The frequency of occurrence of each color scheme ranges from some that are represented by single cases to others that consistently appear in ceramic collections (if even in low frequency). The most notable omissions from this list are the total absence of three-paint polychrome combinations; evidently these were beyond the range of possible variation. Also lacking in the list, except for the black-on-white-on-red color scheme associated with Rincon Polychrome, are polychrome color schemes involving the use of two background field colors.

Chronological Distribution of Color Scheme Variation

There is a strong temporal pattern to the observed occurrences of these color scheme variations (Table 4.2). The available chronological information spans only the early Colonial (Cañada del Oro phase) through the early Classic (Tanque Verde phase) periods; too

Table 4.2

OBSERVED COLOR SCHEMES BY CHRONOLOGICAL TIME PERIOD

	Colonial		Sedentary			Classic	
	E	L	E	M	L	E	L
red-on-brown	X	X	X	X	X	X	X
red-on-white	X	X	X	X	X	X	?
red-on-black		?	X	X	X	X	X
black-on-brown			?	X	X	X	?
black-on-white			X	X	X	?	
black-on-red			X	?	X	X	X
red-and-black-on-brown			?	X	X	X	X
red-and-black-on-white			X	?	X	X	?
black-and-white-on-red			X	?	X	X	X
black-on-white-on-red			X	?			
white-on-brown						X	
red-and-white-on-brown						X	

E = early, M = middle, L = late

little information is available for the Pioneer period and only sketchy information is available for the late Classic period (Tucson phase). The most obvious feature of this pattern is that most of the alternative

42

color schemes first appear during the Sedentary period. Even then, when
the information is available, the distribution indicates that it is
during the middle Rincon when the greatest florescence begins. Only the
red-on-white color scheme definitively occurs earlier than the middle
Sedentary period, lending support to the idea that this color scheme
variant is an attempt to emulate the Gila Basin decorative pattern
(Greenleaf 1975: 50). Most of the alternative color schemes that first
appear in the Sedentary period continue, into the early Classic period.
This information lends support to the idea that the middle and late
Rincon pottery styles are the early developmental stages of what
ultimately emerges as a highly formalized and standardized stylistic
tradition in the Classic period (Whittlesey 1987a, 1988).

Other Considerations on Color Scheme Variation

        Before synthesizing the observed color scheme variation within
the Tucson Basin pottery typology, it is necessary to consider other
color scheme variations that result from Tucson Basin potters decorating
more than one surface of a vessel. At a very general level Tucson Basin
potters produced two formal classes of vessels: unrestricted and
restricted. "Unrestricted vessels" include bowls and scoops.
Restricted vessels are essentially equivalent to traditional jar forms,
though I also include incurved bowls as restricted forms (Deaver 1984:
270). Both these classes provide three possible surfaces for
decoration: the interior, the exterior, and the narrow surface of the
rim (lip) that bridges between the interior and exterior surfaces. Over
the course of time the Tucson Basin potters' tradition dictated the
fields and parts of the fields that were appropriate for decoration.
Bowls were variously decorated on the interior, exterior, or interior
and exterior. Throughout the duration of the Tucson Basin tradition,
two separate design fields were designated on jars: the principal design
field was on the exterior with a less substantial design on the interior
of the rim and neck in the Preclassic phases, and on the exterior of the
neck during the Classic Period. Occasionally during the Preclassic
period, two distinct design fields were designated on the exterior, the
principal design field limited to the body of the vessel and a secondary
design field limited to the neck. Because of the extremely limited area
available for painting, the lip is not considered a significant field of
decoration, but over the course of the Tucson Basin pottery tradition
this field received specific decorative treatments. During the Colonial
period the bowl lips were rarely decorated and jar lips were decorated
as often as not (Deaver 1984: 293, 303, 386-387; Doelle and Wallace
1986: 15; Wallace 1986c: 16; Whittlesey 1986a: 112). Beginning in the
early Sedentary period and continuing in to the Classic period however,
both bowl and jar lips were consistently painted (Deaver 1984: 319, 386-
387; Wallace 1986c: 30, 42, 59; Wallace and Doelle 1986, Table 2.5;
Whittlesey 1986a: 112).

        These notes are important to consider when documenting the color
scheme variations because each decorative field could be decorated in a

separate color scheme. This greatly amplifies the potential range of variation in total decorative color effects. Tanque Verde Red-on-brown bowls provide a good example. The smudged variety of Tanque Verde Red-on-brown was noted in the earliest descriptions and discussions of this pottery (Hawley 1930; Gabel 1931; Fraps 1935; Kelly 1978). These workers often referred to the decorative effect as "red-on-black" or "red-on-gray." Fraps (1935: 4) enumerated four distinct "wares" from Tanque Verde Ruin based on the contrasting color schemes of the interior and exterior of the vessel. Since then, the presence of smudging among Tucson Basin pottery has been widely accepted as a standard attribute of this type, but smudged vessels are in effect polychromatic, with an exterior color scheme of red-on-brown and an interior color scheme of red-on-black. Some of the Tanque Verde Black Paint from the Whiptail ruin with black-on-brown or black-on-white exterior color schemes often had red-on-brown or red-on-black interior designs.

Another example from the Sedentary period that most clearly demonstrates this point is the pottery I have called Sahuarita Polychrome (Deaver 1984: 328-329). This type appears to be a "hybrid" between the decorative and red ware traditions of the middle Sedentary period, much like Rincon Polychrome. So-called Sahuarita Polychrome is characterized by a counter-balanced polychrome design of red and black applied on a brown decorative field. In this feature it strongly resembles Rio Rico Polychrome (Doyel 1977: 36-40, 1988), but the decoration is applied to the exterior of bowls, while the interior is covered by a red slip. I have also included within the definition of Sahuarita Polychrome two varieties: one that has an exterior red-on-brown design and another with a black-on-brown design, both found on vessels with red-slipped interiors. In these examples bichromatic and polychromatic decorated surfaces are contrasted with a monochromatic surface which differs from the background field color of the decorated surface. These two examples indicate the complexity that lies ahead in synthesizing the color scheme information with the current perceptions of the Tucson Basin pottery types.

Significance of the Color Scheme Variation

The decision on whether or not the current typological system should be expanded, adding new typological categories to accommodate the color scheme variation, or whether this variation is best subsumed under existing typological categories as attributes must be based, in part, on the potential significance of the color scheme variants to provide information on the prehistoric Tucson Basin way of life. The intent here is not to explore the full range of the potential significance; this is best left for additional studies and investigations that are beyond the immediate scope of this discussion. Rather, the attempt here is to illustrate that these color scheme variations have value toward understanding the overall cultural development in the Tucson Basin, especially the changes during the middle and late Sedentary period that lead into the Classic period.

A major emphasis of pottery studies since the first archaeological work in the Tucson Basin has been to compare and contrast the Tucson Basin pottery tradition and its developmental sequence with other pottery traditions of the Southwest, most notably the Gila Basin Hohokam pottery tradition. An example of this research is the continuing question of whether the Tucson Basin pottery tradition is a hybrid between the Gila Basin Hohokam buff ware tradition and the Mogollon brown ware tradition (Kelly 1978: 3, 62; Whittlesey 1986), or whether the Tucson Basin pottery tradition is a Hohokam tradition made with locally available raw materials, which impart the observed differences (Deaver 1984: 416-419; Doyel 1977: 31). The color scheme variants that employ a red design on a white-slipped background have been interpreted to represent attempts by the Tucson Basin potters to emulate the Gila Basin tradition (Greenleaf 1975: 50). This inference is supported by the chronological distribution of color scheme variants in Table 4.2 and the discussion of the early, pre-Colonial period Tucson Basin pottery tradition presented below.

During the Colonial and early Sedentary periods the red-on-white color scheme is the only alternative to the typical red-on-brown color scheme that occurs. This is also a time of other pronounced similarities between the Tucson Basin and Gila Basin pottery traditions (Deaver 1984: 416-419). The color scheme variants that appear during the middle Sedentary period, however, are unparalleled in the ceramic developments in the Gila Basin, and in other parts of regional expanse of the Hohokam cultural phenomenon. These color scheme variants, in effect, give the Tucson Basin pottery tradition a unique identity within the larger Hohokam pottery tradition. The Gila Basin cannot be viewed as the source area for these innovations. Where the inspiration for these variations stems from—internal innovations or outside influences--is not known. The use of a blackish-colored paint pigment that maintains its color in an oxidizing atmosphere with a reddish-colored paint may have more than a superficial resemblance to the color scheme typical of northern Sonoran types such as Trincheras Purple-on-red, Nogales Polychrome, and Altar Polychrome. The similarities between Nogales and Altar polychromes with Rio Rico Polychrome are obvious. The black-on-brown, black-on-white, and black-on-red color schemes may be local innovations, reflecting experimentation with the newly incorporated ideas from northern Sonora. Thus the question emerges: "Was northern Sonora the source for inspiration of the color scheme variations?"

The use of the black paint on a white background more frequently than the red paint suggests a northern or northeastern source for these ideas. Regardless, there were dynamic processes at work in the Tucson Basin pottery tradition that are not represented in the remainder of the Hohokam culture area. These color scheme variants were introduced during the middle of the Sedentary period, a time when other aspects of the Tucson Basin culture were also undergoing change (see the earlier discussion of Cortaro Red-on-brown). The changes in Tucson Basin culture seem to be a rejection of the earlier Colonial period, Gila Basin-influenced cultural pattern.

Each of the color scheme variations presented above, as well as the overarching phenomenon of which they are exemplars, are worthy areas of study. Looking for the possible sources of influence in the appearance of these color schemes may aid in identifying the inspiration for changes in other aspects of the Tucson Basin culture.

Synthesizing the Variability

Most studies of Tucson Basin decorated pottery are typological and classificatory; that is, ceramics recovered during archaeological projects are categorized within existing, defined pottery types. Many of these color scheme variants cannot be adequately documented using existing pottery type descriptions and definitions. The issue was not whether there was a need to reevaluate the typological system to accommodate this variation; over the years there have been numerous attempts to create new typological categories to account for variation in the Tucson Basin pottery tradition. Rather, the issue was how to modify the existing typological system.

Four approaches were considered, most of which have been attempted in some fashion. The first approach is to redefine existing type categories to include the color scheme variations as attributes of these types. The second choice is to define new type categories independent of present types but still using the theoretical framework of the existing typological system. A third choice is a compromise between the first two and involves redefining existing type categories to lump some of the observed variation into existing type categories and to define new categories when lumping is not feasible. The most radical choice would be to abandon the present typological system altogether and define a new typology with an explicitly defined theoretical base.

Specifically, whichever tactic is best suited in a particular situation is determined by the research objectives and those attributes of the pottery that have the greatest potential for informing on these research topics. I advocate that the character of typological units should vary with respect to the kinds of research questions being asked. The established Tucson Basin pottery types are best used as dating tools to answer questions about the age of archaeological deposits. The same categories are not equally well suited, however, for documenting intraregional variation in the pottery tradition, or as in this case, documenting the full range of experimentation and technological variation in the pottery tradition. My opinion is that there is value in both the third and fourth tactics presented above, proposing specific modifications to the established typological sequence and defining a different typological perspective. Both approaches must be based on an explicit theoretical foundation.

Recently, attribute analyses have become more common (Wallace 1986a, 1986b, 1986c). In such analyses the various paint and background field colors can be recorded as attributes. This discussion is not on how to record the color scheme attributes during analysis but rather how these attributes should be synthesized into theoretical categories for archaeological inference and interpretation of the past way of life in the Tucson Basin.

Previous Attempts at Modifying the Established Typological Sequence

Researchers have long been sensitive to and aware of variation in the Tucson Basin pottery tradition. They have observed not only variation in the decorative color combination as emphasized here, but variations in design, form, temper, clays, and surface finish, to highlight but a few areas. Variations in these aspects of the pottery tradition have been treated both descriptively and typologically. Prior to the 1970s, archaeological work in the Tucson Basin was scant. After the Tucson Basin type sequence was established from the excavations at Hodges (Kelly 1978), pottery "oddities" that were observed were rarely found in sufficient quantity to warrant serious consideration as new pottery types. Thus Frick (1954: 63) notes a new unnamed polychrome, but the task of defining the new type was left to Doyel (1977), when a sufficient number of examples was found to justify naming a new pottery type, Rio Rico Polychrome. Likewise, Kelly (1978: Table 4.15) and later DiPeso (1956: 351) noted the occurrence of an unidentified polychrome type that Greenleaf (1975) found in sufficient quantities to define as a new Tucson Basin pottery type, Rincon Polychrome.

Occasional studies prior to the 1970s, and most that date from the 1970s and later, have proposed various modifications to the established typological sequence. Greenleaf (1975) and Doyel (1977) added two new polychrome pottery types to the established type sequence. Greenleaf's (1975) naming of Rincon Polychrome parallels the method employed by Kelly (1978): the primary name given to the type is the phase name in which the type occurs. Doyel's (1977) naming of Rio Rico Polychrome does not follow this convention. Doyel applies a tactic more similar to the northern Arizona pottery typology where types are given geographic place names rather than phase names (Colton and Hargrave 1935). Also, Doyel (1977) observed that Rio Rico Polychrome was not chronologically restricted to a single phase, so assigning a phase name as the primary type name would not have been sound. Even if it were restricted to the Rincon phase, as I have suggested (Deaver 1984: 326-327), the potential type name "Rincon Polychrome" was previously used by Greenleaf (1975) for a distinctly different kind of pottery. Although Greenleaf's (1975) and Doyel's (1977) theoretical stances on naming pottery types are slightly different, their decisions are based on accepted methods for defining and naming pottery types.

Other researchers in the Tucson Basin have taken similar typological approaches to accommodate other variations in the pottery tradition. The most frequent approach is to define and name project specific ad hoc categories to classify the odd pottery. These ad hoc categories are often modeled after the established Tucson Basin red-on-brown types, but the actual approach is more similar to the type-variety method of analysis (Wheat and others 1958; Gifford 1960, 1976). DiPeso's (1956) work with the pottery from the site of Palo Parado is an early formulation of the type-variety method. The observed variation is grouped based on similarities and then classed as variants of the established pottery types. Each variant is assigned a name similar to the type name. Thus, for Tanque Verde Red-on-brown, DiPeso (1956: 319) presents the following variants: Tanque Verde Red-on-black; Tanque Verde Red-on-brown Etched; Tanque Verde-Rincon Red-on-brown Transitional; and Tanque Verde Polychrome. Although not segregated as variants, DiPeso (1956: 315-318) also refers to Tanque Verde Red-on-brown (unslipped) and Tanque Verde Red-on-brown (slipped) to distinguish a large number of Tanque Verde Red-on-brown sherds that had a white kaolin slip from those lacking a slip. Each of these variants is distinguished based on a variety of attributes ranging from differences in the color scheme (red-on-black, slipped, unslipped, and polychrome variants), differences in technology (etched variant), and differences in relative age as indicated by differences in the design style and manner of decoration (transitional variant).

This approach by DiPeso (1956) is currently the preferred method of referring to variations of the traditional red-on-brown pottery tradition as exemplified in the pottery descriptions by Ervin (1982), Huntington (1982), Huckell (1978), Whittlesey (1986), Beckwith (1987), and Slawson (1988). None of these latter attempts has explicitly presented the theoretical reasoning for the decision to use a particular method of naming and defining new typological categories. In some cases the same typological name has been applied to two distinct variations. For example, DiPeso's (1956: 319) "Tanque Verde Polychrome" refers to pottery decorated with a counter-balanced red and black design applied on a white-slipped surface. In the Arizona State Museum Type Collection, this same name has been applied to another polychrome variant, first defined by Zahniser (1970: 109), that has white painted lines added to the more typical red-painted design. More recently, Beckwith (1987: 209-210) uses the typological category "Tanque Verde Polychrome Variant" to encompass as many as four distinct decorative treatments. Thus there is neither an explicit theoretical position for judging which variation is significant nor a consistent method for assigning names to the defined variants.

Wallace (1985a, 1986a, 1986c) also uses the type-variety approach to expand the Tucson Basin typological system, but is explicit on his methodological position. Wallace (1985a, 1986c) presents a typological hierarchy, modified after the type-variety method, consisting of pottery type, subtype, and variety, ranging from most general to most specific respectively. This typological hierarchy was created within the context of Wallace's research with Tucson Basin pottery and it is important to view the structure of this hierarchy with respect to the research topics explored by Wallace. The intent, and contribution of Wallace's work has been to identify chronologically distinct subdivisions of Rincon phase pottery so that better chronological resolution can be achieved in dating archaeological deposits (Doelle and Wallace 1986: 27; Wallace 1986c: 1-4). To

integrate the chronologically defined subgroups of Rincon phase
decorated pottery with the current typology he creates the
classificatory group subtype, which falls hierarchically between "type"
and "variety" (Wallace 1986c: 20-21). Thus he names "Early," "Middle,"
and "Late" subtypes of Rincon Red-on-brown.

This is a reasonable approach to the needs of his research, but
Wallace generalizes this typological system to the Tucson Basin type
sequence. He considers technological variation in the paint color and
background field color as "varieties" within each subtype, and coins
typological names such as "Early Rincon Red-on-brown, black paint
variety" (Wallace 1986c: 21). In this respect, Wallace's (1986c: 21)
work reflects the position taken by most other researchers; he and
others accept the opinion that the Tucson Basin pottery types are
primarily cultural horizon markers. This approach clearly views
chronological variation in the pottery as hierarchically superior to the
technological variation which results in the various distinctive color
schemes and suggests that the definitive attribute for defining types is
some chronologically identifiable constellation of traits. I contend
that this position is inconsistent with the full intent of how the
Tucson Basin pottery types were first defined, and with the theoretical
and methodological premises behind the traditional Southwestern
typological system.

I believe that Wallace and other authors have focused too
strongly on just one aspect of the type names. I fear that Wallace's
(1986c: 21) position to subsume all technical variants into a single
type category such as Rincon Red-on-brown will over simplify what may be
a more complex reality, and creates a cumbersome and illogical
typological system. To me, the names "early Rincon Red-on-brown, black
paint variety" (Wallace 1986c: 21) and "late Rincon Red-on-brown, black-
on-white" (Ervin 1982: 25) are contradictory and illogical. I believe
that there is evidence in the way Kelly (1978) formulated and named the
Tucson Basin pottery types and in the traditionally accepted standards
for naming pottery types (Colton and Hargrave 1935, 1937; Gladwin and
Gladwin 1930) for my position of creating additional pottery types
(Deaver 1984).

Wallace (1986c: 21) has criticized my approach toward revising
the Tucson Basin typology because he views variations in the paint color
as "minor technological distinctions." I contend that the issue of
whether or not a technological feature of the pottery is major or minor
is a judgment that must be made within the domain of particular research
issues. Aspects of decoration and vessel form are more critical to
Wallace's research than are technological variants of paint color.
However, the research emphasis of Wallace is more specific than that of
Kelly (1978) or, more generally, of the historic period in Southwestern
pottery studies in which Kelly worked. Colton and Hargrave (1937: 2)
specifically state that "a pottery type is a group of pottery vessels
which are alike in every important characteristic except (possibly)
form." They include the chemical composition of the paint as one of six
characteristics for defining pottery types; style of design is one of

the other characteristics (Colton and Hargrave 1937: 2). The rules for designating pottery types at Gila Pueblo (Gladwin and Gladwin 1930) were essentially the same as those at the Museum of Northern Arizona (Colton and Hargrave 1935, 1937; Colton 1953). Because the red and black paints used in Tucson Basin ceramics are chemically different (see Appendix P), separate type status for red-painted and black-painted pottery would be consistent with these definitions. My opinion is that if we are to continue to use the typological system employed by Kelly then we must continue to follow the rules. Wallace's (1986c) approach modifies these rules to fit his specific research emphasis; within the context of his research this is sound, but it is not equally sound for Wallace to extrapolate his system beyond the confines of his research questions. It is not that the technical variations in paint and background color are "minor" attributes in Wallace's research, they are simply insignificant toward answering the research questions he poses. Yet the color scheme variations are significant when viewed with respect to the rules of the traditional Southwestern typological system (Colton and Hargrave 1935, 1937; Colton 1953; Gladwin and Gladwin 1930), and possibly toward understanding social interactions among the prehistoric Tucson Basin inhabitants.

Wallace (1986c:21) is concerned that an uninhibited splitters approach would unnecessarily complicate the task of learning the Tucson Basin types and obscure the obvious close relationships that exist between the various pottery groups. My concern is that the lumpers position, seemingly advocated by Wallace, would obscure information in the pottery collection that is significant toward reconstructing prehistoric cultural development in the Tucson Basin. I agree that many of the color scheme categories are closely related; I also agree that each of these categories are variations of a larger standard category, or theme. I do not, however, accept that a black-on-brown design is a variant of a red-on-brown design, but rather that both red-on-brown and black-on-brown are each equal variants or expressions of a larger standard category that may best be referred to as "Rincon Phase Decorated" or even "Middle Rincon Phase Decorated," but not "Rincon Red-on-brown." I do not believe that Wallace perceives the black-on-brown pottery as a variant of the red-on-brown pottery, but rather he perceives a more generic category such as "Rincon Phase Decoration." He chooses to use the name of a specific expression of this category (Rincon Red-on-brown) to label the larger, more inclusive concept.

I present two methods of synthesizing the color scheme variants with the established Tucson Basin typology. One position is to redefine existing categories and define new pottery types. This approach follows the position I presented in the synthesis of the ANAMAX pottery (Deaver 1984). The second method is to define a different typological system for the Tucson Basin pottery tradition. This different typological system is based on a particular theoretical perspective of pottery production. This typological system is intended to specify the relationships and structures that seem to have existed in the prehistoric pottery traditions during particular intervals of time. This is a strongly synchronic presentation of the pottery tradition, and is intended to complement Wallace's (1985a, 1986a, 1986c; Doelle and Wallace 1986) more diachronic studies.

Modifying the Traditional Type Sequence

In order to modify Kelly's (1978) typological sequence to reflect variations in color scheme, I think that the established type definitions should be expanded to include variations in surface treatment, which alter the decorative background field color, and to define new pottery type categories to reflect variations in paint pigment. This position is presented in the ANAMAX pottery descriptions (Deaver 1984). Such an approach must consider how the types were originally defined. I argue that the position I have taken and the proposed modifications to the typological sequence are consistent with how the original types were established.

The Tucson Basin pottery types were defined within the constructs of a particular method that was developed within the research needs of that time. Wallace (1985a, 1986c) summarizes the history of Isabel Kelly's (1978) pioneering work with the Tucson Basin pottery, presenting the research emphasis and the importance of the work at Snaketown on the structure of the Tucson Basin pottery types. Of key importance is that Kelly did her work under the auspices of Gila Pueblo. Harold and Winifred Gladwin (1930) list the criteria for designating pottery types that was most certainly used in defining the Tucson Basin pottery types. Two key traits selected were the geographic location where the type occurs and its color combination or surface treatment (Gladwin and Gladwin 1930). These criteria are indicated in the information presented in the labels (type names) assigned to groups of similar pottery.

Each of the pottery type names in the sequence as originally defined by Kelly (1978) is composed of two parts. The first part is the phase name in which the type occurs and of which the type is diagnostic. This phase name is also a geographic place name, so the name of the pottery type is consistent with the rules for designating pottery types set forth by Colton and Hargrave (1935) and Gladwin and Gladwin (1930). This feature of the typology is modeled after the Gila Basin pottery sequence defined at Snaketown (Gladwin and others 1937; Haury 1976) so that there is a one-to-one correspondence between cultural phases and pottery types. Each type name signifies a particular constellation of stylistic, formal, and technological traits that were shared by a group of people during a particular phase in Tucson Basin Hohokam development. For example, the designation "Rincon" encompasses a broad range of ideas (norms) on design, form, and pottery manufacture shared by potters during a particular developmental phase of the Tucson Basin cultural tradition.

The second part of the type name is a descriptive label that denotes the typical decorative color combination and the character of the clay. Thus "red-on-brown" denotes that the Tucson Basin types are characterized by a red-painted design applied on a brown-colored clay body. At the time of Kelly's (1978) work only red-painted pottery was recognized as local Tucson Basin products; she apparently did not recognize the pottery later designated as Rincon Polychrome as a local product. Because of the rules set forth at Gila Pueblo for designating pottery types, had Kelly recognized the polychrome as a local product, or had she recognized the existence of locally produced black-painted pottery she would have been compelled to designate new types. Since Kelly defined the foundation of the Tucson Basin type sequence, polychrome types have been defined (Greenleaf 1975; Doyel 1977); the remainder of the Tucson Basin painted pottery has been more-or-less assumed to have been painted with red paint.

Prior to Kelly's work the pottery from the Tucson Basin was referred to as red-on-buff (Gladwin and Gladwin 1929: 119; Gabel 1931; Fraps 1935) apparently as an acknowledgment that this material was considered part of the "red-on-buff" culture. The later "red-on-brown" label connotes the idea presented by Kelly (1978: 3, 62) that the Tucson Basin pottery had strong affinities with the Mogollon brown ware tradition. Thus the "-brown" part of the type label could be seen as an abbreviation for "brown ware," which serves to distinguish the Tucson Basin pottery from the Gila Basin buff wares with connotations of affiliation with the Mogollon culture.

The content of these type labels indicates that there are at least three levels of information being communicated. First is the association of a particular group of pottery with a particular phase of development in the Tucson Basin cultural sequence--expressing shared ideas about design, form, and technology. Second is the decorative color combination typical for this group of pottery, specifically the color of the paint. Third is that the foundation of the Tucson Basin pottery tradition is distinct from the Gila Basin Hohokam tradition and is more similar to the Mogollon pottery tradition as is indicated by the kind of clay body (brown ware) preferred. Thus, to integrate the observed color scheme variation into the existing typology would necessitate evaluation with respect to each criterion, specifically the second criterion. Based on the second criterion each color scheme resulting from the use of a distinct paint color or combination of paint colors would warrant type status.

The color of the background is not as clearly indicated in the traditional Tucson Basin type names nor in the Gila Pueblo list of criteria for designating pottery types (Gladwin and Gladwin 1930). Variations in the surface finish such as polishing and smudging have traditionally been considered as part of the range in variation of the normal red-on-brown surface finish (Kelly 1978). There is thus a clear traditional precedent for Wallace's (1986c: 21) position to subsume technological variation within the phase-specific types when it involves the surface treatment, but not such a clear traditional precedent for his proposition to consider differences in the paint color as "minor" technological distinctions. In fact, such a position is contradictory to the rules for designating pottery types on which the Tucson Basin types were defined (Colton and Hargrave 1935, 1937; Gladwin and Gladwin 1930).

The position that each difference in the paint color or combination of paint colors should warrant type status and that each difference in the background field color should warrant varietal status may be consistent with the traditional theoretical foundation of the Tucson Basin pottery type sequence, but a diligent adherence to this position would require a significant increase in the number of typological categories (Table 4.3). Such a large increase in the number of types is considered impractical and undesirable (Wallace 1986c: 21). Many of the proposed "type" categories are represented by only a few sherds or even a single sherd. There is a common opinion that a pottery type should not be defined from a single sherd, or from a small collection of sherds. This opinion probably stems from the view that a pottery type represents what a large group of people (in this case the Tucson Basin Hohokam) considered as normal or "appropriate" ways of decorating pottery. If a particular pottery expression is archaeologically represented by only a few examples, such divergences from the normal concept are considered anomalies, aborted attempts at innovation or experimentation by one or a few potters that never became culturally acceptable. This view point is concerned with normal or typical means of decorative expression at a particular interval of time. It may be this deep-seated presumption that suppressed the investigation of the full-range of variation present in Tucson Basin pottery.

I am interested in this range of variation because it is not constant over time. The variation seen during the latter part of the Rincon phase and continuing in the Classic period does not occur during the earlier horizons, or at least the variation in the pottery tradition is not expressed in the same way. Whittlesey (1986, 1987a, 1988) has shown that, in terms of variation in design, the Colonial period pottery is more diverse than the pottery of the Classic period. This must be contrasted with the color scheme information in Tables 4.2 and 4.3 which indicate that in terms of decorative color schemes the Classic period is more diverse than the Colonial period. These observations lead me to conclude that the relationship of the pottery tradition to the larger encompassing cultural system has changed between the late Colonial and the middle Sedentary periods.

From a practical stance I agree with Wallace (1986c: 21) that it may be counterproductive to name a new pottery type based on each documented paint color variation, combination of paint colors, or even the use of contrasting decorative color combinations on separate decorative fields. Yet I believe that the use of a black paint in a bichromatic color scheme occurs in sufficient quantity and over a sufficiently large area during the Rincon and Tanque Verde phases to warrant type status. It is the addition of this element into the pottery tradition that is one of two important keys in the explosion of alternative color schemes in the Sedentary period. Thus I propose two new pottery types: Rincon Black-on-brown and Tanque Verde Black-on-brown, one of which, Rincon Black-on-brown, has been previously defined

Table 4.3

POSSIBLE TUCSON BASIN TYPES AND VARIETIES BASED ON
PAINT AND SURFACE COLORS

Phase	Paint Color "Type"	Surface Color "Varieties"	Color Scheme	Established Types Represented
Cañada del Oro	red	unslipped white slipped	red-on-brown red-on-white	Cañada del Oro Red-on-brown
Rillito	red	unslipped white slipped	red-on-brown red-on-white	Rillito Red-on-brown
Rincon	red	unslipped, unsmudged white slipped smudged	red-on-brown red-on-white red-on-black	Rincon Red-on-brown
	black	unslipped white slipped red slipped white and red slipped	black-on-brown black-on-white black-on-red black-on-white-on-red	 Rincon Polychrome
	red and black	unslipped white slipped	red-and-black-on-brown red-and-black-on-white	Rio Rico Polychrome
	black and white	red slipped	black-and-white-on-red	Rincon Polychrome
Tanque Verde	red	unslipped, unsmudged white slipped smudged	red-on-brown red-on-white red-on-black	Tanque Verde Red-on-brown
	black	unslipped white slipped red slipped white and red slipped	black-on-brown black-on-white black-on-red black-on-white-on-red	
	white	unslipped	white-on-brown	
	red and black	unslipped white slipped	red-and-black-on-brown red-and-black-on-white	
	red and white	unslipped	red-and-white-on-brown	Tucson Polychrome
	black and white	red slipped	black-and-white-on-red	

(Deaver 1984: 322-326). In addition, in 1982 (Deaver 1982) I proposed the type names "Tanque Verde Polychrome" and "Saguaro Polychrome". These proposed Classic period polychrome types are discussed below to explain the reasons that these two type names were proposed.

Rincon Black-on-brown (new type)

This type was originally documented during the Los Morteros ceramic analysis but was not defined as a distinct Rincon phase decorative type until the ANAMAX pottery collection was analyzed (Deaver 1984: 322-326). At Los Morteros it was originally classified as "Unidentified Decorated." Since the completion and publication of the ANAMAX analysis, other occurrences of this type have been documented.

Decoratively, this type seems to differ from the contemporaneous Rincon Red-on-brown in two features: (1) the color of the paint and (2) a greater incidence of a white-slipped variant. Rincon Black-on-brown pottery has been documented in the pottery collections at the West Branch Community (Wallace 1986c: 37, Fig. 2.12 b), the Tanque Verde Wash Site (Wallace 1986a: 151), at sites along the Santa Cruz River within the San Xavier Reservation (Doelle and Wallace 1986: 27, 29), at the Hodges Ruin (Whittlesey 1986, Table 6.15), at the Observatory Site (Ervin 1982; Deaver and Tagg 1984: 20), at sites in the Rincon Mountains (Simpson and Wells 1984: 108), and at a seasonally occupied site in the Avra Valley (Deaver 1989c). Where the information is available, it seems that this type does not appear until the middle of the Sedentary period (Deaver 1984: 326; Wallace 1986a: 151, 1986c: 37, Doelle and Wallace 1986: 27; Deaver and Tagg 1984: 20), but it may first appear during the early Sedentary period, as early as A.D. 900 (Deaver 1984: 326). Certainly Rincon Black-on-brown post-dates the Colonial period. No examples of black-paint pottery have been attributed to the Colonial period. Even at two large Colonial period sites in the Avra Valley recently excavated by the Arizona State Museum, no examples of black-paint pottery were identified (Deaver 1988, 1989a). Wallace (1986c: 37) observed that the the black paint frequently occurs with a white slip. Although Wallace does not quantify this relationship, at ANAMAX nearly 49 percent of the Rincon Black-on-brown pottery had a white slip (Deaver 1984: 324). This attribute is strong evidence that the Tucson Basin potters treated this decorative expression differently from the more typical Rincon Red-on-brown. With further investigation additional differences from Rincon Red-on-brown may be seen in the range of forms or the preferred stylistic attributes associated with Rincon Black-on-brown pottery.

Tanque Verde Black-on-brown (new type)

As Rincon Black-on-brown pottery appears to mirror the main decorative, formal, and technological features of Rincon Red-on-brown, so Tanque Verde Black-on-brown mirrors the same range and preferences in design, form, and technology as Tanque Verde Red-on-brown. Figure 4.1

Figure 4.1. Examples of Tanque Verde Black-on-brown from Hodges (a,d,e) Loma Alta (b), and Los Morteros (c).

illustrates some examples of Tanque Verde Black-on-brown vessels. At present the only known distinction is the use of a black paint. This type has the same range of variation as Tanque Verde Red-on-brown. Much of this type has a white slip applied prior to decoration, and many pieces exhibit smudged interiors. An interesting phenomenon that is associated with this type is that because Tanque Verde phase potters decorated both sides of bowls, some of the Tanque Verde Black-on-brown sherds exhibit red-on-white, red-on-brown, and red-on-black interiors. Technically these may be considered polychromes, but for now they are simply acknowledged as part of the range of decorative variation possible for Tanque Verde Black-on-brown.

According to Bruce Huckell, Tanque Verde Black-on-brown was first observed at Whiptail Ruin (AZ BB:13:2 [ASM]) where it was referred to as Tanque Verde Black Paint. Since the identification of this type at Los Morteros it has been documented at a large number of sites throughout the Tucson Basin (Deaver 1982; Simpson and Wells 1984: 108; Doelle and Wallace 1986: 32; Whittlesey 1986: Table 6.15, 1987: Table 9.2; Beckwith 1987: 209; Slawson 1988: 141). In addition to the published occurrences, whole vessels of this type have been recovered from the Hodges Ruin (Fig. 4.1a,d,e), from the Loma Alta Site (Fig. 4.1b), and Los Morteros (Fig. 4.1c). I have seen sherds of this type in site collections from throughout the Tucson Basin, the site of Cerro Prieto, sites in the Papaguería, and from near Arivaca, Arizona. In proportion to Tanque Verde Red-on-brown this type is not frequent, but the observed occurrences indicate that it is geographically and temporally coincident with Tanque Verde Red-on-brown pottery.

The initial question about this type was whether or not the paint was indeed different from the more typical red paint. A hematite paint will be either red or black depending on the nature of the firing atmosphere; however, the occurrence of both the red and black paints on the same sherd as in Tanque Verde Polychrome (see below; DiPeso 1956: 319; Hayden 1957: 223) and Rio Rico Polychrome (Doyel 1977: 36-41) argues for a mineralogical difference in the paints. As an initial test, several sherds were refired at temperatures up to 700 degrees centigrade in an electric kiln under oxidizing conditions, only one sherd showed any observable reddening of the paint. It was thus originally presumed that this black paint was a manganese oxide or iron-manganese mixture (Shepard 1956: 40-42). As a second test, some of the black paint scraped from a sherd was determined to be strongly attracted by a magnet. This test suggested a large proportion of iron in the paint. Shepard (1956: 42) notes that some 40 paints from Maya and Pueblo pottery have iron-manganese ratios between 0.06 and 2.0. Finally, chemical analysis of the red and black paints by Susan Brantley (Appendix P) indicates that there is a clear distinction between the red and black pigments in the manganese content; however, the manganese in the black paint is not proportionately dominant. Therefore, it seems that the large proportion of the pigment is iron. Additional assay of the black and red paints is necessary to identify what minerals are being used and where the potential raw resources were obtained. The black mineral in Tanque Verde Black-on-brown should be the same as that used in other related oxidized wares in southern Arizona such as Rincon Black-on-brown, Rincon Polychrome, Rio Rico Polychrome, Babocomari Polychrome, and Santa Cruz polychrome. DiPeso (1951: 125) inferred that the dark pigment in Babocomari Polychrome was magnetite although he did not present the information on which that conclusion was based. His conclusion that the dark pigment in Babocomari Polychrome was magnetite, and by inference, the possibility that the black pigment in Rio Rico Polychrome, Rincon Polychrome, Rincon Black-on-brown, Tanque Verde Polychrome, Tucson Polychrome, and Tanque Verde Black-on-brown is also magnetite should be considered. It was anticipated that if the paint were magnetite it would have oxidized to red in the refiring experiments. Shepard (1956: 38) notes; however, that "the oxidation of magnetite begins at 400 degrees centigrade in air but proceeds to completion very slowly because the ferric oxide that is formed acts as a protective coating and prevents further oxidation." Thus, although the temperature during the refiring experiment was sufficient to begin oxidation of magnetite to hematite, the length of the refiring may not have been sufficient to cause observable changes in the paint color.

Tanque Verde Polychrome (new type)

DiPeso (1956: 319) first applied the name Tanque Verde Polychrome to six sherds from Palo Parado. These sherds were decorated in typical Tanque Verde style except that the design was executed using counter-balanced red and black paints on a white-slipped background. He further noted the occurrence of 76 sherds of a similar type that he referred to as Tanque Verde-Rincon Polychrome (transitional) (DiPeso 1956: 334). Hayden (1957: 223) added a footnote to Danson's (1957) type description of Tanque Verde Red-on-brown to mention two sherds decorated with red and black paints. This type subsequently has been recorded at Los Morteros and at sites on the San Xavier Reservation (Doelle and Wallace 1986: 34; Beckwith 1987: 210). The available descriptions indicate that this type has two varieties, an unslipped (Hayden 1957: 223; Doelle and Wallace 1986: 34; Beckwith 1987: 210) and a white-slipped variety (DiPeso 1956: 319). Tanque Verde Polychrome would seem to be a Classic period continuation of the Rio Rico Polychrome tradition; support for this proposition is the transitional polychrome that DiPeso (1956: 334) documented. Also, Tanque Verde Polychrome is probably closely related to Santa Cruz Polychrome (Sauer and Brand 1931; Brand 1935; DiPeso 1956: 331) and Babocomari Polychrome (DiPeso 1951: 123-129, 1956: 336), which have similar color schemes and decorative motifs. The name "Tanque Verde Polychrome" has also been used occasionally to refer to another polychrome decorated with red and white painted designs. This latter polychrome ceramic is referred to as Saguaro Polychrome.

Saguaro Polychrome (new type)

Zahniser (1970: 109) describes an unusual variant of Tanque Verde Red-on-brown that is decorated in typical red-painted design with white lines added. Although he does not name this "Tanque Verde Polychrome," it has become known by this name and was so classified in the Arizona State Museum Type Collections in 1980. Rules of priority require that the name "Tanque Verde Polychrome" be applied to the red and black decorated version described by DiPeso (1956: 319) and Hayden (1957: 223). Therefore, a new name is proposed for the polychrome pottery described by Zahniser (1970: 109). The name Saguaro Polychrome is suggested; the name being taken from Saguaro National Monument where the type was first recorded. Sherds of this type are very rare, but examples have been found at Los Morteros, the San Xavier Bridge Site (Beckwith 1987: 210), Tanque Verde Village (AZ BB:14:1), and at Ash Hill (AZ Z:12:6). Thus the type has a wide geographic range.

Unlike Tanque Verde Polychrome (DiPeso 1956: 319), Saguaro Polychrome is not decorated in a balanced design. Rather the decoration seems most appropriately referred to as a red-on-brown design with white paint added. From this perspective it is interesting that the use of the red and white paint colors are not integrated into an equal relationship as are the red and black paint colors. Zahniser (1970: 109) alluded to the similarity with St. John's Polychrome, but there is also a general similarity with Tanque Verde Red-on-brown, white-on-brown variety (Beckwith 1987: 209), Sells White-on-red (Scantling 1940: 32; DiPeso 1957: 309), Tucson Polychrome (Danson 1957: 226-229), and Sells Polychrome (DiPeso 1956: 309). This type may not represent an attempt to copy the White Mountain Redware tradition as much as a logical consequence of the decorative experimentation during the Sedentary and Classic periods.

Problems Associated with Modifying the Traditional Type Sequence

Table 4.4 presents a proposed scheme for modifying the existing Tucson Basin type sequence including the new types I present above. The organization of categories in this table is based on my conclusion that differences in the paint color or paint combination warrant distinct type status whereas differences in surface color should be given no more than varietal status. I did not diligently adhere to this procedure, however. Note that under Rincon Polychrome I include pottery that exhibits both black-painted designs and black-and-white-painted designs; this is in keeping with the type definition for Rincon Polychrome (Greenleaf 1975). Also in this scheme, those sherds exhibiting an exterior red-on-brown, black-on-brown, and red and black-on-brown design with a red-slipped interior surface are not considered as variants of Rincon Polychrome as suggested by Wallace (1985a: 128, 1986a: 167, 1986c: 78) or Sahuarita Polychrome as I have suggested (Deaver 1984: 328-329). Wallace's criterion for designating Rincon Polychrome is any sherds or vessels that if not painted would be classified as Rincon Red (Wallace 1986a: 167, 1986c: 78). To account for this in Table 4.4 it would be necessary to elevate the attribute "red slip" as equivalent to paint color so that types are designated either based on paint color or the presence of a red slip. It would seem, following this reasoning, that the attribute "white slip" might be a viable criterion for designating types. I do not agree with the latter suggestion, for reasons expressed later.

59

Table 4.4

PROPOSED TYPES AND VARIETIES FOR THE TUCSON BASIN TYPE SEQUENCE
BASED ON THE EXISTING SEQUENCE

Type	Varieties	Decorative Color Scheme
Cañada del Oro Red-on-brown	unslipped white slipped	red-on-brown red-on-white
Rillito Red-on-brown	unslipped white slipped	red-on-brown red-on-white
Rincon Red-on-brown	unslipped, unsmudged white slipped smudged exterior decorated with red-slipped interior	red-on-brown red-on-white red-on-black red-on-brown
Rincon Black-on-brown	unslipped white slipped red slipped ? exterior decorated with red-slipped interior	black-on-brown black-on-white black-on-red black-on-brown
Rincon Polychrome - Black Paint - Black and White Paint	white and red slipped red slipped ? red slipped	black-on-white-on-red black-on-red black and white-on-red
Rio Rico Polychrome	unslipped white slipped exterior decorated with red-slipped interior	red-and-black-on-brown red-and-black-on-white red-and-black-on-brown
Tanque Verde Red-on-brown	unslipped, unsmudged white slipped smudged exterior decorated with red-slipped interior	red-on-brown red-on-white red-on-black red-on-brown
Tanque Verde Black-on-brown	unslipped, unsmudged white slipped smudged	black-on-brown black-on-white black-on-brown or black-on-white exterior, red-on-black interior
Tanque Verde Polychrome	unslipped white slipped	red-and-black-on-brown red-and-black-on-white
Saguaro Polychrome	unslipped	red-and-white-on-brown
Tucson Polychrome	red slipped	black-and-white-on-red
Tucson Black-on-red	red slipped	black-on-red
Unamed Type - White Paint	smudged	white-on-brown exterior red-on-black interior
Unamed Type - Black and White Paint	red slipped	black-and-white-on-red

The attempt to incorporate the various color scheme variations into the existing typological system by defining as few new types as possible confounds the relationships among much of the pottery pieces (notably those that exhibit the use of a red-slip), but also leaves unaccounted for two Classic period examples that are each represented by a single sherd. One of these is decorated in the same color scheme as Tucson Polychrome, but is associated with the Tanque Verde phase and is apparently distinct from Tucson Polychrome (Beckwith 1987: 209). Therefore, this approach toward typologically categorizing the observed color scheme variations is not entirely suitable for my interests. The following is an alternative perspective on the nature of the Tucson Basin pottery tradition that I believe is more appropriate for exploring and documenting variation in the pottery tradition.

A Different Perspective on the Tucson Basin Pottery Tradition

I first applied a type-variety typological system during the ANAMAX pottery analysis (Deaver 1984) and again, to a limited degree, in the preceding discussion. Wallace (1986c: 21) has criticized this approach because it would require splitting of the Tucson Basin pottery into categories such as those in Table 4.4. He suggests that this system would obscure the close relationship that exists between many of these "types." I agree with this assertion. Many of these paint color "types" are closely related to one another and share many attributes of decoration, form, and technology that the typological system presented above does not illustrate. I propose that a different typological system is necessary to document and study the range in variation as well as demonstrating the close relationships between the multitude of alternative color schemes.

The typological system I propose is based on a particular theoretical perspective, a perspective that I believe is implicit in Wallace's (1986c: 21) decision to subsume pottery designs decorated in two distinct colors under a single heading and a perspective that probably underlies all pottery typologies. To repeat, Wallace's (1986c: 21) example category was "Early Rincon Red-on-brown, black paint variety." Wallace thus considers, typologically, black-painted pottery as a variety of red-painted pottery. It is this premise in his typological system that I find illogical. Wallace (1986c) recognizes that all Rincon phase decorated pottery is generically related in many attributes of form, technology, and design. Thus, each of the decorative color schemes can be viewed as variant expressions of a more generic category. I perceive that both the red-painted and black-painted pottery are equivalent expressions of a more encompassing abstract category, and I find it confusing to select the name of one specific expression to label the larger more inclusive category.

I would like to further point out that Wallace (1986c) does not propose that Rincon Polychrome or Rio Rico Polychrome be subsumed within the "Middle Rincon Red-on-brown" subtype as distinct varieties. There are aspects of form and design peculiar to Rincon Polychrome that are

not shared by the bichromatic pottery or by Rio Rico Polychrome;
however, both Rincon Polychrome and Rio Rico Polychrome are nonetheless
expressions of the same body of knowledge from which red-on-brown,
black-on-brown, and the other bichrome and polychrome color schemes are
derived. In principle, I agree with Wallace that all decorated pottery
is generically related, and I perceive that some of the various
expressions of the decorated pottery are more closely related than
others, but I disagree in terms of how particular variant expressions
are selected for type or varietal status and how the typological
categories should be labeled. Neither the additions to the existing
typological sequence that I propose above nor Wallace's (1986c) attempts
to modify the existing typological sequence are adequate to document the
range of decorative variation that occurs in the Tucson Basin decorated
pottery tradition. Nor does either approach adequately portray the
relative similarities between each distinct expression.

     Two basic things are necessary for pottery production: raw
materials and know-how. I believe that in the manufacture of pottery
there was an interaction between the potters' knowledge and the
environment, both leaving their distinctive marks on the pottery. The
material resources in a geographic area are finite; the environment thus
restricts the choices available to the potters. It is the potters
knowledge about how to make clay pots that determines which of the
available resources are appropriate for particular needs, and if
necessary, how to modify these materials to produce suitable clay pots.
Therefore, the attributes observable on pottery result from two
independent domains: one that consists of the knowledge held by a
potter on how to manufacture an appropriate clay pot, and the other that
consists of those attributes imparted to the raw materials by
environmental processes beyond human control. Either of these domains
are valuable areas for archaeological investigation, but are not equal.

     Differences in the decorative color schemes represent decisions
by the potter as to which of the available resources to use. Similarly,
differences in the use of sand, micaceous sand, or crushed rock as
temper may indicate conscious choices made by the potter. But the
specific mineralogical or chemical composition of the tempers, clays, or
pigments that allows us to trace the procurement or production areas of
the raw materials are accidents of nature. I contend that the potters
were consciously aware of concepts akin to such categories as "red
paint," "black paint," "sand temper," or "crushed rock temper," but were
not aware of the special mineralogical or chemical patterns in each of
these categories, whereby we are able to identify the various locales
where sand was procured. Thus Wallace's (1986c: 21) implication that
color scheme variation is equivalent to variation in the chemical and
mineralogical composition of tempers is false. From the perspective
presented here they fall into different domains. Typological schemes
can be constructed based on elements contained within either domain
specifically or on elements in both domains. Which attributes are most
suitable for developing the typological units depends on the specific
research questions and objectives of a particular study. Whether or not

variations in temper should be used to assign type status depends on the typological stance proposed.

In the early studies of northern Arizona pottery types, differences in temper were key attributes used to define new pottery types because tempers were regionally specific and identifiably distinct and could be used to identify the production source for specific pieces of pottery. Thus, trade and regional interaction could be inferred (Colton and Hargrave 1937). Traditionally, Hohokam pottery types have not been distinguished on the basis of temper variation, but recently Heidke (1988) has indicated that it may be possible to identify intraregional stylistic variation by identifying the production source for pottery through temper analysis. The patterns in the mineralogical composition of the temper provide a means of discerning intraregional variation in the expressed pottery knowledge.

I am not concerned here with detailed chemical, physical, or mineralogical analyses of the clays, tempers, or paints nor with the variation within each of these variables; I am concerned with documenting the knowledge Tucson Basin potters had at particular intervals of time about how to manufacture culturally acceptable ceramic vessels. Pottery knowledge is comprised of ideas that were organized into a structured system. No single pot represents the expression of all ideas, but rather each pot represents an expression of a highly specific, selected set of ideas. The similarities between one pot and another, which lead to an analytical grouping of these vessels as representatives of a single classificatory category, argue that there are archaeologically discernable patterns in how the individual pottery ideas were selected and organized in the individual potter's mind and in the collective potters' mind. My concern is to use the available archaeological data to reconstruct the ancient pottery ideas and the underlying structure of how these ideas were organized as determined from the patterns in the distribution of these ideas. I have restricted my scope to the Tucson Basin and will not attempt to follow up on Heidke's (1988) work to identify intraregional differences in the expressed pottery knowledge.

The character of the pottery tradition during each chronologically recognizable period of time is illustrated using inverted tree diagrams. Theoretically, the bottom nodes of these diagrams could be individual pots, if each pot had unique characteristics. However, I am concerned here with documenting the range of various decorative color schemes and thus the bottom nodes represent groups of pottery that share specific attributes of design style, paint color, and surface color. The top node in each diagram represents the total of all pottery knowledge expressed during each chronological period. Each lower node represents a point where particular aspects of this knowledge were partitioned. In the discussions that follow, the nodes are named according to convenience. Because the number of nodes and levels of nodes differ from one time period to the next, due to the increasing complexity in the decorative tradition, it is not possible to assign the equivalent names to nodes from one chronological period to the next. The only exception is the application of the terms "tradition" and "ware."

Tradition is used to embody all pottery knowledge that is expressed during the particular chronological period. This body of knowledge seems to have been divided into as many as three groups that are typically referred to as wares: decorated, plain, and red-slipped. I also identify a fourth ware during the Sedentary and Classic period that I refer to as painted red ware. The following discussions focus specifically on the decorated wares and painted red wares; discussion of the plain and red wares is interjected when relevant. For each of the chronological periods considered I assume that all decorated pottery exhibits a more or less homogenous body of ideas about design style, form, and technology (with exception to those aspects which are manipulated to produce alternative decorative color schemes), so that the concept of "early Rincon decorated," for example, will indicate a host of decorative, formal, and technological ideas that are different from similar ideas represented by the concepts of "Colonial decorated" or "middle Rincon decorated". For a full discussion of changes in the design style, vessel forms, and technology that occur over time the reader is referred to Deaver (1984), Wallace (1985a, 1986b, 1986c); Doelle and Wallace 1986), and Whittlesey (1987a, 1988).

Pre-Colonial Period Tucson Basin Pottery Tradition

Very little is known about Tucson Basin pottery from the time preceding the Colonial period. Work has been restricted to a few sites scattered across the basin that represent a period of cultural development in the Tucson Basin broadly coeval with the Pioneer period Hohokam cultural development in the Gila Basin. Although the pre-Colonial period cultural developments in the Tucson Basin are traditionally referred to by the phase names associated with the Gila Basin cultural development (Kelly 1978), it may not be entirely appropriate to apply the phase concepts of Vahki, Estrella, Sweetwater, and Snaketown to the coeval Tucson Basin cultural developments or even the concept of Pioneer period. The ceramic content of the pre-Colonial period contexts in the Tucson Basin are generically similar to the Gila Basin Pioneer period but exhibit notable dissimilarities, so using the ceramics as a means of cross-dating the early Tucson Basin cultural developments with the Gila Basin Hohokam sequence is problematical. Also, the ongoing debate over the absolute antiquity of the Gila Basin Pioneer period phenomena makes it difficult to equate the early Tucson Basin cultural developments with the contemporaneous phases in the Gila Basin using absolute chronometric methods. Despite these difficulties and the scant information available from the pre-Colonial period cultural developments in the Tucson Basin, there is enough information to speculate on the character of the Tucson Basin pottery tradition during this broad time range and thus set the stage for developments that occur later in the chronological sequence.

64

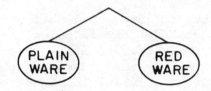

Figure 4.2. Conceptual model of structure of early Pre-Colonial period Tucson Basin pottery tradition.

The earliest evidence of pottery in the Tucson Basin comes from the site of El Arbolito, AZ EE:1:153 (ASM), in the Corona de Tucson area (Huckell 1987). Radiocarbon dates from this site have lead Huckell (1987: 121) to conclude that the age of this site predates A.D. 600, possibly even A.D. 450. The ceramic collection is particularly interesting because of the implications it has toward the possible cultural identity of the earliest ceramic-producing inhabitants in the Tucson Basin. First, only plain and red-slipped pottery were recovered (Fig. 4.2); there is no evidence for decorated pottery contemporary with the earliest component at this site. In this respect the pottery tradition represented at El Arbolito shows a strong affinity to early pottery traditions of the Southwest, and is similar to the early stages of both the Gila Basin Hohokam tradition and the early Mogollon tradition. The early Gila Basin (Vahki phase) pottery tradition is characterized by crushed-micaceous schist temper which imparted a micaceous sheen to both the plain and red-slipped pottery (Haury 1976). The pottery from El Arbolito also showed some mica but this was apparently a component of the stream sand selected for temper and was not characterized by a micaceous sheen (Huckell 1987, Table 5.3). Thus there is only a generic similarity with the early Gila Basin tradition.

My opinion is that the difference in the tempering agents indicates that the early Tucson Basin potters' knowledge as to how to produce suitable clay pots was different from the knowledge held by the contemporary Gila Basin potters. The difference between selecting stream sand for temper or crushing micaceous rock for temper may be a culturally meaningful attribute because this represents a difference in technique (Colton and Hargrave 1937: 2). This difference in technique may indicate that the pottery traditions of the Gila Basin and Tucson Basin were distinct, or at least distinguishable, at that time. One could argue that micaceous rocks were not available for the potters and thus the difference reflects locally available resources; however, during the Colonial period a large proportion of the Tucson Basin plain and decorated pottery was tempered with crushed micaceous rock even in areas where it was not locally available (Deaver 1984, 1988, 1989a, 1989b; Heidke 1988: 396). It would thus seem that the potters at El

Arbolito were not constrained to use crushed micaceous rock as temper as were the potters in the Gila Basin.

Technologically, then, the El Arbolito pottery bears a stronger similarity with the Mogollon tradition. There is other evidence that indicates a similar conclusion. The sherds from El Arbolito indicate a restricted array of vessel forms dominated by jars, particularly incurved forms (seed jars) (Huckell 1987: 148). Huckell (1987: 149) notes that this form is rare among the documented pottery collections from Hohokam sites but is more common at early Mogollon sites. This seems to imply a strong Mogollon affiliation. Regardless of the cultural label we attach to this early pottery tradition, the pottery collection from El Arbolito indicates that the early Tucson Basin pottery tradition was characterized by sand-tempered plain wares and red wares (see also Deaver 1989b).

Information from the Dairy Site, AZ AA:12:285 (ASM), supports the inference that the earliest local pottery tradition is distinct from the earliest Gila Basin Hohokam tradition. The Dairy Site contains a cultural sequence from the earlier Colonial period to an early component represented ceramically by plain wares and red wares (P. Fish and others 1987; Beckwith 1984). The inference that the plain ware/red ware component is early is probably based on analogy to the early Hohokam and early Mogollon pottery traditions. The only case of stratigraphic superpositioning at the site supports the inference that the plain ware-red ware component is early; a Snaketown phase roasting pit overlies a house associated with the plain ware-red ware component (P. Fish and others 1987). Several unpublished radiocarbon dates from the early component, which are on file with the Archaeology Division, Arizona State Museum, suggest that this component may be contemporary with or only slightly later than El Arbolito. The oldest type of decorated pottery recovered from the Dairy Site is Estrella Red-on-gray, which is represented by several sherds from a single, partially reconstructible vessel. There is also a significant amount of Sweetwater Red-on-gray representing multiple vessels (Beckwith 1984). This information indicates that the prehistoric occupation at the Dairy site was at least as early as the Sweetwater phase in the Gila Basin, possibly even the Estrella phase.

The Dairy Site collection presents an interesting situation. The Estrella and Sweetwater red-on-gray pottery is tempered with crushed micaceous rock, in contrast to the associated plain and red-slipped pottery which are predominantly sand-tempered, as are the plain and red-slipped wares associated with the early component. I have suggested that these decorated pottery types are intrusive to this site from the Gila Basin and not part of the local pottery tradition (Deaver 1989b). Thus the local pottery tradition represented at the Dairy Site would be similar to that at El Arbolito. The array of vessel forms is different however (Beckwith 1984), although this difference may be less real than it seems. The discussion of vessel shapes seems to include pottery from all chronological components, thus the collection of plain ware rims spans more recent time periods than does the collection of plain ware rims at El Arbolito. Although the absolute or relative frequency of incurved jars are not reported for the Dairy Site, this class of vessels does occur (Beckwith 1984).

The speculation that the early Tucson Basin pottery tradition is characterized by sand-tempered plain wares and red wares leads to the question as to what happened between this early time period and the later Colonial period. By the Colonial period red wares were no longer made and decorated pottery was locally produced. Also, a large proportion of decorated and plain pottery were manufactured using crushed-micaceous-rock-tempered clays (Deaver 1984, 1988, 1989a). In short, there is a strong Gila Basin influence on the local pottery tradition. The evidence from El Arbolito and the Dairy Site would suggest that the changes in the local pottery tradition that gave rise to the Colonial period pattern emerged during the stage immediately preceding the Colonial period, equivalent to the Snaketown phase in the Gila Basin.

Another pre-Colonial period site recently excavated in the Avra valley dates from this time period and provides provocative evidence for changes in the Tucson Basin pottery tradition. The Hawk's Nest Site, AZ AA:12:484 (ASM), appears date to primarily to the Snaketown phase, with a short term early Colonial reoccupation (Ravesloot and others 1989). The dominant decorated pottery is Snaketown Red-on-buff/brown. This pottery appears to be comprised of three groups based on variation in the temper and clay (Deaver 1989b). One group contains sherds that exhibit a sand-tempered, brown ware clay. A second group consists of sherds with a buff ware clay tempered with crushed micaceous rock (schist). The final group contains sherds that appear to have a brown ware clay tempered with crushed micaceous rock. The pottery collections from El Arbolito and the Dairy Site indicate that the the sand-tempered Snaketown pottery at Hawk's Nest is locally produced whereas the schist-tempered pottery is imported. However, the plain pottery is about equally split between sand and crushed-micaceous-rock temper (Deaver 1989b).

Either half of the plain pottery was imported from the Gila Basin as well or local production of crushed-micaceous-rock tempered plain pottery had begun. It may be that the group of Snaketown sherds exhibiting a brown ware clay with crushed micaceous rock temper are also locally made. Thus the late Pioneer Tucson Basin pottery tradition is characterized by three wares: plain, decorated, and red (Fig. 4.3). As well as the addition of a decorated ware to the extant plain and red ware tradition, the basic pottery technology is beginning to change with an increasing proportion of locally produced pottery made with crushed-micaceous-rock-tempered clay. I perceive these features as evidence of an increasing overprinting of the Gila Basin pottery tradition on the indigenous Tucson Basin tradition. There is a greater proportion of bowls at Hawk's Nest than at El Arbolito. The dominant jar is a flaring-necked form; only a single sherd from an incurved jar was found

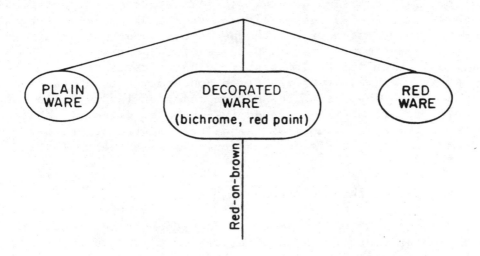

Figure 4.3. Conceptual model of structure of late Pre-Colonial period Tucson Basin pottery tradition.

(Deaver 1989b). It is tempting to associate the change in the array of vessel forms with the increasing Gila Basin influences; this is a comparison that should be pursued in future research.

The early Tucson Basin pottery tradition appears to be characterized by sand-tempered plain ware and red ware pottery that is independent of the Gila Basin. This time period is represented by the site of El Arbolito and the early plain ware-red ware component at the Dairy Site. This distinction is maintained until sometime toward the latter part of the Gila Basin Hohokam Pioneer period. During the middle of the Pioneer period Gila Basin decorated pottery begins to appear in the Tucson Basin as trade ware; the local tradition is still characterized by sand-tempered plain wares and red wares. This situation is represented by the Estrella and Sweetwater components at the Dairy Site. By the Snaketown phase, however, the Gila Basin Hohokam influence has increased so that Tucson Basin Potters were absorbing ideas from the Gila Basin. This is suggested primarily by the introduction of a locally produced decorated ware, Snaketown Red-on-brown, which has a distinct Gila Basin design style and was made with both sand and crushed-micaceous-rock-tempered clays. This is the earliest evidence of local decorated pottery (Fig. 4.3). The decline and eventual cessation of the red ware production may be another trend influenced by the Gila Basin. The overprinting of the local tradition is virtually complete by the early Colonial period, when the Tucson Basin pottery tradition is no more than a regional expression of the Gila Basin Hohokam tradition (Masse 1982; Deaver 1984: 416-419).

These changes described for the Tucson Basin pottery tradition are based on admittedly weak data, but are intriguing in the connotations that they have for the early growth and development of prehistoric Tucson Basin culture. This model of ceramic development supports Kelly's (1978) observations that Tucson Basin pottery has strong underlying affinities with the Mogollon pottery tradition even though the demonstrable characteristics of the current pottery collections, which are predominantly Colonial period and later, indicate strong affinities with the Gila Basin Hohokam. This scenario also harkens back to DiPeso's (1956) O'Otam model of Tucson Basin cultural development, where a Gila Basin-derived Hohokam cultural pattern was imprinted over an indigenous O'Otam cultural pattern. As new data are unearthed from early sites these speculations can be evaluated further.

Colonial Period Pottery Tradition

Although the early end of the development is speculative, there is little question that the Colonial period tradition in the Tucson Basin is strongly influenced by the Gila Basin Hohokam tradition. I have not presented a detailed picture of all the elaborations in the Tucson Basin pottery tradition that may have occurred prior to the Colonial period. It is sufficient to say that the changes and elaborations in the pottery tradition prior to the Colonial period occurred in the basic technological knowledge of how to make pottery, in the array of suitable vessel forms, and in the emergence of a Tucson Basin decorated tradition that had strong affinities with the Gila Basin. This latter feature is particularly interesting because the Tucson Basin decorated tradition is only distinguishable from the Gila Basin tradition in aspects of technology (surface polishing and use of brown-firing clay) and a more restricted use of the design style and vessel form than the Gila Basin "parent" tradition (Kelly 1978).

Yet in the basic technology there is a dual use of both sand and crushed-micaceous rock as the dominant tempering materials in both the plain and decorated pottery. This might suggest that the Gila Basin pottery ideas were fully accepted where there were no conflicting indigenous Tucson Basin ideas to replace or modify them (design style), but only partially accepted where there were indigenous ideas already in place (the basic notion of how to temper the clay). There also seem to be differences in degree as to the completeness with which these traits are accepted across the Tucson Basin. At ANAMAX about 53 percent of the plain ware attributed to the Rillito phase was tempered with a crushed micaceous rock (Deaver 1984, Fig. 4.69), whereas about 88 percent of the contemporary decorated pottery was tempered with crushed micaceous rock (Deaver 1984, Fig. 4.67). In the Avra Valley during the Rillito phase however, there is a much greater proportion of crushed-micaceous-rock-tempered plain ware. A visual inspection of the tempering materials in rim sherds from the sites of Fastimes (AZ AA:12:384 [ASM]), and Water World (AZ AA:16:94 [ASM]) indicates that over 90 percent of the plain ware rims exhibited crushed-micaceous-rock temper. The proportion of decorated pottery with crushed-micaceous-rock temper from these sites approximates that observed at ANAMAX. Thus, by the Colonial period

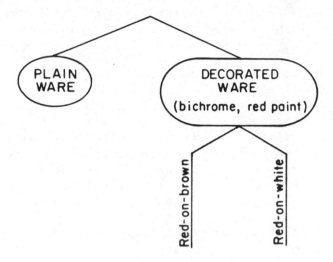

Figure 4.4. Conceptual model of structure of Colonial period Tucson Basin pottery tradition.

there seems to be a pronounced Gila Basin overlay on the Tucson Basin pottery tradition.

Variations in the decorative color schemes begin to appear in the early Colonial period (Fig. 4.4). The Colonial period notions of what constitutes an appropriate decorated vessel in terms of design style and form were expressed in either a red-on-brown or red-on-white color scheme. The use of a whitish-colored slip or wash has been documented for both Cañada del Oro Red-on-brown (Deaver 1984: 286, 292) and Rillito Red-on-brown (Deaver 1984: 298; Doelle and Wallace 1986: 17; Whittlesey 1986, Table 6.15; Beckwith 1987: 223). The theoretical effect is to produce a red-on-white design scheme, but in actuality the effect was merely to lighten the background field color to a cream or tan color. The use of a white slip on Tucson Basin pottery was first noted by Greenleaf (1975: 50) for Rincon phase pottery; he inferred that this was an attempt by the local potters to create the effect of the Gila Basin pottery. The use of a white slip to lighten the background color is a hallmark trait that appears during the Snaketown phase in the Gila Basin (Haury 1976: 214) and may be one other aspect of the Gila Basin pottery tradition introduced into the Tucson Basin tradition. The use of a white slip persists throughout the duration of the Tucson Basin pottery tradition even though in later periods it seems that it is no longer used to emulate the Gila Basin pottery tradition.

Frick (1954: 53) has indicated that some Rillito Red-on-brown pottery may have been smudged. Blackening of the background field color is common on Rillito Red-on-brown sherds, but is apparently accidental (Wallace 1985a: 97). I have seen sherds that appear to have been intentionally smudged, but have not seen any whole or partially restored vessels that exhibit all-over smudging. Until the intent of smudging

can be demonstrated using whole vessels I prefer to explain blackened
sherds as the result of imperfect firing controls.

Early Sedentary Period Pottery Tradition

The developments in the Tucson Basin pottery tradition that
occurred during the Sedentary period are traced with respect to
Wallace's (1986c) tripartite chronological subdivision of Rincon Red-on-
brown. I do not agree that the Sedentary period is represented by a
single phase of development, therefore, I will use the terms Early
Sedentary, Middle Sedentary, and Late Sedentary rather than Early
Rincon, Middle Rincon, or Late Rincon. The conceptual configuration of
the Early Sedentary period pottery tradition (Fig. 4.5) resembles the
Colonial period tradition (Fig. 4.4) apart from changes in design style
and vessel form that are used to temporally identify this time period.

Three phenomena occur during the Early Sedentary that
distinguish the pottery tradition from the earlier Colonial tradition.
Two of these phenomena do not affect the decorative color scheme and
thus are not shown in Figure 4.5. The first phenomenon is that there is
a reversal of the trend begun in the late Pioneer period in the dominant
tempering material. Stream-rolled sand becomes increasingly dominant at
the expense of the use of crushed micaceous rock (Deaver 1984; Heidke
1988). This seems to be a reversion back to the traditional
technological ideas seen in the El Arbolito and Dairy Site ceramic
collections. The second phenomenon, closely associated with the first,
is a curious shift in the treatment of the vessel lip. Prior to the
Early Sedentary period, the lips of bowls were typically not decorated
and jars were decorated as often as not, but beginning in the Early
Sedentary period both bowl and jar lips become more commonly painted so
that by the middle of the Sedentary period unpainted lips are unusual
(Deaver 1984: 386). These two phenomena represent changes in the basic
technological and decorative knowledge, which I assume to be constant
for all color scheme variants.

The third phenomenon is an addition to the color scheme
possibilities. The basic decorative knowledge during the Early
Sedentary period was expressed in red-on-brown, red-on-white, or red-on-
black color schemes (Fig. 4.5). The first two of these represent
continuations of the variations first expressed in the Colonial period,
but the red-on-black color scheme is unprecedented. This color scheme
also represents the first observable divergence between the Gila and
Tucson Basin pottery traditions; there is no Gila Basin analogue for
smudged, decorated pottery. Kelly (1978: 62) suggested that smudging is
one of the Mogollon affinities in Tucson Basin pottery, but there is a
fundamental difference between Mogollon smudged wares and the Tucson
Basin smudged pottery. In the Mogollon area, with only rare exception,
smudging is not applied to painted surfaces (Deaver 1984: 317).
Smudging may be no more than a local innovation that derived from the
poor firing control exhibited in Early Sedentary pottery (Deaver 1984:
317). Even if it is a trait borrowed from the Mogollon, it is a newly

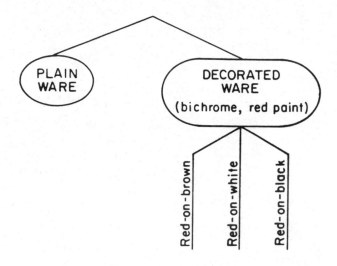

Figure 4.5. Conceptual model of structure of Early Sedentary period Tucson Basin pottery tradition.

borrowed characteristic that is incorporated into the local tradition in a unique fashion and does not indicate a fundamental Mogollon affinity for Tucson Basin pottery tradition.

Originally, Doyel (1977: 36-37) suggested that Rio Rico Polychrome may date as early as A.D. 850. This would place the first appearance of this type in the latter part of the Rillito phase. I have argued that this type is probably associated with the middle of the Rincon phase after A.D. 1000 (Deaver 1984: 326-327) based on its absence at two large late Colonial and early Sedentary period sites in the Rosemont Mountains. More recently, Doyel (1988: 355) has reevaluated the chronological associations of this type and proposes dates of A.D. 950 to 1100. I still contend that the use of panels, rectilinear scrolls, and opposed triangular-flagged lines (Doyel 1988, Fig. 21.3) suggest a middle or late Rincon phase association for this type. Clearly more information on this type is needed. If Doyel (1988) is correct on the age, Rio Rico Polychrome could be associated with the Early Sedentary period. This would necessarily expand our conceptualization of the Early Sedentary pottery tradition (Fig. 4.6), with Rio Rico Polychrome being seen as the source for the black pigment that is used in a bichromatic color scheme in the Middle Sedentary Period.

Middle Sedentary Period Pottery Tradition

At about A.D. 1000 there is a veritable explosion of new ideas and experimentation in the Tucson Basin pottery tradition (Fig. 4.7). Red ware pottery again becomes part of the tradition; there is no

72

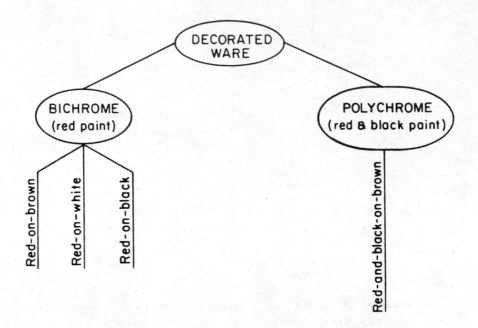

Figure 4.6. Conceptual model of structure of Early Sedentary period Tucson Basin pottery tradition if Rio Rico Polychrome dates to this time period.

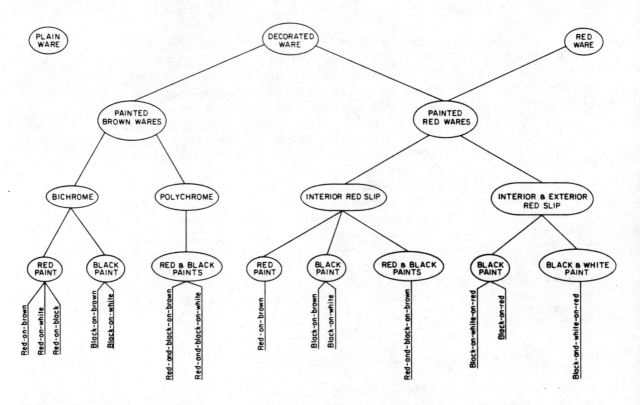

Figure 4.7. Conceptual model of structure of Middle Sedentary period Tucson Basin pottery tradition.

conclusive evidence for local red ware production in the Tucson Basin since the late Pioneer period. It is the addition of the red ware ideas as well as the use of a black paint that are key features in the increased variation in the pottery tradition. Although the red ware and black paint ideas may be the elements used to create the multiple color schemes, the fact that this phenomenon occurs at all argues that there are changes in the larger cultural tradition that allow this variability to be expressed. This expansion is correlated with a radical shift in the design style. If one wishes to follow DiPeso's (1956) O'Otam reassertion model, these color schemes might be seen as evidence of the Tucson Basin asserting a cultural identity independent of the Gila Basin; however, the developments in the design style, seen in the preference for panelled and plaited rectilinear decoration parallel developments in the Gila Basin as well.

Still, the various color schemes of the Middle Sedentary Tucson Basin pottery tradition are unparalleled in the Gila Basin pottery tradition. It is curious that this increase in variability occurs during a time period when there is a rapid decrease in the importation of Gila Basin buff wares into the Tucson Basin (Wallace 1985a: 131, 1986a: 102, 1986c: 176; Doelle and Wallace 1986: 37; Wallace and Holmlund 1984), which is offset by an apparent increase in local production of pottery (Heidke 1988: 394). The appearance of red-slipped pottery in the ceramic tradition indicates that the Middle Sedentary is not solely a time of reversion back to ancestral ideas about pottery manufacture, but a period where there is an influx of new ideas.

I have divided the Middle Sedentary Period decorated pottery into two groups, which are labeled in Figure 4.7 as "painted brown" and "painted red" ware. These labels are not the most desirable but convey the meaning that I intend. The painted red ware ceramics are a group of pottery that exhibit a merging of both painted and red ware ideas. The most obvious distinction between the painted red ware group and the painted brown ware group is that the former all characteristically have red-slipped surfaces (either on which the decoration is applied or on the opposite surface) and the latter lack the use of red-slip. The painted brown wares are the continuation of the preceeding decorated pottery tradition with the addition of the use of a black paint in polychrome and bichrome color schemes.

Before explaining the structure of the "painted red ware" grouping, it will be helpful to relate the "painted red ware" nodes in Figure 4.7 with traditional type names. The original description of Rincon Polychrome is equivalent to the node labeled "interior and exterior red slip" (Greenleaf 1975: 67-73). Greenleaf (1975: 67-73) noted both black-on-white-on-red and the black-and-white-on-red varieties of Rincon Polychrome. More recently Wallace (1985a: 128, 1986a, Table 6.17, 1986c: 87), Doelle and Wallace (1986: 34), and others (Ervin 1982: 41; Huntington 1982: 114) have included those expressions that I have grouped under the node "interior red slip" as variants of Rincon Polychrome. Thus in Wallace's scheme, Rincon Polychrome would be equivalent to my node "painted red ware". In fact it is from Wallace's work (1985a: 128) that I have adopted the term "painted red ware".

It is based on the conceptual structure of the diagram in Figure 4.7 that I chose to propose the type Sahuarita Polychrome (Deaver 1984: 328-329), reserving the label Rincon Polychrome for the interior and exterior red slip node that corresponds to Greenleaf's (1975: 67-73) original type description. There are attributes associated with the "interior red slip" node that are distinct from the "interior and exterior red slip" node. Doelle and Wallace (1986: 35) also included a piece of pottery that is decorated in a red-and-black-painted design on a white-slipped surface as a variant of Rincon Polychrome. This sherd, however, lacks a red slip and thus I have included it under the node "painted brown ware".

Painted Red-Slipped Ware. Red-slipped pottery reflects a new set of ideas introduced into the Tucson Basin pottery tradition. The ideas were more than just the concept of applying a red slip to a vessel surface, however, there are also associated vessel forms that are unique (Wallace 1985a, 1986b, 1986c). The painted red ware group is particularly intriguing because it indicates a merging of the red ware concepts and Decorated Ware concepts. Painted red-slipped wares are distinct from painted brown wares in that the painted red-slipped wares exhibit a host of red ware ideas that are not expressed among the painted brown wares. There is thus an intimate link between the red wares and the painted red-slipped wares (Wallace 1986a: 167-176, 1986c: 96-98) and the exchange of ideas does not seem to "leak" across to the painted brown wares.

The vessel forms attributable to the introduced red ware ideas seem to covary with the use of a red slip. Thus, Rincon Polychrome, as the term is applied by Wallace (1986b, 1986c), exhibits these red ware forms in a painted pottery expression. However, these red ware forms are not documented for the painted brown wares. The painted red-slipped ware grouping differs from the painted brown ware grouping in the overall array of forms as well. Wallace (1986c: 82) notes that Rincon Polychrome jar forms are rare and there is a preference for bowl forms.

The division between painted brown wares and painted red-slipped wares seems to represent more than just a heuristic division of the pottery, and is one that is based on a covariation of traits. It would seem that Tucson Basin potters associated a particular set of forms with red slipping and that when a red slip was not used, it was not appropriate to use the Red Ware vessel forms. Also, the use of a red slip seems to have carried with it certain prescriptions as to which of the potentially available decorated ware forms could be used.

There are other attributes that distinguish the painted red-slipped ware group from the painted brown ware. Associated with the painted red ware group is the use of a white paint. Although a white slip occurs among the painted brown wares and painted red wares, no examples of the use of a white paint are known that would fall in the painted brown ware group. Also, one particular contrast between the painted red-slipped wares and the painted brown wares is that, in the former, although the design ideas are drawn from the same body of knowledge as those expressed among the painted brown ware group, they are not expressed in the same way (Wallace 1986c: 84-85). This is seen particularly in the examples of this group defined as Rincon Polychrome by Greenleaf (1975). Rather it seems that Rincon Polychrome exhibits bits of the Rincon decorated style but not the entire configuration of the style as is typically expressed in the bichrome group of the painted brown wares.

The pottery grouped as painted red-slipped ware can be further divided into interior red slip and interior and exterior red slip (see Fig. 4.7). The salient difference between these two groups is that the painted design and the red slip are are applied to opposite surfaces in the interior red slip group (Deaver 1984: 328-329; Deaver and Tagg 1984: 20; Wallace 1986c: 87). The interior red slip group is represented by sherds only, and Wallace's (1986c: 87) caution that a red slip might be applied somewhere on the decorated surface should be heeded, especially with regard to the black-on-white color scheme. Still, this group seems distinct at this level from interior and exterior red slip. Two color scheme expressions among the interior red slip group, the red-on-brown and red-and-black-on-brown exhibit the use of a red paint. This idea is not expressed on any examples that have both an interior and exterior red slip. Thus the larger grouping, painted red-slipped wares, must contain the attributes of red, black, and white paint. The subgroup interior red slip exhibits only the use of the red and black paints whereas the interior and exterior red slip group exhibits only the use of the black and white paints. It may be the use of the red paint that prescribes against the use of the red slip on the surface that was to have been decorated. But this alone cannot account for the use of a black paint on an unslipped surface.

It was noted previously that the group of painted red-slipped wares exhibited a peculiar application of the available decorated ware ideas. This assessment is based on pottery associated with the interior and exterior red slip group. Pottery associated with the interior red slip group seems to exhibit a decorative style more typical of bichrome pottery. Yet, because of the nature of the examples this observation cannot be further substantiated.

Painted Brown Wares. The differences between this group of decorated wares and painted red-slipped wares is explicated above. The two key attributes are an absence of a red slip and the absence of the use of a white paint. I divide this group into two subgroups which are labeled as bichrome and polychrome in Figure 4.7. Note that these labels are somewhat unsatisfactory because the pottery previously discussed as painted red-slipped wares are all technically polychromatic. The labels bichrome and polychrome as used here are simple conventions for characterizing the differences between the various painted brown ware expressions.

The node labeled polychrome is for all intents and purposes the traditional type Rio Rico Polychrome (Doyel 1977: 36-41, 1988). This node represents the knowledge of applying a red and black paint together in a single design. The design style is still clearly derived from the ideas available in decorated ware, but undoubtedly modifications to the typical bichrome style are necessitated by the use of two contrasting paints in a balanced design scheme. I have included in this grouping a single sherd described by Doelle and Wallace (1986: 34) that exhibits a red and black design on a white slipped background, which they classified as a Rincon Polychrome variant. This sherd lacks any evidence of a red slip and thus does not fit Wallace's definition of Rincon Polychrome (Wallace 1986a: 167, 1986c: 78). To consider this single sherd as a variant of Rincon Polychrome would destroy the clear distinction between Rio Rico Polychrome and Rincon Polychrome; Rio Rico Polychrome could then be considered as no more than this variant without the white slip. Doelle and Wallace (1986: 34) note that the use of the red and black paints differs from Rio Rico Polychrome in that the two paints are not used in a balanced design. Nonetheless, this does not automatically exclude it from the type Rio Rico Polychrome, and require that it be classified as Rincon Polychrome. In this example Doelle and Wallace (1986: 34) appear to be using the category of Rincon Polychrome as a catch-all for any pottery that cannot otherwise be distinguished as a red-on-brown or Rio Rico Polychrome. I prefer to classify this sherd as "Rio Rico, white-slipped variety," and additionally note the variation in the use of the red and black paints.

The second group of painted brown wares is bichrome pottery. The knowledge represented by this node can be expressed in either red- or black-painted designs. Traditionally, the type Rincon Red-on-brown would be associated with the node I have labeled as red paint, however, Wallace (1986c: 21) associates this type name with the bichrome node. Above I have stated that I find Wallace's use of the term red-on-brown to include black-painted pottery illogical; Figure 4.7 illustrates why: red paint and black paint are equal nodes. Red paint is not superior hierarchically to the black paint, though I concur that in terms of prehistoric ceramic production the red-painted pottery was numerically and developmentally the dominant decorated pottery produced.

Associated with the red-paint node are three possible color scheme expressions which result from manipulation of the color of the vessel surface. The three possible surface treatments are: (1) unslipped, unsmudged, (2) white slipped, unsmudged, and (3) unslipped, smudged. These surface treatments result in red-on-brown, red-on-white, and red-on-black color schemes respectively. Associated with the black-paint node are only two possible color scheme expressions. The black-paint pottery is associated with either and unslipped, unsmudged surface or a white-slipped, unsmudged surface, resulting in a black-on-brown and black-on-white color schemes. The attributes "+ black paint" and "+ smudge" are mutually exclusive. The red-paint and black-paint pottery share a uniform design style, array of forms, and construction technology, but they differ in two aspects. The first, as mentioned above, is that black-paint pottery is not smudged. The second is that the black-paint pottery is white-slipped more often than the red-paint pottery (Deaver 1984: 324; Wallace 1986c: 37). Thus the red-paint and black-paint pottery are very similar, but are not identical.

Late Sedentary Period Pottery Tradition

The most notable differences between the Late Sedentary pottery and the pottery of the Middle Sedentary period are the changes in the design style and vessel forms. During the Late Sedentary period there appears to be an eventual cessation in the production of red wares and the closely related painted red wares (Wallace 1986a: 171, 1986c: 90). Certainly by the Classic period red wares were no longer locally produced. Thus the configuration of the Late Sedentary pottery tradition appears similar to the Middle Sedentary period (Fig. 4.7), with a gradual proportional decrease in the quantity of red wares and painted red wares.

Early Classic Period Pottery Tradition

The Early Classic period pottery tradition, for the most part, indicates a continuation of the color schemes introduced in the Middle Sedentary period, but with a nearly complete cessation of locally produced red wares (Fig. 4.8). The only red ware pottery associated with the Classic period was imported from the Papaguería, from the San Carlos area, and probably from the Gila Basin. Painted red wares, however, still appear to be part of the pottery tradition. This group of pottery is represented by two sherds recovered during the excavations at the San Xavier Bridge Site (AZ BB:13:14 [ASM]) (Beckwith 1987: 209-210). One sherd exhibits an Early Classic red-on-brown design on the exterior of a bowl with an interior red slip (Beckwith 1987: 209). This sherd is similar to the red-on-brown expression of the Middle Sedentary period interior red slip node of the painted red wares. The other sherd from the San Xavier Bridge Site is decorated with black and white painted designs over a red slip (Beckwith 1987: 209). In color scheme this sherd is similar to Tucson Polychrome but was identified as a Tanque Verde Polychrome Variant (Beckwith 1987: 209). This sherd is also similar to the black and white paints node under the painted red wares of the Middle Sedentary period (Fig. 4.7). These two sherds bear closer similarities with analogous Middle Sedentary color scheme. Because red wares are no longer locally produced, the painted red wares seem anomalous. They may be no more than isolated continuations of the similar pottery expressions in the Middle and Late Sedentary period, but it is interesting that in the Papaguería locally produced red wares (Sells Red) and locally produced painted red wares (Sells White-on-Red and Sells Polychrome) were still produced coeval with the Early Classic period pottery of the Tucson Basin.

78

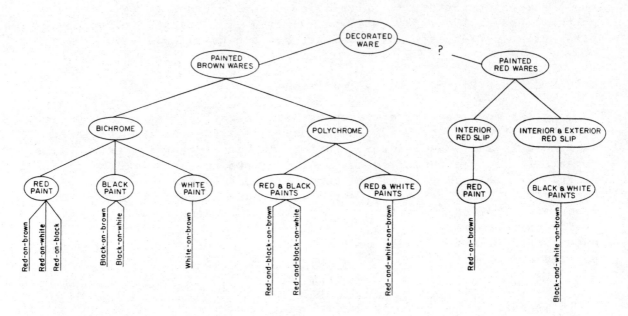

Figure 4.8.   Conceptual model of structure of Early Classic period
Tucson Basin pottery tradition.

There are some notable changes that occur in the painted brown
wares. This group of pottery also shows strong similarities with the
painted brown ware group of the Middle and Late Sedentary period, but
white paint is added to the inventory of possible paint colors. Thus
one additional bichrome expression, White-on-brown, and one additional
Polychrome expression, Red and White-on-brown, result. During the
Middle and Late Sedentary period the use of a white paint is restricted
to the painted red wares. The use of a white paint among the painted
brown wares apparently represents a shift in the application of this
idea.

Another important change in the painted brown wares is not
represented in Figure 4.8. The change is a shift in the location of the
primary design field on bowls from the interior to the exterior, and the
adoption of a secondary design field on the bowl interior. Because of
this, each Classic period bowl could be decorated in multiple color
schemes. In fact, this seems to become a major source of variability.
Tanque Verde Black-on-brown sherds from Los Morteros and Whiptail Ruin
exhibited red-on-brown, red-on-black, or simply black smudged interiors.

There are seven decorative color schemes that could be used for
the exterior design: (1) red-on-brown, (2) red-on-white, (3) black-on-
brown, (4) black-on-white, (5) red and black-on-brown, (6) red and
black-on-white, and (7) red and white-on-brown. Note that a red-on-
black exterior design is not considered possible.

Each of these color schemes could be coupled with any of eleven interior color schemes: (1) red-on-brown, (2) red-on-white, (3) red-on-black, (4) black-on-brown, (5) black-on-white, (6) red-and-black-on-brown, (7) red-and-black-on-white, (8) red-and-white-on-brown, (9) brown, (10) black, and (11) white. Note that I have included brown, black, and white monochromatic color schemes.

Thus there are 77 possible combinations of color schemes that could occur on Classic period bowls. When the same decorative color scheme is used for both designs, or when the interior surface color is the same monochromatic color scheme as the background field color of the exterior design, then the vessel is bichromatic. But when the interior color scheme is different from the exterior decorative color scheme, or when the interior monochromatic color scheme differs from the background field color of the exterior design, then the vessels are technically polychromatic. Given these definitions, it would seem that the majority of Early Classic period bowls are in fact polychromes.

This type of variation may not seem to be of any major consequence, but we must recognize that similar elaboration is not present in the Gila Basin tradition. The closest analogue for this phenomenon of Tanque Verde decorated pottery is San Carlos Red-on-brown in the Mogollon tradition, yet the similar range of variation is not expressed for this type either. Whittlesey (1987a, 1988) has shown that there is a rigid standardization of Tanque Verde design style. This extreme standardization of design style stands in obvious contrast to the variability that exists in the decorative color schemes, and in the contrasting color schemes of bowl interiors and exteriors.

Late Classic Period Pottery Tradition

Little is actually known about locally produced Tucson phase pottery. Much of the work done at sites dating to this time period was completed three or more decades ago. I anticipate that much of the color scheme variation seen in the Early Classic continued into the Late Classic period (Fig. 4.9). One notable change in the local pottery is represented by the painted red ware group. Although a generically similar group of pottery occurred in the Middle and Late Sedentary periods and in the Early Classic period, the pottery represented by painted red wares in the Late Classic period is distinctly different from the earlier analogues. This category of pottery is represented by the Tucson Polychrome series, consisting of Tucson Polychrome (Danson 1957) and Tucson Black-on-red (Franklin 1980). These types clearly represent a different pottery tradition, but there is the possibility that these types were locally produced in the Tucson Basin at the sites where they were found (Danson 1957: 226). A question for further study is whether the Tucson Polychrome pottery series is indeed locally produced and represents an introduction of new ideas that were melded into the local pottery tradition, much as the red-slipped pottery was melded into the Middle Sedentary period tradition.

80

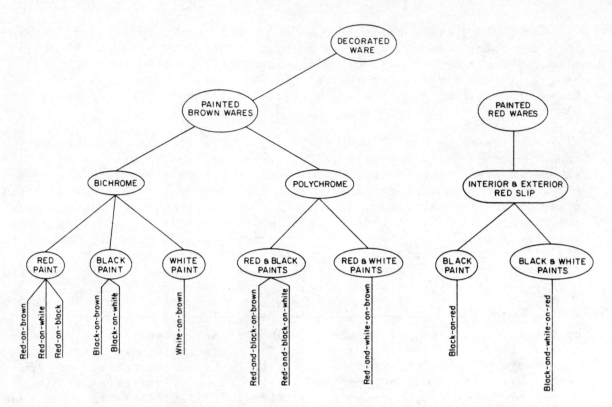

Figure 4.9. Conceptual model of structure of Late Classic period Tucson Basin pottery tradition.

Summary

I have presented a rather lengthy discussion of the variation in the decorative color scheme observed in pottery produced in the Tucson Basin. The argument I have tried to present is that the study of color scheme variation offers significant information concerning the overall cultural development of the Tucson Basin. Probably of greatest importance is the simple observation that the variation in the decorative color schemes produced by the Tucson Basin potters gives the Tucson Basin pottery tradition a unique identity. In sum, the Tucson Basin pottery tradition appears to have been influenced over the course of history by various other pottery traditions. The first external influences seem to emanate from the Gila Basin. Prior to the late Pioneer period the Tucson Basin pottery tradition appears to be distinct from the Gila Basin. Yet, by the late Colonial period the Tucson Basin pottery tradition is little more than a regional expression of the Gila Basin Hohokam pottery tradition. Beginning in the Sedentary period, the Tucson Basin pottery tradition exhibits new features that are unparalleled in the Gila Basin, most notably the application of smudging to a red-painted design to create a red-on-black design field. This color scheme is unparalleled in any other pottery tradition of the Southwest. The divergence from the Gila Basin tradition continues into the Middle Sedentary where there is an influx of new ideas into the pottery tradition represented by Rincon Red, Rincon Black-on-brown, Rio Rico Polychrome, and a suite of polychrome pottery that represents a merger of the local decorated ware knowledge with the knowledge represented by Rincon Red. From this point the variation in the decorative color schemes continues more or less unabated into the Classic period.

I have also presented the argument that our current conceptualizations of the Tucson Basin pottery sequence are not adequate for documenting the range of variation in the pottery, nor for unambiguously illustrating the relationships between the numerous color scheme variants that have been observed. I presented a different typological scheme for documenting the range of color scheme variation and illustrating which particular pottery is more similar or less similar to other pottery. This scheme is basically an attribute approach, expressed in a tree-diagram. Each node in the diagram represents a group of pottery that shares a common set of attributes. I further infer that these nodes represent a group of ideas about pottery manufacture that are distinct from other hierarchically equivalent nodes. This typological scheme can be equated with the established Tucson Basin pottery types, but each established type would represent a different level of the typological scheme proposed here. The type name Rincon Polychrome as used by Wallace (1985a, 1986a, 1986c) represents a hierarchically higher node in the diagram than the type name Rincon Red-on-brown. I do not advocate that this typological scheme is necessarily better than that represented by the established pottery types. Rather, I advocate that a different typological scheme is necessary in order to explore the potential significance of how the Tucson Basin pottery knowledge was structured and how the pottery ideas were expressed. The established types have their place in Tucson Basin archaeological studies, but they are not entirely adequate for pursuing the answers to different types of research questions.

I have also presented here the rationale for designating several new pottery types: Rincon Black-on-brown, Tanque Verde Black-on-brown, Tanque Verde Polychrome, and Saguaro Polychrome. The criteria on which these types are designated are the same as those on which the original Tucson Basin pottery types were designated by Kelly (1978).

Finally, I have not intended this discussion as a resolution. Rather, I have presented my perceptions of the Tucson Basin pottery tradition that has emerged from my work over the past decade. This discussion is intended for contemplation, discussion, debate, and further research.

Chapter 5

FEATURE DESCRIPTIONS

Richard C. Lange

Table 5.1 lists the feature types and assigned time periods for
the 65 entities at Los Morteros that were given individual feature
numbers or, in a few instances, were combined under one feature number.
Locations of features are shown in Figure 5.1. Houses were the most
numerous feature type identified by the testing. A further tabulation
of the location and feature type by feature number is provided in
Appendix D. Temporal assignments for most of the features are
tentative; determinations often had to be made on the basis of only a
few diagnostic sherds in the profile wall, or even more tenuously from
the sherds recovered from the backdirt--a mixture of overburden and fill
from the feature.

A few comments about the feature types and temporal divisions
are necessary to explain Table 5.1. "Cremations" are isolated or
clustered vessels containing burned human remains, while "crematories"
are the location of the burning. "Possible canals" may be natural
drainages or deep fill areas, something that could only be determined by
excavation. This is also true of the "possible houses"; they may be
borrow pits or trash areas rather than houses. The term "hornos" was
restricted to large (at least 1-m in diameter by 1-m deep), plastered
pits presumed to have been used in processing foods. Smaller pits,
sometimes called "roasting pits," are included in the "pits" category.
These are small, generally unlined, and rarely show evidence of burning
or heating.

Under the labels used for temporal placement, "Rillito-Rincon"
includes features that can be dated to either phase. "Preclassic ?"
includes two features that can tentatively be dated to this period.
Similarly, "Tanque Verde ?" indicates a tentative assignment of a
feature to this phase.

Table 5.1

FEATURE TYPES AND CHRONOLOGICAL PLACEMENT

Feature Type	Chronological Placement								
	Rillito-Rincon	Rincon	Preclassic?	Late Rincon-Early Tanque Verde	Tanque Verde-Cortaro	Tanque Verde	Tanque Verde?	No Date Possible	Total
Cremation						6			6
Crematory						3			3
Canal						2	1		3
Possible Canal			1				1		2
Possible Walk-in-Well						1			1
House	5	3	1	2		6	2	12	31
Possible House		1						4	5
Isolated Vessel					1				1
Horno		2				1	1	1	4
Pit	1			1		4		3	9
Sherd Pile								1	1
Totals	6	6	2	3	1	22	5	21	66

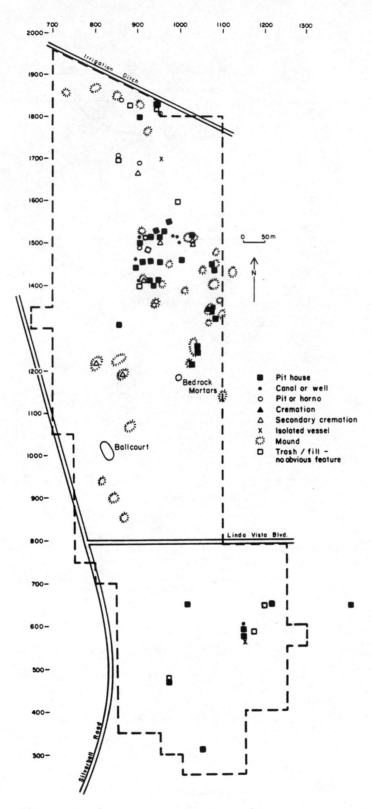

Figure 5.1. Locations of features discovered by testing.

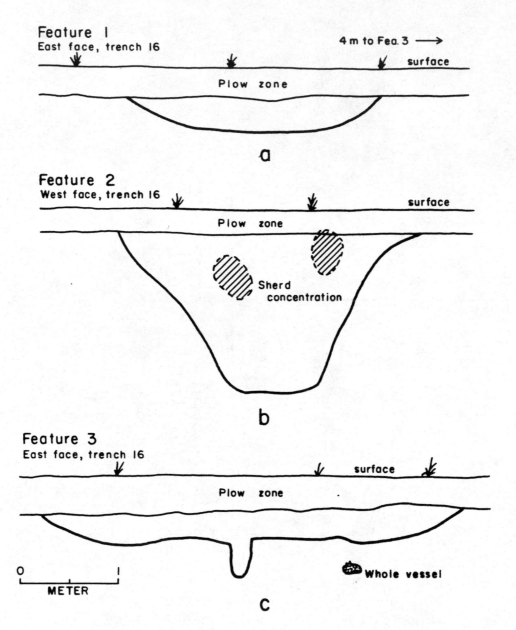

Figure 5.2. Profiles of Features 1, 2, and 3.

Features 1 and 2: Pits

Features 1 and 2 occur in the profile walls of Trench 16 at N600 E1100 (Fig. 5.2). Trench 16 was oriented north-south and appears to have exposed a cluster of cultural features and debris. A shell bracelet fragment, numerous large sherds, and ground stone were all recovered from the back dirt piles.

Table 5.2

CERAMICS FROM FEATURES 1 AND 2

Type	Nos. from Trench Backdirt	Nos. from F. 1	Nos. from F. 2
Rillito Red-on-brown	2	–	–
Rillito-Rincon Red-on-brown	6	–	3
Rincon Red-on-brown	3	–	–
Cortaro Red-on-brown	–	–	1
Indeterminate Red-on-brown	43	1	3
Indeterminate Red-on-buff	6	–	–
Buff ware	2	–	–
Indeterminate red ware	1	–	–
Plain ware (micaceous variety)	108	3	35
Plain ware (nonmicaceous variety)	143	–	4
Total	314	4	46

As can be seen in Table 5.2, ceramics recovered from the features are mostly plain ware (micaceous variety.) The decorated wares are largely indeterminate Tucson Basin Red-on-brown wares, but those that could be identified are Preclassic in age (Rillito-Rincon Red-on-brown).

Feature 1 is a shallow basin or pit that contained loose fill, a few sherds, and pieces of charcoal. Found in the east wall of Trench 16, it is probably the remaining upper portion of Feature 2. The intervening part of the feature was probably excavated by the backhoe. Feature 2 is a deep, conical but flat-bottomed pit, with concentrations of sherds and charcoal in the fill. Maximum length along the profile wall at the top of the feature is approximately 4 m while maximum depth is about 1.8 m below surface. The feature was not formally plastered and showed no evidence of having been subjected to high temperatures. It would seem to be a borrow, trash, or storage pit rather than an oven horno (oven) or large roasting pit.

Feature 3: House

Feature 3 occurs in the east wall of Trench 16, approximately 4 m south of Feature 1 (Fig. 5.2). Feature 3 is a shallow house basin with no evidence of formally plastered floor, walls, or wall curbs. The fill is dark, loose soil with sherds present throughout the fill. The length of the feature in the profile wall is 4.4 m, and the depth below surface (to the floor) being 0.6 m to 0.7 m. One posthole is visible near the center of the house. The ceramics recovered (Table 5.3) do not permit a firm dating of the house, but based on the collections from nearby features and the general trench backdirt it would seem to date to the Preclassic period.

Table 5.3

CERAMICS FROM FEATURE 3

Type	Nos. from Trench Backdirt	Nos. from F.3
Rillito Red-on-brown	2	-
Rillito-Rincon Red-on-brown	6	-
Rincon Red-on-brown	3	-
Cortaro Red-on-brown	-	-
Indeterminate Red-on-brown	43	4
Indeterminate Red-on-buff	6	-
Buff ware	2	-
Indeterminate red ware	1	-
Plain ware (micaceous variety)	108	42
Plain ware (nonmicaceous variety)	143	-
Total	314	46

Feature 4: House?

Feature 4 is located at roughly N1300 E850 (Trench 37). It consists of a relatively thick (50 cm) fill area with charcoal, sherds, and a flake in the vicinity of the feature (Fig. 5.3). This was only a small portion of what is probably the lip of a house basin exposed in

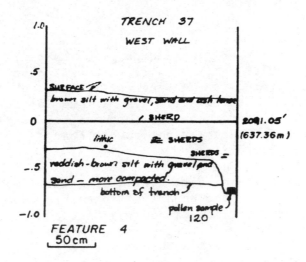

Figure 5.3. Profile of Feature 4.

the west wall of the extreme north end of the trench. A pollen sample
(No. 120) was recovered from immediately above the floor. Dating is
insecure (Table 5.4), but the trash in the vicinity of the feature seems
to indicate a Classic period (Tanque Verde phase) house. There is no
evidence of formal plastering of the wall or floor. The floor is about
90 cm below ground surface (true elevation: 636.61 m).

Table 5.4

CERAMICS FROM FEATURE 4

Type	Nos. from Trench Backdirt	Nos. from F.4
Tanque Verde Red-on-brown	8	2
Indeterminate Red-on-brown	7	2
San Carlos Red ware	1	–
Plain ware (micaceous variety)	21	4
Plain ware (nonmicaceous variety)	8	2
Total	45	10

Feature 5: Houses

Feature 5 is the designation given to a cluster of features located near N1390 E930 (Fig. 5.4a). Several superimposed house floors or basins were exposed in the side walls of Trench 38, varying in depth from 0.55 m to 1.2 m below surface. Maximum length in the profile wall is 6.4 m. There appear to be two to three houses represented. No orientations of the houses or noticeable changes in architecture can be discussed from the profile.

Diagnostic ceramics recovered from the trench backdirt and profile walls indicate the houses all probably date to the Preclassic period, that is the Rillito-Rincon transition or the Rincon phase (Table 5.5). The profile shows numerous ash and clay lenses as well as laminated silts, sands, and cobbles. Walls and floors of the houses are indicated by clay curbs and lenses, with the deepest and most prominent floor and curb indicating a slant-wall pit house. This floor is at an elevation of 635.52 m (true elevation).

Feature 6: House

Feature 6 is an adobe-walled house located near N1490 E900 in Trench 40 (Fig. 5.4b). The walls are indicated by large blocks of adobe--at the north end measuring 18 cm by 25 cm, but slightly irregular in shape; and at the south end 38 cm by 34 cm, and rectangular. The interior distance between walls along the profile wall is 4.4 m. The floor is 45 cm below present ground surface (at true elevation 635.84 m) and has a compacted or thinly plastered surface. Two pollen samples (Nos. 107 and 108) were taken from this surface. Only one sherd (indeterminate red-on-brown) was exposed in the fill of the house (Table 5.6). Based on architectural evidence and the ceramics recovered from the trench backdirt, the house seems to date to the Tanque Verde phase.

Feature 7: House?

Immediately to the south of Feature 6 is another fill area, Feature 7, that is interpreted to be a house (Fig. 5.4b). The fill area runs 2.4 m along the profile wall, but the house is not well-defined at the south end, that is, there is no distinctive edge to the house basin. The fill contains charcoal flecks, lenses of white ash, and several artifacts. Six pollen samples were recovered from various surfaces in the fill and on the floor of the feature. The floor is 60 cm to 70 cm below the present surface, at an elevation of 635.52 m. Diagnostic ceramics recovered from the fill and disturbed layers above the house indicate a late Preclassic or early Classic period occupation (Table

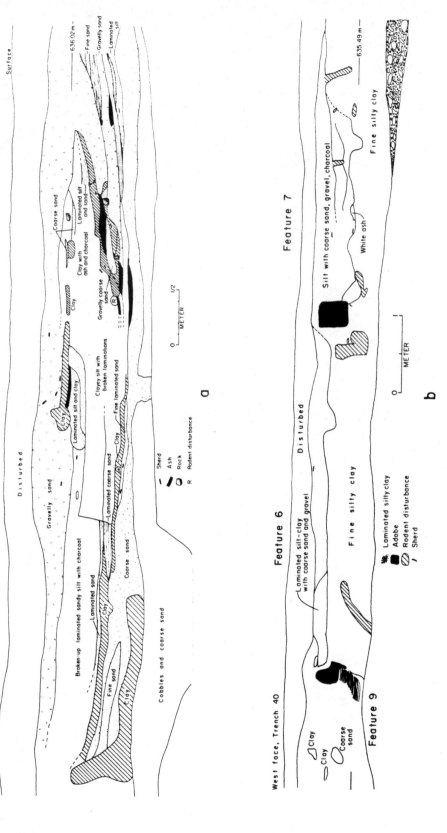

Figure 5.4 Profiles of Feature 5(a), 6(b), 7(b), and 9(b).

Table 5.5

CERAMICS FROM FEATURE 5

Type	Nos. from features	Nos. from Trench Backdirt	Nos. from Screening
Rillito-Rincon Red-on-brown	1	3	17
Rincon Red-on-brown	1	3	4
Tanque Verde Red-on-brown	–	3	1
Indeterminate Red-on-brown	3	20	94
Rincon Polychrome	–	1	–
Sacaton Red-on-buff	–	6	8
Indeterminate Red-on-buff	–	5	10
Buff ware	–	9	18
Rincon Red	–	5	18
Indeterminate red ware	–	2	–
Plain ware (micaceous variety	16	147	414
Plain ware (nonmicaceous)	1	15	83
Total	22	219	667

Table 5.6

CERAMICS FROM FEATURE 6

Type	Nos. from Trench Backdirt
Rillito-Rincon Red-on-brown	6
Rincon Red-on-brown	4
Tanque Verde Red-on-brown	22
Indeterminate Red-on-brown	34
Sacaton Red-on-buff	2
Indeterminate Red-on-buff	1
Buff ware	7
Plain ware (micaceous variety)	186
Plain ware (nonmicaceous variety)	49
Total	311

5.7). The relationship of Features 6 and 7 is unclear. From the profile wall, there is no indication that Feature 6 and Feature 7 overlap each other in any way.

Table 5.7

CERAMICS FROM FEATURE 7

Type	Nos. from Trench Backdirt
Rillito-Rincon Red-on-brown	5
Cortaro-Tanque Verde Red-on-brown	1
Tanque Verde Red-on-brown	6
Indeterminate Red-on-brown	22
Indeterminate Red-on-buff	3
Buff ware	6
Rincon Red	1
Indeterminate red ware	1
Plain ware (micaceous variety)	74
Plain ware (nonmicaceous variety)	40
Total	159

Feature 8: Pit

Feature 8 appears to have been intruded into the post-occupational fill of Feature 6. Feature 8 is a small, plaster-lined fire or roasting pit with outward slanting sides and a flat bottom. It was visible only in the east wall of Trench 40. The maximum diameter at the top edge of the feature is 40 cm. Maximum height is 30 cm while the maximum depth below surface is 40 cm; elevation is 635.90 m. The pit was full of charcoal, ash, and fire-cracked rock. Approximately half of the feature remained in the trench wall. The feature was excavated and radiocarbon and archaeomagnetic dating samples were removed. The archaeomagnetic dating confirms the Tanque Verde phase date for the feature (A.D. 1215-1255 [DuBois]; AD 1160-1210 [Sternberg/McGuire]), while the radiocarbon analysis provided an obviously anomalous date (2670 $\pm$ 200 B.P.; Sample A-2299, University of Arizona Radiocarbon Laboratory, Department of Geosciences). The date range interpreted from the Sternberg-McGuire Southwest Curve is judged to be the most reliable

94

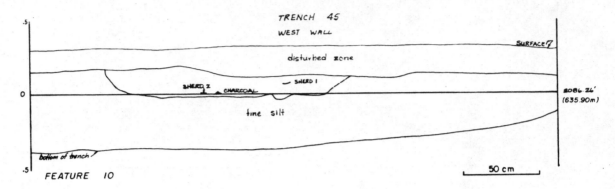

Figure 5.5. Profile of Feature 10.

dating of this feature (Sternberg 1982), placing it in the early Tanque Verde phase.

Feature 9: Fill Area

Feature 9 is an area of cultural fill with several chunks of clay or adobe located just south of Feature 6 (Fig. 5.4b). It may be a house, but this cannot be confirmed from the trench profile.

Feature 10: House

Feature 10 is a house exposed in the profile of Trench 45, located at N1445 E995 (Fig. 5.5). A 3.2-m length of the house basin is exposed in the trench, with the floor 30 cm to 40 cm below the surface (elevation: 635.90 m). The fill consists of an ashy, grey-brown soil, several sherds, charcoal, and some stone artifacts. No interior house features are visible in the profile and the orientation of the house is uncertain. The walls and floor of the house are not formally plastered. The sherds recovered do not permit even a tentative dating of the feature (Table 5.8).

Feature 11: House

A relatively deep house basin occurs near N1445 E940, in Trench 46. The floor is somewhat irregular, shows some internal features such as postholes, and lies about 90 cm below the surface (elevation at floor: 635.63 m) (Fig. 5.6). Feature 11 is also quite large, running

Table 5.8

CERAMICS FROM FEATURE 10

Type	Nos. from Trench Backdirt
Indeterminate Red-on-brown	2
Plain ware (micaceous variety)	7
Total	9

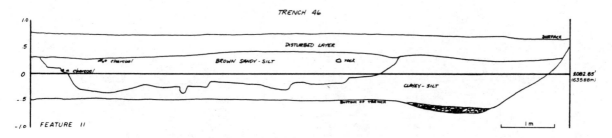

Figure 5.6. Profile of Feature 11.

Table 5.9

CERAMICS FROM FEATURE 11

Type	Nos. from Trench Backdirt
Rillito-Rincon Red-on-brown	2
Rincon Red	1
Plain ware (micaceous variety)	3
Total	6

6.7 m along the profile wall. No ceramics were recovered from the fill of the house, but those recovered from the general trench backdirt indicate a Preclassic occupation of the house (Table 5.9).

Feature 12: House

Trench 48 was excavated expressly to test a section of the vegetation anomaly in the area of N1520 E950. A pit house (Feature 12), 3.9 m in length, was exposed in the profile (Fig. 5.7). The floor is compacted or thinly plastered, but no formal walls were evident. The floor is about 65 cm below surface (elevation: 635.63 m). About 30 cm of fill is in the house basin, consisting of finely laminated sand, silt, and ash lenses. A hearth in the house was sectioned by the trench and contained a small amount of ash. Only three micaceous sherds were associated with the feature (Table 5.10), and the diagnostics recovered from the trench backdirt do not permit placement of the feature chronologically.

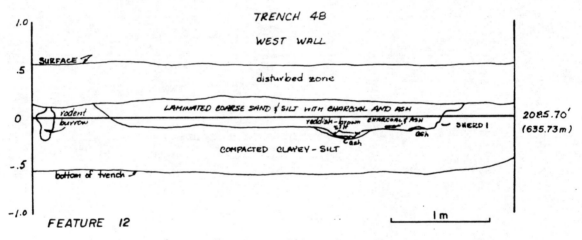

Figure 5.7. Profile of Feature 12.

Feature 13: Pit

Feature 13 is a small, rock-filled pit located at N1695 E900 in Trench 51. The pit is irregular in shape with a maximum width of 0.9 m and a maximum depth below surface of 0.9 m (Fig. 5.8). Elevation of the top of the pit is 634.96 m, while the elevation at the bottom is 634.46 m. It does not appear to be a formally prepared pit. Fine sand occurs in the bottom of the pit, which contrasts with the surrounding clayey silt. Ceramics associated with the feature or surrounding fill area and trench backdirt indicate an early Classic period or earlier date for the

Table 5.10

CERAMICS FROM FEATURE 12

Type	Nos. from Trench Backdirt
Tanque Verde Red-on-brown	1
Indeterminate Red-on-brown	1
Santa Cruz Red-on-buff	1
Plain ware (micaceous variety)	10
Total	13

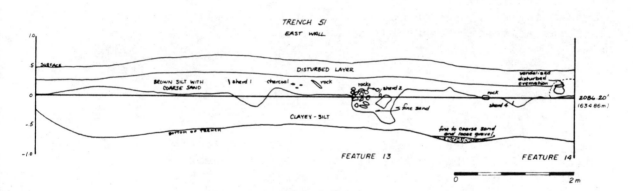

Figure 5.8. Profiles of Feature 13, and 14.

use of the feature (Table 5.11). Food processing (roasting) is the inferred function.

Feature 14: Cremation Vessel

Approximately 2.7 m south of Feature 13 (Fig. 5.8) was an isolated Tanque Verde Red-on-brown cremation vessel (jar, black paint variety)—Feature 14, IN 542. No evidence of a pit or burning was found. It appears to be a secondary burial of the material. The vessel was broken and had been dug out of the profile wall when found by

Table 5.11

CERAMICS FROM FEATURE 13

Type	Nos. from Backdirt, feature fill
Cortaro Red-on-brown	2
Tanque Verde Red-on-brown	2
Indeterminate Red-on-brown	1
Plain ware (micaceous variety)	17
Plain ware (nonmicaceous variety)	9
Total	31

archaeologists. Some bone and some of the vessel were recovered, but no attempt at vessel reconstruction was made.

Feature 15: House

Two features were identified in the walls of Trench 52. One extends 4.8 m along the profile at N1439 E890 (Feature 15). It is a relatively deeply buried house with a large, bell-shaped or globular pit located in the floor at one edge of the house basin (Fig. 5.9). The floor is 0.9 m below ground surface (elevation: 634.76 m) and the bottom of the pit is 2.0 m below that--dug into loose sand and cobbles. Long laminations in the house fill indicate a slow infilling of the house after abandonment.

Stone and ceramic artifacts were found in the fill of the house basin and deep pit. Diagnostics indicate a Preclassic Rillito-Rincon occupation of the house (Table 5.12). One pollen sample (No. 110) was taken at the bottom of the deep pit and one other (No. 109) was taken from the surface of the floor near the center of the house basin.

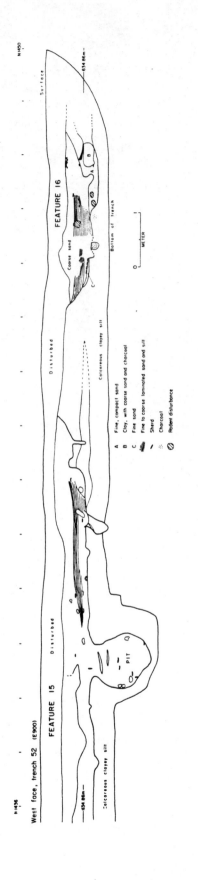

Figure 5.9. Profiles of Features 15 and 16.

Table 5.12

CERAMICS FROM FEATURE 15

Type	Nos. from Trench Backdirt	Nos. from Bell Pit	Nos. from Feature Profile
Rillito Red-on-brown	3	-	-
Rillito-Rincon Red-on-brown	10	2	3
Rincon Red-on-brown	5	-	-
Cortaro Red-on-brown	3	-	-
Tanque Verde Red-on-brown	1	-	-
Indeterminate Red-on-brown	30	-	5
Santa Cruz Red-on-buff	-	-	1
Sacaton Red-on-buff	1	-	-
Indeterminate Red-on-buff	8	3	1
Buff ware	2	-	2
Rincon Red	1	-	-
Plain ware (micaceous variety)	78	29	50
Plain ware (nonmicaceous)	42	-	6
Total	154	37	68

Table 5.13

CERAMICS FROM FEATURE 16

Type	Nos. from Profile and Backdirt
Indeterminate Red-on-brown	1
Plain ware (micaceous variety)	22
Plain ware (nonmicaceous variety)	4
Total	27

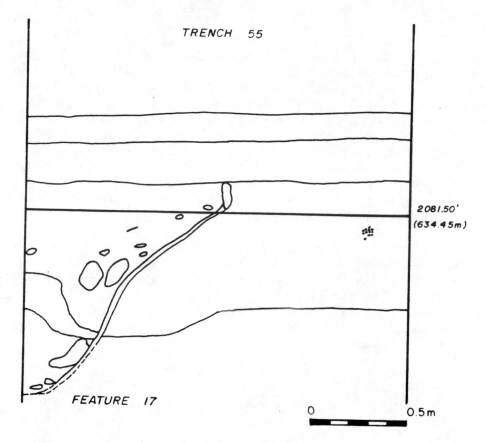

Figure 5.10. Profile of Feature 17.

Feature 16: House?

The second feature in Trench 52 (Feature 16) is also probably a house basin (Fig. 5.9). It may also be a large shallow pit (3.2 m long in the profile wall). The fill in the basin is noticeably striated with long, thin laminations of silt and fine sand. The floor is at an elevation of 635.63 m. Small pockets of charcoal and sand occur in certain areas of the fill. The ceramics recovered from the profile are almost wholly undecorated (Table 5.13), thus not providing a means for chronological placement of the feature. If Feature 16 is not a house, it is likely to be the borrow area for mud and adobe for Feature 15 or other nearby houses.

Feature 17: Horno

Feature 17 is located at N1800 E950.5 (Trench 55). The feature was exposed at the extreme northern end of the backhoe trench and, reflective of its nutrients and water-holding ability, a large bush is growing over the center of the feature. The feature seems to be a large roasting pit or horno, like Features 52 and 60. The top diameter could be as much as 4 m with the bottom diameter less than 2 m. The top of the feature is 35 cm below surface, the bottom, 1.45 m below surface (Fig. 5.10). At the top of the pit rim is a heavy, blackened, clay collar. The middle and upper sides of the pit are lined with a thin greyish-white plaster. The bottom is not plastered, but shows hard, fired sand and soil.

The fill of the horno consists of some medium-sized fire-cracked rock, small fire-cracked pebbles, and lenses of clay, sand, and silt with charcoal, often quite black and ashy. Chronological placement is not possible due to the absence of diagnostic ceramics (Table 5.14), but the potential for radiocarbon or archaeomagnetic dating should be quite good. Two pollen samples (No. 100 and IN 806) were removed from this feature before backfilling.

Table 5.14

CERAMICS FROM FEATURE 17

Type	Nos. from Feature Profile
Plain ware (micaceous variety)	2

Feature 18: House?

This feature is in the east wall of Trench 56 at N1795-1800 E900 (Fig. 5.11). It is defined by a slightly darker and sandier soil than the surrounding matrix, with occasional pieces of charcoal, pebbles and coarse sand. Feature 18 is interpreted as a house basin, but neither the floor nor side walls are plastered. Some vandalism occurred in the southern portion of the profile, exposing several sherds. The house basin is about 5 m long in the profile wall, with the floor at 90 cm

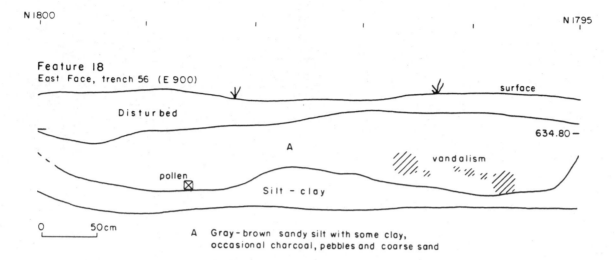

Figure 5.11. Profile of Feature 18.

below surface (634.25 m). A pollen sample (No. 132) was taken from just above the floor of the basin. Ceramics recovered from the trench profile walls and feature indicate a Tanque Verde phase (Classic period) use of the feature (Table 5.15).

Table 5.15

CERAMICS FROM FEATURE 18

Type	Nos. from Trench Backdirt and Feature
Tanque Verde Red-on-brown	2
Tanque Verde-Cortaro Red-on-brown	1
Indeterminate Red-on-brown	2
Red ware	1
Plain ware (micaceous variety)	3
Plain ware (nonmicaceous variety)	9
Total	18

104

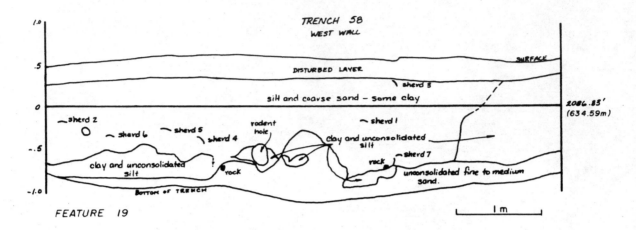

TRENCH 58
WEST WALL

Figure 5.12. Profile of Feature 19.

Table 5.16

CERAMICS FROM FEATURE 19

Type	Numbers
Tanque Verde Red-on-brown	2
Indeterminate Red-on-brown	2
Plain ware (micaceous variety)	1
Plain ware (nonmicaceous variety)	2
Total	7

Feature 19: Canal?

Trench 58 cut into a very long and deep zone of fill (Fig.
5.12). The fill is a mixture of silt and coarse sand with small pockets
of laminated clays. The fill also contains sherds in random
orientations and charcoal flecks. The deposit is designated Feature 19
and runs 5.8 m along the west wall of the trench. The best
interpretation seems to be that this is a longitudinal section through a

canal. There are some irregularities of the bottom, but these can be accounted for by collapse of the side walls. The bottom is approximately 1.2 m below surface (635.22 m). Features 27 and 28, also interpreted as canals, occur immediately to the north of Feature 19. Feature 19 may be a portion of one of these features, or may split into these features in the area between the backhoe trenches. Ceramics recovered from the fill indicates a Classic period (Tanque Verde phase) use of the canal (Table 5.16).

Feature 20:   Isolated Vessel

Feature 20 was assigned to a large Cortaro Red-on-brown bowl that unfortunately was damaged by the backhoe during excavation of Trench 62 (N1700 E950) (Fig. 5.13). The bowl was located at N1690 E950, 80 cm to 90 cm below surface (633.90-634.00 m). The bowl was upside down in a loose matrix of medium to coarse sand with a few pebbles. A mixed cobble and sand layer rises to about the same level 1 m north of the bowl. It is possible that the bowl was left along the edge of a stream course in the floodplain and was buried by a flooding episode. The ceramics recovered from the vicinity of Feature 20 indicate an early Classic period use of the area (Table 5.17).

Feature 21:   House

Trench 67, located in the south field, cut through a feature containing a dense accumulation of sherds and ash (Fig. 5.14). Feature 21 is interpreted to be a house basin, which contained at least 3 to 4 large vessels now smashed in the fill in four concentrations. No attempt has yet been made to reconstruct these vessels. The location of the house can be given as N475-485 E895-905. The length of the feature along the profile wall is 4.8 m. Several irregularities in the floor may indicate small pits or postholes. The floor is about 90 cm below the plowed surface, while the basin fill is 70 cm thick from floor to the bottom of the disturbed layer. The basin fill is capped by a hard-packed, grey, ashy layer that is 2 cm thick. Ceramics recovered from the trench wall and backdirt, as well as what was on the surface, indicate an early Rincon phase date for this structure (Table 5.18).

Feature 22:   Canal

Feature 22 is a canal recorded as a result of profiling the south wall of Trench 77. It is located at N1500 E900-902 (Fig. 5.15a). Maximum width at the top of the canal is 1.9 m, while the depth of the

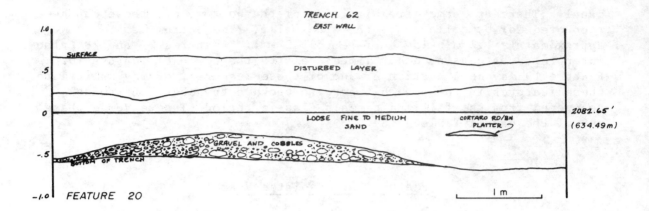

a

b

Figure 5.13.   Profile and photograph of Feature 20.
Diameter of vessel is 43 cm.

Table 5.17

CERAMICS FROM FEATURE 20

Type	Nos. from Trench Backdirt
Cortaro Red-on-brown	6
Cortaro-Tanque Verde Red-on-brown	6
Tanque Verde Red-on-brown	5
Indeterminate Red-on-brown	97
Indeterminate Red-on-buff	1
Buff ware	3
Rincon Red	1
Indeterminate red ware	2
Plain ware (micaceous variety)	219
Plain ware (nonmicaceous var.)	<u>289</u>
Total	629

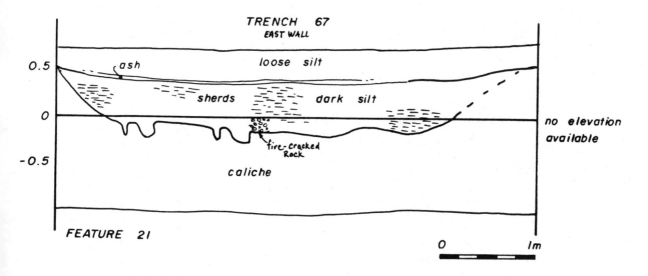

Figure 5.14. Profile of Feature 21.

Table 5.18

CERAMICS FROM FEATURE 21

Type	Nos. from Surface Collection	Nos. from Trench Wall and Backdirt
Rillito-Rincon Red-on-brown	1	4
Rincon Red-on-brown	1	2
Indeterminate Red-on-brown	7	15
Indeterminate Red-on-buff	1	2
Buff ware	2	2
Indeterminate red ware	-	2
Plain ware (micaceous variety)	36	297
Plain ware (nonmicaceous variety)	10	50
Total	58	374

Table 5.19

CERAMICS FROM FEATURE 22

Type	Numbers
Tanque Verde Red-on-brown	1
Indeterminate Red-on-brown	1
Plain ware (micaceous var.)	6
Plain ware (nonmicaceous var.)	3
Total	11

feature, from the disturbed zone to the bottom, is 80 cm (634.72 m elevation. The feature contains numerous sherds and pockets of various grades of unconsolidated sand and silt. Many show fine laminations of the sediments. Ceramics recovered from the feature indicate a Classic

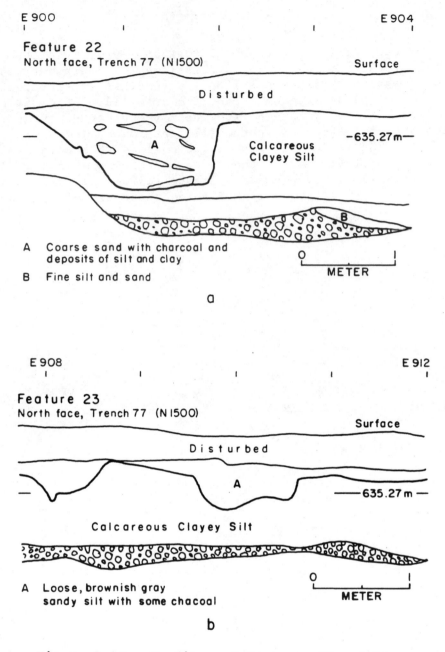

E 900   E 904

Feature 22
North face, Trench 77 (N 1500)   Surface

Disturbed

−635.27 m−

Calcareous
Clayey Silt

A Coarse sand with charcoal and
    deposits of silt and clay

B Fine silt and sand

0   1
METER

a

E 908   E 912

Feature 23
North face, Trench 77 (N 1500)

Surface

Disturbed

A

−635.27 m −

Calcareous Clayey Silt

A Loose, brownish gray
    sandy silt with some chacoal

0   1
METER

b

Figure 5.15. Profiles of Features 22 and 23.

period (Tanque Verde phase) or earlier date for the canal (Table 5.19).
A pollen sample (No. 121) was taken from the bottom of the canal.

Feature 23: Pit

Feature 23 is located at N1500 E909.5-910.65 in the south wall of Trench 77 (Fig. 5.15b). It is classified as a pit but could be a portion of a house basin. The floor is somewhat irregular and there is no evidence of plastering on the bottom or walls of the pit. A pollen sample (No. 122) was recovered from near the floor of the pit. Orientations of the sherds in the fill are random and could indicate trash fill. The feature length is 1.2 m along the profile wall and contains 40 cm of fill below the disturbed plowzone layer. The bottom of the pit is 75 cm below ground surface (635.15 m). Diagnostic ceramics seem to indicate a Tanque Verde phase use of the feature (Table 5.20).

Table 5.20

CERAMICS IN FEATURE 23

Type	Numbers
Tanque Verde Red-on-brown	1
Tanque Verde Red-on-brown white slip variety	1
Plain ware (micaceous variety)	7
Plain ware (nonmicaceous variety)	4
Total	13

Feature 24: Pit

Originally noted at N1500 E913 in the south wall of Trench 77, Feature 24 was a small pit, but was noted as not having any cultural material. This feature could not be relocated during the detailed profiling and mapping phase.

<u>Feature 25:   House</u>

Feature 25 is a house basin located at N1495-1505 E922-927 in the south wall of Trench 77. The interior fill has several areas of chunks of clay/adobe—possibly roof and wall fall—but otherwise no artifacts were visible. Several areas of laminated sediments occur just above floor level (Fig. 5.16a). At the edges of the house basin are

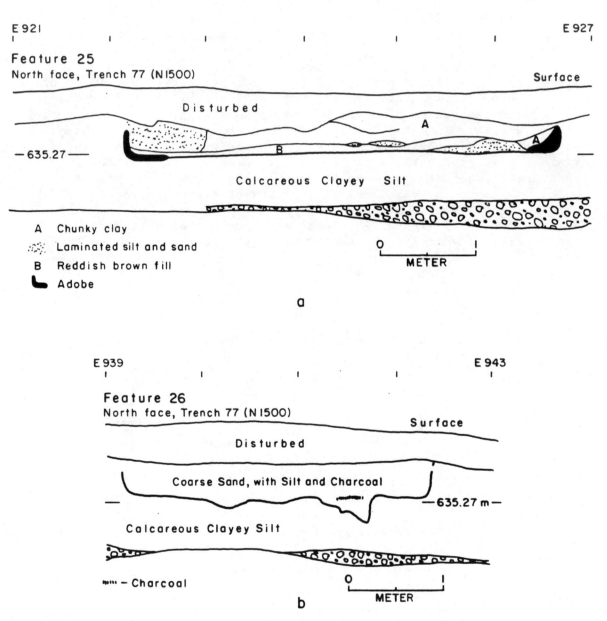

Figure 5.16.   Profiles of Features 25 and 26.

small "curbs" of adobe, and at one end, a small patch of plaster on the floor. A pollen sample (No. 123) was recovered from immediately above this surface. The floor is 60 cm below surface (25 cm to 30 cm below the disturbed zone) at a true elevation of 635.27 m. The house length exposed in the trench wall is 4.55 m. The absence of diagnostic ceramics precludes temporal placement of the feature.

Feature 26: House

Another house basin (Feature 26) was mapped in the south wall of Trench 77 (Fig. 5.16b). The house is located at N1495-1505 E939-943, with a maximum length of 3.2 m in the profile. Sherds, coarse sand, silt, and charcoal flecks characterize the fill in the house. The floor elevation is 636.27 m which is 80 cm below the surface and 40 cm below the disturbed plowzone layer. The only pit visible in the profile, shows a concentration of charcoal and is possibly an ash pit associated with a hearth. The juncture of the floor and walls shows a thin adobe/plaster rim, rising 25 cm up the basin walls but providing only a minimal plastered surface on the floor. A pollen sample (No. 124) was recovered from just above one of the plaster curbs. Evidence for the walls was found in both faces of the backhoe trench. From the angle of the plaster surfaces, it is possible to say that most of the house is on the south side of Trench 77. Temporal placement of this feature is also not possible due to the absence of diagnostic ceramics (Table 5.21).

Table 5.21

CERAMICS FROM FEATURE 26

Type	Numbers
Indeterminate red ware	1
Plain ware (micaceous variety)	2
Plain ware (nonmicaceous variety)	2
Total	5

Feature 27: Canal

Feature 27 is a cross-section of a canal located at the east end of Trench 77, at N1500 E986.5-989. It is visible in both faces of the backhoe trench, but is considerably wider in the north wall. Feature 28, another canal cross-section, is located 3 m to the west.

Feature 27 shows numerous laminated zones near the bottom of the canal. The width of the canal at the top appears to be about 2.8 m and 2.2 m at the bottom (Fig. 5.17). The bottom of the canal is 60 cm below the bottom of the disturbed layer, 1.1 m below surface (elevation 635.12 m). Pollen sample No. 126 was recovered from the bottom of the canal. The fill consists of various grades of sand, a few rocks and pebbles, and some clay. The canal was excavated into a very silty matrix. Ceramics recovered from the profile/feature fill indicate a Tanque Verde phase date for this feature (Table 5.22). Feature 27 may be related to Feature 19 (7 m to the south) as a fork or continuation of the canal.

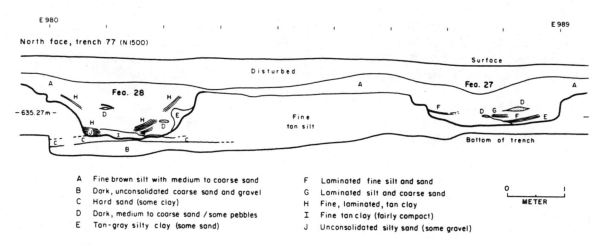

Figure 5.17. Profiles of Features 27 ad 28.

Feature 28: Canal

Feature 28 is associated in some manner with the two nearby canal segments, Features 19 and 27. Feature 28 is located approximately 3 m west of Feature 27, and, as with Feature 27, may be a fork from or continuation of Feature 19. Feature 28 is also visible in both walls of Trench 77, and like Feature 27 is much wider in the north wall than in the south wall. In the north wall, this canal is 2.7 m wide at the top and 1.55 m wide at the bottom (Fig. 5.17). Elevation at the bottom is 634.77 m; it is 1.05 m below the disturbed layer and 1.4 m below the present surface. The fill of Feature 28 also contrasts with the

Table 5.22

CERAMICS FROM FEATURE 27

Type	Numbers
Tanque Verde Red-on-brown	2
Cortaro-Tanque Verde Red-on-brown	1
Plain ware (micaceous variety)	1
Plain ware (nonmicaceous variety)	1
Total	5

surrounding silty matrix, and contains pockets of clay, laminated sands and clays, and pockets of various grades of sand.

Some of the laminated lenses indicate that the canal filled in while in use and was reduced in dimensions to 2.2 m at the top, 0.85 m at the bottom, and 0.85 m in depth (below disturbed layer). A hard-packed sand and heavy clay developed in the canal bottom. Ceramics recovered from the canal fill again indicate a Classic period use of the canal (Table 5.23). The Tanque Verde Red-on-brown sherds are associated with the latest series of laminations, raising the possibility that the original canal could date to a earlier period.

Table 5.23

CERAMICS FROM FEATURE 28

Type	Numbers
Cortaro-Tanque Verde Red-on-brown	1
Tanque Verde Red-on-brown	3
Indeterminate Red-on-brown	3
Sells Red	1
Plain ware (micaceous variety)	1
Plain ware (nonmicaceous variety)	1
Total	10

Feature 29:   Horno

Trench 81, located near N1834-49 E868, cut into an area of
cultural fill designated as Feature 29 (Fig. 5.18). From the fire-
cracked rocks, charcoal and ash noted in the fill of the feature, it has
been classified as an horno. Detailed depths and dimensions are not
available for this feature, only initial sketches and dimensions. In
the portion of the feature exposed these indicate an horno with a
sloping wall, and a bottom approximately 50 cm to 75 cm below the
surface and about 1 m in width, disappearing into the south end of the
trench. Detailed measurements were not done because the trench was
excavated to over 3 m in depth into very loose sand and cobbles and was
backfilled immediately for safety reasons. Some sherds associated with
the feature were noted as being Tanque Verde Red-on-brown, indicating a
Classic period placement for this feature. If the feature is an horno,
it does not exhibit the formal plastering and high temperature
conditions noted for Features 17, 52, and 60.

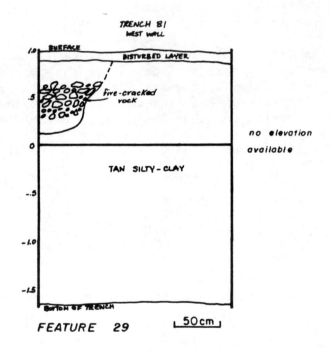

Figure 5.18.   Profile of Feature 29.

Feature 30: House

Feature 30 is a house located during profiling in both the north
and south faces of Trench 84 (Fig. 5.19). Approximate grid coordinates
for the house are N1397 to 1406, E924 to 933, and floor elevation

116

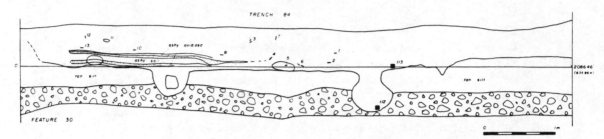

Figure 5.19. Profile of Feature 30.

averages 635.90 m. The profiles showed the existence of several floor
features (pits and post holes), a clearly defined floor, and relatively
high numbers of artifacts in the profile walls. Along with Feature 39,
this was the first feature to be excavated at Los Morteros by the
University of Arizona field schools. Two semesters of work were done on
this house--the first semester concentrating on the area north of Trench
84 (directed by Ed Stasky), the second, on the area to the south
(directed by Denise Shay).

During the first field season excavators sought to maintain
tight control over the locations of materials in the structures.
Because Feature 39 had already been excavated, Feature 30 was the only
true test of this strategy. The area containing the feature was gridded
off into 1-m by 1-m units based on the general Los Morteros grid. These
were to be excavated in 10-cm levels, one-half level at a time, with all
materials (artifacts, charcoal, rock, etc.) to be point provenienced and
mapped.

Although controlling each unit was not too difficult, those in
charge felt that controlling the overall excavation of the house was
difficult using this strategy. Accurate excavation of the levels by the
students was not easy, resulting quickly in only patches (1-m by 1-m
areas) of level surface after the excavation of one or two levels. This
made it almost impossible to keep track of internal features or
deposits, and even of the edge of the house that extended from unit to
unit.

With the experience gained working on the north half of the
house, it was hoped many of the problems could be controlled for during
excavation of the south half. Just as excavations began, the definition
and interpretation of Feature 30 was clouded by an unfortunate incident.
Between field days, vandals removed the tarps and protecting frames and
dug into areas on the north and south side of Trench 84, but
particularly on the south side. It was never really possible to get
back full provenience control of portions of the excavations after this
happened. Definition of the edge of the house basin was never possible
on the south side.

Portions of Feature 30 contained quantities of charcoal, ash, and fire-stained soil leading to the strong likelihood that the structure had burned. Also recovered were shell, bone, macrobotanical remains, ground stone, and other lithics. Ceramics were also abundant. It was initially thought that most of the artifacts were trash fill into the abandoned house. The amount of burned material and the ability of a patient and skilled volunteer to assemble three large vessels (Appendix O: Figs. O.1-O.5) changed the interpretation. Many of the pieces of the vessels came from near the assumed edge of the house basin; presumably, the vessels were along the interior wall. This is unclear due to the vandalism. Presently, the best interpretation is that the house burned while occupied, with numerous artifacts in place.

Several burned areas at floor level were located near the west edge of the house basin, just north of the backhoe trench. Because no formal hearth was found, this area was sampled. In the case of Feature 30, the hearth may have been removed by the backhoe. This burned floor area produced archaeomagnetic date ranges of A.D. 890-1070, and 1140-1340. This is in line with the available ceramic data, indicating a Rincon phase date for the house (see Table 5.24).

No definite entryway was located, although some large pieces of caliche/adobe near the northeastern edge of the house might have been the location of the entry. This is not where the fire-staining on the floor indicates the hearth may have been, and thus where the entryway should be.

Feature 31: House?

Feature 31 is a 2.2 m length of cultural fill identified in the south wall of Trench 84 (N1398-1402 E935-938). Interpreted as a house basin, the fill consists of oxidized and ashy soil, charcoal, coarse sand and silt, and a few sherds. Several pits or postholes seem to be visible in the floor of the house (Fig. 5.20). A pollen sample (No. 111) was recovered from the floor of the house basin (elevation: 635.78 m) at a level 90 cm below surface, and 65 cm below bottom of disturbed zone. One slanted, unplastered side wall is visible in the profile, rising 35 cm and possibly higher above the floor. Very little artifactual material was seen in the profile. The two sherds recovered indicate a possible late Rincon/early Tanque Verde phase date for the occupation of the feature (Table 5.25).

Feature 32: Crematory

A corner of a crematory was exposed at N1400-1402 E920.5-923 in the north wall of Trench 84 (Fig. 5.21). The elevation of the bottom of the feature is 635.61 m. Human bone and several sherds were poked out

118

Table 5.24

Ceramics from Feature 30

Type	Numbers
Rillito Red-on-brown	5
Rillito-Rincon Red-on-brown	106
Rincon Red-on-brown	449
Cortaro Red-on-brown	8
Cortaro-Tanque Verde Red-on-brown	3
Tanque Verde Red-on-brown	32
Tucson Red-on-brown	2
Indeterminate Red-on-brown	543
Rincon Polychrome	2
Indeterminate painted	1
White ware	1
Indeterminate corrugated	1
Santa Cruz Red-on-buff	3
Sacaton Red-on-buff	101
Indeterminate red-on-buff	226
Buff ware	137
Rincon Red	27
San Carlos Red	2
Sells Red	22
Indeterminate red ware	44
Wingfield Plain	37
Plain ware (micaceous variety)	6,273
Plain ware (nonmicaceous)	2,267
Indeterminate brown ware	21
Other	2
Total	10,315

of the wall by vandals one weekend. Further clearing of the profile revealed heavy ash deposits, a thick, highly oxidized plaster rim and more bone. It was decided that this highly visible feature should be excavated for its own protection and preservation.

The disturbed zone was stripped back from the edge of the trench by shovel, then finer horizontal layers were removed by troweling until the rim of the crematory pit could be fully defined. The long axis of the crematory pit was oriented west-northwest to east-southeast. The pit measured 1.7 m long by 0.9 m wide by 0.6 m deep. Excavation proceeded by five horizontal levels, and materials recovered were bagged by arbitrary 10-cm levels.

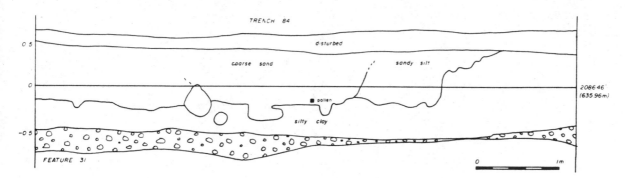

Figure 5.20. Profile of Feature 31.

Table 5.25

CERAMICS FROM FEATURE 31

Type	Nos. from Profile
Cortaro Red-on-brown	1
Plain ware (nonmicaceous variety)	1
Total	2

Initially, all fill was screened through eighth-inch mesh. A chance discovery of a very small pyramidal clay bead lead to screening of all fill through window screen and subsequent flotation of all fill to separate and recover the macrobotanical remains. Materials recovered included human bone; sherds from two vessels and miscellaneous other sherds; numerous small beads of clay, shell, or bone; a shell bracelet fragment; a shell ring fragment; and a perforated slate disc. All of these materials had been through the cremation fire.

The human bone, skeletal remains of an adult male, was analyzed by T. Michael Fink (see Appendix K) as Cremation #3. The two vessels included a Tanque Verde Red-on-brown bowl (IN 555, Fig. 5.22) and a plain ware (non-micaceous variety) lug-handled jar (IN 536, not pictured). The heaviest concentration of bone occurred in the level 30 cm to 40 cm below the pit rim. There was no bone in the lowest level, but some fragments were scattered through the upper levels. There is

120

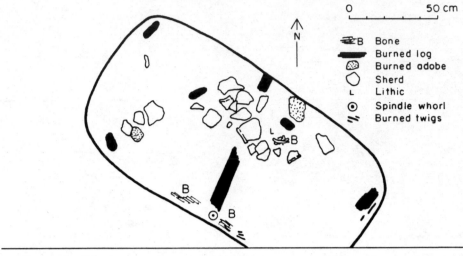

Trench 84

Legend:
- ⊜B Bone
- Burned log
- Burned adobe
- Sherd
- L Lithic
- ⊙ Spindle whorl
- Burned twigs

0   50 cm

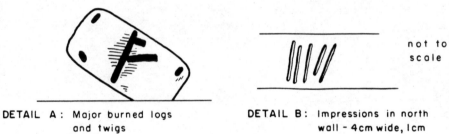

DETAIL A: Major burned logs and twigs

DETAIL B: Impressions in north wall – 4cm wide, 1cm deep

not to scale

a

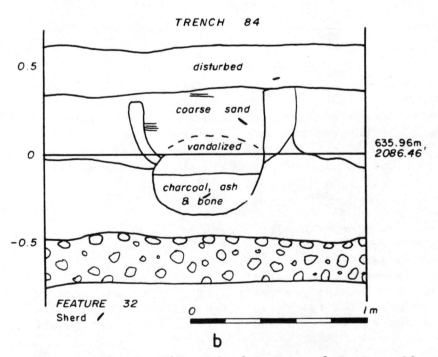

TRENCH 84

disturbed

coarse sand

vandalized

635.96m, 2086.46'

charcoal, ash & bone

FEATURE 32
Sherd /

0   1m

b

Figure 5.21. Profile and plan maps of Feature 32.

Figure 5.22.   Photograph of vessel from Feature 32.
Diameter of vessel is 28 cm.

evidence that the body was placed on a pyre above or near the top of the
pit.   Several large burned pole fragments were found near the bottom,
oriented vertically or nearly vertically.   These may be the ends of
beams placed across the top of the pit, or vertical supports for a
platform built inside the pit.   A smaller timber (5 cm to 10 cm in
diameter) was found along the short mid-line axis, running from pit wall
to pit wall.   The bottom of the crematory was filled with carbonized and
uncarbonized twigs, brush, and small branches, up to 5 cm in diameter.
Along the north wall of the pit was a series of vertical grooves,
probably impressions in wet plaster of small twigs or reeds used to line
the interior of the pit.

Distribution of the sherds from the two vessels indicates that
they were either placed on the pyre with the body and broke in the heat
and collapse of the pyre, or that they were thrown into the fire and
broke on impact.   The first explanation appears to be the best: the jar
exhibited warping characteristic of being in place in a fire for a
prolonged period, both vessels occurred near each other in the eastern
half of the pit, and bone was found below, among, and above the sherds.
Cranial fragments were concentrated in the east-central portion of the
pit, suggesting a similarity to other eastward facing cremations
considered typical of Hohokam cremation patterns (Haury 1976: 170).
Fragments and larger pieces of the long bones are found along the north
and south walls parallel to the east-west mid-line.   The slate disc was
found near the long bones along the south wall at the north-south mid-
line.

Much of the macro-botanical material was corn (including several
varieties), but also recovered were cotton seeds, Trianthema seeds, and
hedge hog cactus seeds (see Appendix I).   Mesquite was the dominant wood
used, followed by little-leaf palo verde, blue palo verde, and ironwood.
It is presumed that these items were mostly intended as fuels, but the
range of corn species and variety of smaller seeds suggests the

possibility of food offerings included in the cremation vessels or with the primary fuel materials. Corn can also serve as a fuel capable of producing a very high-temperature fire.

Radiocarbon and archaeomagnetic dating samples were recovered from the crematory. The radiocarbon sample was analyzed at the University of Arizona, Department of Geosciences 14C Dating Laboratory (Lab No. A-2300) and was counted for 5,000 minutes to decrease the standard deviation. Results indicated a date of 750 ± 50 B.P. (A.D. 1150-1200). The archaeomagnetic results have been interpreted two ways. One is based on an interpretation of the DuBois curve and produces a conforming date of A.D. 1180-1220. This dating was based on a visual inspection and comparison of the sample plot and curve. Sternberg (1982) has modified the curve, substantiated it clearly, and provided a statistical means for deriving a dating interpretation. The paleomagnetic results were also tested against the Sternberg-McGuire curve and yielded a dating interpretation at the 95 percent level, two standard deviations, of A.D. 1030-1170, a range slightly earlier than that suggested by the radiocarbon date. These dates and the associated Tanque Verde ceramics, certainly place the use of this feature in the early Tanque Verde phase.

Feature 33: Canal?

Feature 33 is located at N1400 E890-895, in the west end of Trench 84. It is a large canal or a remnant of a drainage. Several large mesquite trees grow in the path of this feature, following a supposed course around the point of the terrace where the ballcourt is located, and curving back toward the Tucson Mountains as it heads toward Rillito Peak to discharge into the Santa Cruz River (see Fig. 1.1). Estimated width of the feature at the top of its banks is 5.5 m, while the bottom is at least 1 m below the disturbed zone (1.3 m below surface). The bottom of the trench (at 1.3 m below surface, 635.33 m) may not have exposed the bottom of Feature 33. The feature is full of laminations and sand pockets typical of a canal. The few sherds recovered from the profile are largely non-diagnostic. The single diagnostic sherd recovered (Rincon Red) could indicate a Preclassic date for the feature, with abandonment before the Classic period (Table 5.26). This is far from conclusive. More discussion of this matter is included in the section dealing with the overall distribution of features at Los Morteros.

Feature 34: House

In the long east-west trench (No. 87) located at N650 between E925 and E1400, a house was located at E1375-1380. An ash lens was

Table 5.26

CERAMICS FROM FEATURE 33

Type	Numbers
Rincon Red	1
Plain ware (micaceous variety	13
Total	14

visible just below the plowzone (15 cm to 20 cm deep) in the south trench wall and the house basin and a hearth were identified in the north wall. The hearth had been sectioned by the backhoe, revealing that it had been replastered several times.

Two other features were identified in Trench 87, but were not assigned Los Morteros feature numbers. One, in the area between E1150 and 1200, showed concentrations of charcoal and ash with a lot of large sherds, ground stone, and cracked rock. The ash lense in the north trench wall was approximately 4.5 m long. The other feature, located about E960, was marked by an ashy lense 3 m to 4 m long in the north wall. No profile maps were drawn because the trench had to be backfilled immediately after excavation. It is also not possible to firmly place any of these features chronologically due to the absence of diagnostics in the profiles.

Backdirt collections, obtained at intervals along Trench 87, coincide to some extent with the locations of features and provide indications of possible temporal placements into the Preclassic period (Rillito-Rincon phases, Table 5.27). This is consistent with the broad interpretation of predominantly Preclassic occupation of the site in the area south of Linda Vista Boulevard.

Feature 35: House

Trench 92 intersected two features, one of which (Feature 35) is a house structure with heavy adobe block walls at N1445 E915 (Fig. 5.23). It appears the walls are resting on the floor and exterior occupation surface, that is, no basin edges are visible in the profile.

Table 5.27

CERAMICS FROM TRENCH 87

Type	E965	E1050-1100	E1150-1200
Rillito Red-on-brown	-	-	1
Rillito-Rincon Red-on-brown	-	-	5
Rincon Red-on-brown	-	2	-
Cortaro Red-on-brown	-	-	2
Indeterminate Red-on-brown	-	2	24
Indeterminate Red-on-buff	-	-	4
Buff ware	-	-	4
Rincon Red	-	-	3
Plain ware (micaceous variety)	7	2	168
Plain ware (nonmicaceous)	-	9	62
Total	7	15	273

The trench appears to have cut through the house near one corner. The walls are made of puddled adobe ranging in dimension from 20 cm by 20 cm to 30 cm by 50 cm. Just outside one of the adobe walls in the south trench profile is a small pit lined and filled with sherds (Feature 41). This pit seems to be associated with the house as an exterior storage cist. Sherds from the pit support an architecturally derived Classic period date for the house, probably early Tanque Verde phase (Table 5.28). Surface collections from this area of the site also indicate a mixed or transitional Rincon to Tanque Verde occupation. The house floor elevation is 635.82 m, 50 cm to 70 cm below ground surface. Pollen samples, Nos. 130 and 129, were collected, respectively, from the house floor (Feature 35) and from the bottom of Feature 41.

Feature 36: House

Feature 36 also was located from the south trench face of Trench 92 at N1445 E920. It is located 2.25 m east of Feature 35, and runs 4.2 m long along the trench face (Fig. 5.23). No heavy adobe walls are evident, but the compacted, mostly unplastered surface and edges of a shallow house basin are visible. The east edge of the house basin has been replastered on the upper portion of the basin. The floor elevation is 635.77 m, 40 cm below the disturbed zone and 75 cm below present

125

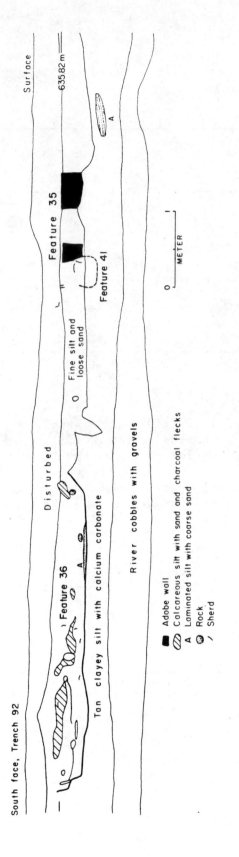

Figure 5.23. Profiles of Features 35, 36, and 41.

Table 5.28

CERAMICS FROM FEATURES 35 AND 41

Type	Nos. from Feature 35	Nos. from Feature 41
Cortaro Red-on-brown	-	3
Cortaro-Tanque Verde Red-on-brown	-	3
Indeterminate Red-on-brown	1	3
Plain ware (micaceous variety)	-	10
Plain ware (nonmicaceous variety)	2	43
Total	3	62

ground surface. The fill in the house basin shows areas of laminated sediments, pockets of laminated coarse sand and charcoal, some rodent disturbance, and a few sherds. The sherds in the fill provide some evidence of a Classic period date for the house (Table 5.29). A small floor depression and reddened soil lenses in the north trench wall may indicate the area of the hearth. Pollen samples Nos. 127 and 128 were collected from the floor near and inside the depression in the north wall.

Table 5.29

CERAMICS FROM FEATURE 36

Type	Numbers
Rillito-Rincon Red-on-brown	1
Tanque Verde Red-on-brown	1
Plain ware (micaceous variety)	2
Plain ware (nonmicaceous variety)	2
Total	6

Feature 37: House

Feature 37 seems to be a house basin in the west wall of Trench
95 (Fig. 5.24a). The house is located at N1515 E940, has a length of
6.2 m in the wall, and is defined by an unplastered shallow basin
containing a tan brown sandy soil. The feature was excavated into clay
and unconsolidated silt. An orange-brown silt lens in a depression near
the center of the house indicates the hearth area. No other mottling or
floor features are evident. Only one sherd, a micaceous plain ware,

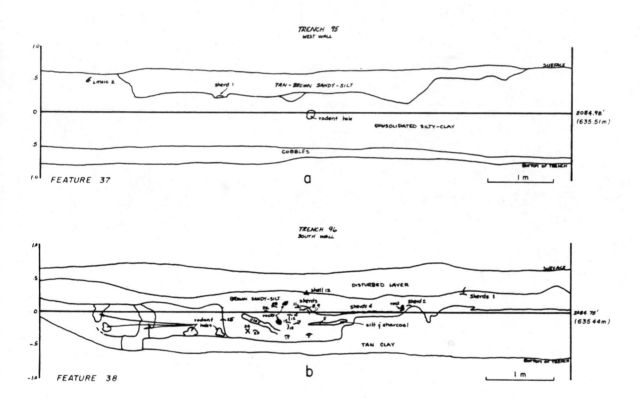

Figure 5.24. Profiles of Features 37 and 38.

was recovered from the profile wall, making temporal placement
impossible. The floor is 30 cm to 35 cm below the plowzone, at an
elevation of 635.81 m.

Feature 38: House

A small portion of a house was discovered in the south wall of
Trench 96 at approximately N1545 E965 (Fig. 5.24b). The profile reveals

a 2.8 m length of mixed fill containing sherds, charcoal, bone, lithics, and laminated lenses. The edges of the basin are unplastered, with one edge very steep. The floor level is at an elevation of 634.99 m, one meter below present ground surface and 70 cm to 75 cm below the bottom of the disturbed zone. This is a deeper basin than is normally observed at Los Morteros. Ceramics recovered from the profile wall suggest a Tanque Verde phase date for this house (Table 5.30).

Table 5.30

CERAMICS FROM FEATURE 38

Type	Numbers
Tanque Verde Red-on-brown	3
Indeterminate Red-on-brown	3
Indeterminate painted	1
Sells Red	1
Plain ware (micaceous variety)	12
Plain ware (nonmicaceous variety)	9
Total	29

Feature 39: House

Feature 39 was originally discovered in a test pit that was part of the testing pattern around Mound 1. Because this westernmost corner of a house was the only substantive feature discovered during that testing, and believing our access to that property could be limited, Richard Lange and William Deaver returned the next day to further explore this feature.

The initial step was to locate and follow out the wall edges. Overburden was removed and initially a narrow trench was used to follow the estimated course of the walls. The walls were not plastered but could be readily identified by the contrast of the interior fill and exterior sterile soil. Once the wall was located, the larger unit (2 m by 2 m) was cleared down to the level at which the wall edge was identified. Following out the walls in this manner left a natural balk in the center of the house. Once the house had been outlined, it was decided to leave this balk for stratigraphic control and for profiling

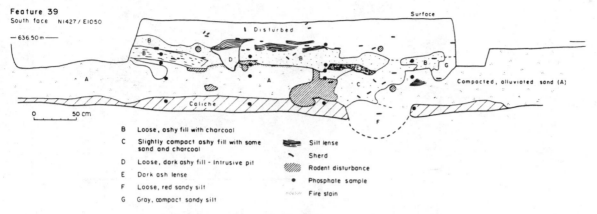

Figure 5.25. Profile of Feature 39.

(Fig. 5.25). Within the outlines of the walls, excavation was then carried to floor level by troweling and careful shovel scraping.

At the completion of the testing, numerous sherds had been recovered from the fill (although no screening was done), a figurine head was found just above floor off the east end of the balk, and several floor features (shallow pits, ash pits, post molds, and burn-stained areas) had been found. These were mapped the next day (Fig. 5.26). Also, two small test pits were excavated at opposite ends and on opposite sides of the balk. One, relatively shallow, revealed continued cultural fill below the "floor" level just mapped and defined. The other, on the west end, went deeper, revealing a deep fill area. Time precluded any further exploration and the house was backfilled. No entryway or hearth were found.

Shortly thereafter, contact was made with the new owners of the property (Mssrs. Waddell and Haskins), and they consented to allowing further investigations on their property. That fall (1980), the first field school classes from the University of Arizona worked on the property, re-opening the excavation of Feature 39 while concurrently beginning the excavation of Feature 30 on the adjacent McGinnis property. The prospect of a second floor or second feature below what had been defined in Feature 39 was the principal reason for returning. The floor elevation is approximately 636.20 m, and the house is located in the area N 1424-1430 E 1071-1075.

The balk was left in place and the previously exposed area of the house was re-excavated. A larger buffer area was excavated around the outside of the house, revealing several exterior post holes. A narrow trench was excavated along the north face of the balk, to deepen the visible profile. Detailed excavations in 1-m by 1-m units began in the area of the house south of the balk. These procedures yielded the same conclusion: there was no second floor. Artifact recovery was

130

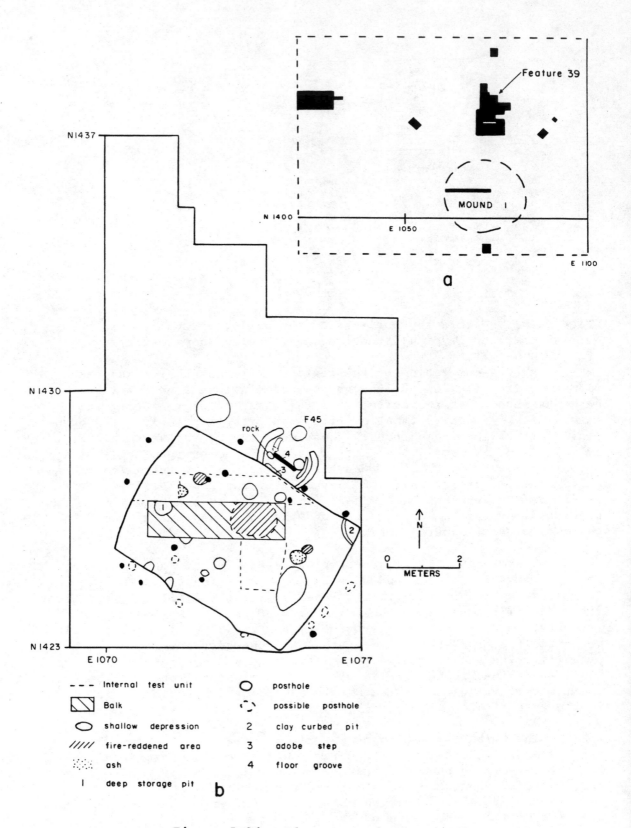

Figure 5.26. Plan maps of Feature 39.

negligible to nonexistent. The house floor features disappeared, or in
the case of post holes continued down, but no new ones were discovered
on the lower "floor." And, from the profile, there was no clear-cut
surface to either "floor." What it seemed to be was a zone (5 cm to 10
cm thick) of extreme mixing by rodent activity. Burrows crisscrossed
the excavated levels.

Eventually, the balk was removed. A slate or schist effigy
pendant (Fig. O.10c), was recovered, but no formal hearth was found. A
heavily reddened area was found in the house where the hearth could be
expected. Archaeomagnetic dating samples removed from this area
indicated date ranges of A.D. 870-1070, 1220-1450 (both from sample
LM004) and A.D. 940-1090, 1060-1380 (LM005). These ranges, coupled with
the ceramics recovered (Table 5.31), indicate a Tanque Verde date for
the house. They do not aid in placing the occupation to early or late
in this phase.

The profile trench north of the balk revealed a small adobe
curbing in the northeast corner of the structure. No pit was found, and
the floor surface continued into the corner. The profile trench also
identified the adobe foundations of the entryway, which was further
defined by the removal of additional overburden from the north side of
the house.

Two sets of semi-circular arms made of adobe formed the
entryway. The interior arms are similar in size to each other and the
exterior arms are similar to each other. The interior arms are below or
at the bottom of the outer arms. It is thus supposed that the interior
arms formed one entryway, the outer arms another. The lower entryway
was earlier, and was later remodeled to a bigger doorway. One of the
lower arms was cut by a floor groove and there seems to be an adobe
step, or lip, to the house basin associated with the upper-outer
entryway.

A small puddling pit occurred in and below the first entryway.
A similar puddling pit (labeled Feature 45), possibly post-dating the
occupation of the house, occurred at or slightly above the level of the
entryway and in the middle of it. There was no adobe "floor" to the
entryway.

Outside, near the northwest corner of the house, was a shallow
pit that contained a few sherds and small rocks. Inside, the deep fill
area in the northwest corner was excavated, revealing a sub-floor
storage pit with sides that expand outward as the pit gets deeper. No
particular items or concentrations of artifacts were recovered in the
pit's fill. A few sherds, charcoal flecks, and soil mottled by ash and
fire staining were present throughout the fill.

It was thought that the excavation of Feature 62 (to the
northwest of Feature 39) might show a "courtyard" group of structures in
this area north of Mound 1. This group consisted of Features 39 and 62
and possibly others. It appears, however, that Feature 62 faces west,
away from this potential grouping.

Table 5.31

CERAMICS FROM FEATURE 39

Type	Count
Rillito Red-on-brown	1
Rillito-Rincon Red-on-brown	12
Rincon Red-on-brown	29
Cortaro Red-on-brown	13
Cortaro-Tanque Verde Red-on-brown	59
Tanque Verde Red-on-brown	153
Indeterminate Red-on-brown	502
San Carlos Red-on-brown	2
Indeterminate painted	13
Indeterminate Black-on-white	1
Indeterminate corrugated	3
Casa Grande Red-on-buff	1
Indeterminate red-on-Buff	23
Buff ware	6
Rincon Red	1
Gila Red	1
San Carlos Red	2
Sells Red	2
Indeterminate red ware	32
Wingfield Plain	4
Plain ware (micaceous variety)	1,705
Plain ware (nonmicaceous variety)	1,356
Other	2
Total	3,923

Feature 40

This feature number was voided, and the feature assigned number 62.

Feature 41: Pit

Feature 41 is discussed in the description of Feature 35.

Feature 42: Trash Fill

Feature 42 is the designation assigned to a trash fill area in Trench 94, N1485 E925 (Fig. 5.27). The feature is visible over a 4 m length in the south wall of the trench. The fill consists of small clay chunks, loose sandy silt, and flecks and pieces of charcoal. The floor of the feature is highly irregular, with possibly three pits near the east end of the feature. The elevation of the floor averages 635.49 m, the bottom of the pits is approximately 634.79 m. No temporal placement of the feature is possible from the profile wall ceramics (Table 5.32). Tentatively, the fill area is interpreted to be a house, but it may have been a borrow area that became filled later with some trash and soil from nearby occupation surfaces.

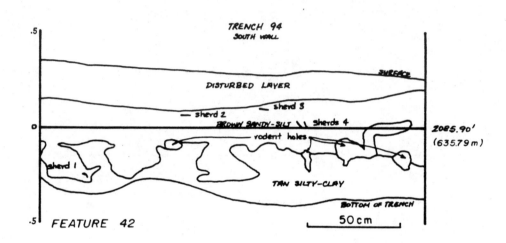

Figure 5.27. Profile of Feature 42.

Feature 43: House?

Feature 43 was assigned to a possible house basin located at the north end of Trench 72, N650 E850. Field notes indicate a concentration of fine white ash, charcoal and sherds--probably representing several vessels. Surface collections from N650 E850 and collections made from the trench backdirt indicate a Preclassic occupation in this area of the site (Table 5.33). No formal profile was measured and drawn, and no attempt has yet been made to reconstruct the vessels represented.

Table 5.32

CERAMICS FROM FEATURE 42

Type	Feature
Indeterminate Red-on-brown	2
Plain ware (micaceous variety)	16
Plain ware (nonmicaceous variety)	2
Total	20

Table 5.33

CERAMICS FROM FEATURE 43

Type	Surface	Backdirt
Rillito Red-on-brown	-	1
Rillito-Rincon Red-on-brown	-	5
Rincon Red-on-brown	-	2
Tanque Verde Red-on-brown	-	2
Indeterminate Red-on-brown	6	16
Indeterminate Red-on-buff	1	2
Buff ware	1	-
Rincon Red	-	2
Indeterminate red ware	1	2
Plain ware (micaceous variety)	19	188
Plain ware (nonmicaceous variety)	6	24
Total	34	244

Feature 44: Sherd Concentration

Near the eastern edge of Mound 1 (N1413 E1080), a concentrated pile of sherds was discovered during testing of the mound area. Dimensions of the stack were approximately 1 m by 1 m. This was assigned feature number 44. The stack contains ceramics from multiple time periods and so cannot be assigned to a particular time (Table 5.34). William L. Deaver has stated that the feature is similar to sherd and rock clusters recorded by the Arizona State Museum's Salt-Gila Project in the Apache Junction and Florence areas. No specific function was attributed to these features.

Table 5.34

CERAMICS FROM FEATURE 44

Type	Feature
Rillito-Rincon Red-on-brown	1
Rincon Red-on-brown	15
Tanque Verde Red-on-brown	14
Indeterminate Red-on-brown	18
Sacaton Red-on-buff	2
Indeterminate Red-on-buff	4
Plain ware (micaceous variety)	186
Plain ware (nonmicaceous variety)	89
Total	329

Feature 45: Pit

Feature 45 is discussed under the description for Feature 39.

Feature 46: Pit

Feature 46 is a pit discovered in the vicinity of Mound 1. It was defined in one portion of a 4-m by 4-m unit (northwest corner is

N1448 E1072). Feature 46 was recorded as a pit. No further information
is available because the feature was not further defined.

Feature 47: Crematory

Feature 47 was excavated in relation to testing of the
vegetation anomaly (Chapter 6) by Henry Wallace and James Holmlund. The
following is abstracted from summary notes made by James Holmlund.

Feature 47 is a cremation pit measuring 180-cm long by 76-cm
wide, oriented slightly northwest to southeast (Fig. 5.28). It is
defined by cremated bone and charcoal in the pit and fill above the pit,
and an oxidized (reddened) rim of soil forming the pit wall. Depth of
oxidation ranges from 2 cm thick along the northwest side of the pit to
8 cm thick near the southeast corner.

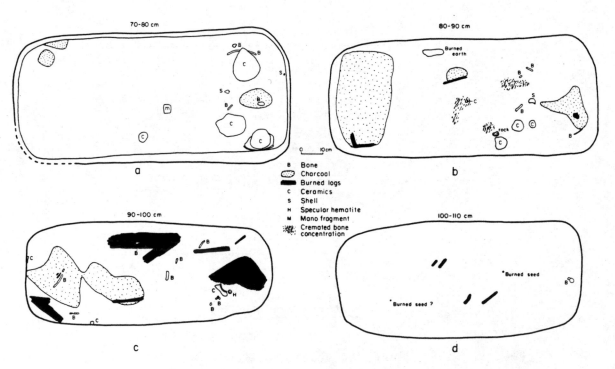

Figure 5.28. Plan map of Feature 47.

The feature is located at N1520-1522 E1024-1026 and was found to
be 50 cm deep. The elevation at the rim is approximately 635.80 m. The
crematory was divided into quarters along the axes of the pit for
purposes of bagging materials and was excavated in 10-cm levels.

The upper 10 cm of fill contained numerous clumps of burnt clay and soil, some charcoal, and very little cremated bone. A large burnt log was noted lying 10 cm to 30 cm from the east end of the pit. Just west of this log was found a shell "cache" containing burnt, broken Laevicardium shell fragments and a whole (burnt) Conus shell. A burned bone awl was also found with the shell materials. Five large sherds of a plainware jar were also found in the eastern end of the pit. Several Olivella shells were recovered from around the sherds. A Tanque Verde Red-on-brown sherd was found in the northeast corner and a mano fragment occurred near the center. The fill was relatively charcoal-free until near the bottom of this level.

The level 10 cm to 20 cm below the rim of the pit contained a much higher concentration of charcoal--particularly in the eastern end. At the western end, the charcoal is denser toward the bottom of the level. Although there are fewer clumps of burnt clay and soil, cremated bone increases in quantity, especially below the 15-cm level. Bone was located in two distinct areas of the pit, one at the center of the pit and extending south contained several vertebral fragments. The second concentration occurs slightly south of center in the northeast quadrant. This contained fragments of the mandible and long bones. Very little bone occurred in the west end of the pit.

Two more Laevicardium shell fragments were found below the area of the "cache" in Level 1. Three more sherds were found near the edge in the southeast quadrant. A small lump of specular hematite was found near the concentration of vertebral fragments, but it disintegrated and could not be collected. Two rocks were also recovered from the level-- one in the north pit wall in the northwest quadrant and one near the sherds in the southeast quadrant.

Charcoal was very prevalent in this level (10 cm to 20 cm), with a large mass in the western one-quarter of the pit that was otherwise sterile. It was determined that the large log noted in the eastern portion of the pit in Level 1 was probably standing vertically at this level.

The next level (20 cm to 30 cm) shows a shift in the concentration of materials. Although large logs occur in the southwest corner, north-central, and east-central areas of the pit, the charcoal and bone concentration shifts from the east to the west-central area. Some bone does occur in the east half of the pit, as do a flake, another lump of specular hematite, and a jar rim sherd. A Tanque Verde Red-on-brown sherd occurs along the south wall in the southwest quadrant and a plainware sherd occurs in the wall in the northwest corner.

Smaller burnt twigs and a few carbonized seeds were found in the next level (30 cm to 40 cm). It was noted that there was less charcoal and minimal amounts of bone in this level. One sherd was recovered from the northwest quadrant.

The level 40 cm to 50 cm below the rim reached the bottom of the crematory. Very little charcoal was present in the fill, but there was a small concentration of bone in the southwest quadrant. No features were noted in the floor; it appeared to be hard-packed or hard-fired and relatively flat.

Feature 47 is dated to the Tanque Verde phase based on the diagnostic sherds recovered in the fill. Radiocarbon samples were taken but have not been analyzed. The bone materials also have not been examined in detail. The upper levels of the pit show materials concentrated toward the east end. This is similar to the treatment of remains in Feature 32 (Los Morteros) and to the numerous cremations recovered at the Rabid Ruin (see Arizona State Museum Library Archives A-1155) where treatment seems even more formalized. Frequently, materials were scooped together into the eastern portion of the pit and a vessel was inverted over them.

Feature 48: Crematory

Feature 48 (Fig. 5.29) was a crematory pit similar to and located near Feature 47, located very nearby. Feature 48 is at N1518-1520 E1026-1025. Feature 48 also seems to date to the Tanque Verde

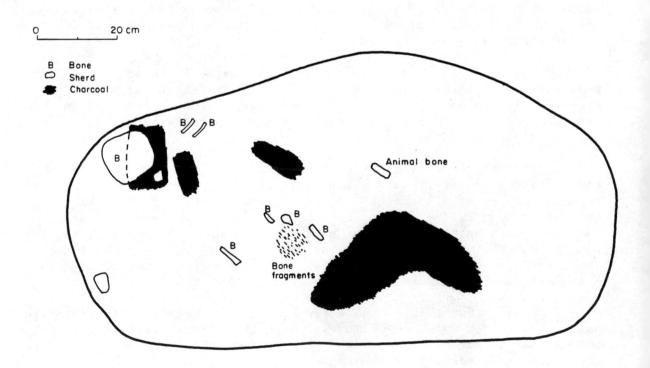

Figure 5.29. Plan map of Feature 48.

phase. Very little remained of the feature, its upper fill having been mixed into the disturbed/plow zone. In elevation, the bottom of Feature 48 is above the bottom of Feature 47.

Bone and charcoal had been noted in the fill above where it was eventually possible to define the edges of the pit. Excavating in a fashion similar to Feature 47 (in quarters by 10-cm levels), only two levels were excavated before reaching the floor of the crematory. The pit was also oriented northwest to southeast, and measures 135-cm long by 75-cm wide.

In the first 10-cm level, charcoal concentrations were found in the south-central and northwest quadrant areas. The bone fragments and sherds were located in the western half of the crematory.

In the second 10-cm level (10 cm to 20 cm below the rim), charcoal was concentrated in the upper portion of the level, although in the northwestern quadrant, charcoal and bone were noted throughout the level. A projectile point (Classic period style) and a flake were recovered from the southwest quadrant at this level.

As with Feature 47, further analyses of the materials recovered have not been done.

Feature 50: House

Feature 50, a very small house approximately 2 m in diameter, with an unusual collection of artifacts, was discovered during the testing of Mound 8. This puts its location south of Mound 1, on the O'Daniels/Waddell portion of the site (see Figure 1.2). It has a well-formed and well-plastered hearth, as well as a heavily plastered floor. These two attributes would themselves make this house unusual, irregardless of its size, for the range of houses found during the testing at Los Morteros. An article specifically discussing this feature and its artifacts is in preparation and so it will not be discussed further here.

Features 52 and 60: Hornos

Features 52 and 60 are two large hornos found as a result of the test trenching of Mound 27. Feature 52 was discovered by the trenching, and Feature 60 was discovered during the process of defining Feature 52. Although these may not be the only features associated with Mound 27, it became apparent that the source of the ashy soil and fire cracked rock in Mound 27 was from these two (and conceivably other) hornos at the center of the mound.

Features 52 and 60 were either heavily plastered or were excavated into a matrix different from most other areas of Los Morteros. The hornos and surrounding soil is a compacted, caliche-like soil. The high temperatures and presumably repeated use of these features has given them a thick black rind, partially due to the firing conditions and partially due to the organic materials processed in the hornos. Both hornos have inward sloping upper shoulders that then drop nearly vertically to a flat bottom.

Feature 52 is roughly circular (Fig. 5.30), about 2.2 m in diameter at the top, and 1.2 m in diameter at the bottom. Feature 52 was filled with fire-cracked rock and ashy soil, to the point of being mounded up in the center, above the top of the lip. The rock varied from fist-sized and smaller spalls to basketball-sized boulders. Most of the rock appeared to be the volcanic rhyolite and andesite available on the slopes just west of the site. Several of the larger boulders were on the floor of the feature but did not seem to be placed in any particular arrangement.

Feature 60 is roughly circular (Fig. 5.30), but elongated north to south. It measures 3.1 m north-south by 2.7 m east-west at the top, and 2.3 m by 2.0 m at the bottom. When first exposed, the fill was concave, dropping toward the center of the horno, and no rocks were visible. Excavation revealed a ring of rock around the inside of the horno, just below the rim. Otherwise the fill was loose, ashy, and silty. Three large rocks and one slightly smaller rock, all spalled from the intense heat of the crematory fire, were evenly spaced around the bottom of the horno. These rocks probably supported the basic structure of the fire, foods, and rocks placed into the horno to sustain the heat and cook the foods.

The one horno being filled with rock (F.52) and one being essentially empty (F.60) raises the possibility that these hornos were used simultaneously in the food-cooking operation. The rocks could have been heated in one horno, while food was stacked into the other. The rocks could then have been transferred to the food-filled horno to complete the cooking process with a minimum heat loss.

The large numbers of sherds found in the hornos (Table 5.35) may also indicate the use of these features for firing large ceramic vessels. Or the sherds represent trash thrown into the hornos or their use as heat-retaining items.

The archaeomagnetic dating results from these features are somewhat unclear (Feature 52: A.D. 970-1090, 1060-1150 [LM 014] and A.D. 1000-1090, 1060-1220, 1200-1250 [LM 015]; Feature 60: A.D.950-1070, 1150-1360 [LM 016] and A.D. 1000-1090, 1060-1170 [LM 017]). They can be interpreted, however, as supporting the contemporaneity of the use of these features (in the period A.D. 1000 to 1200). Contemporaneity of the features is also suggested by the ceramics recovered from them (Tables 5.34 and 5.35). The archaeomagnetic dates tend toward an interpretation of a Pre-classic, Rincon phase use, while

141

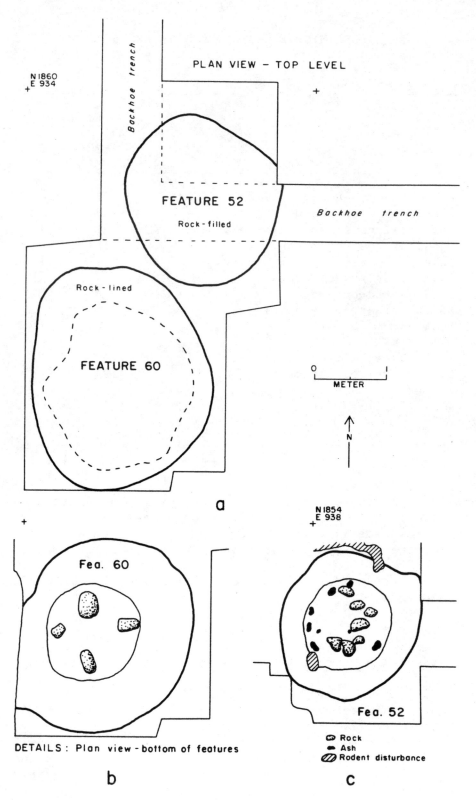

Figure 5.30. Plan maps of Features 52 and 60.

Table 5.35

CERAMICS FROM FEATURES 52 AND 60

Type	Feature 52	Feature 60
Rincon Red-on-brown	1	
Cortaro Red-on-brown	2	8
Cortaro-Tanque Verde Red-on-brown	11	12
Tanque Verde Red-on-brown	28	212
Indeterminate red-on-brown	7	11
San Carlos red-on-brown		1
Sacaton Red-on-buff	4	1
Indeterminate red-on-buff	5	1
Buff ware		15
Gila Plain	1	2
Plain ware (micaceous variety)	112	391
Plain ware (nonmicaceous)	124	686
Total	295	1340

the ceramics indicate a Tanque Verde phase use. The alternative is that dates for the Tanque Verde phase should be placed prior to A.D. 1200. The radiocarbon date is even earlier than any of the date ranges suggested by the archaeomagnetic samples (see Appendixes M and N).

Results from flotation samples taken from Features 52 and 60 are listed in Appendix I.

Features 53 through 59: Houses and Cremation Vessels

Features 53 through 59 were recorded in conjunction with testing in and around Mound 7. Five of these features are houses, several of which are superimposed. One feature was recorded as a stone-lined pit (Feature 54). No further information is available on these features. Supervision of work at these features and analysis of materials was not directly controlled by the Los Morteros Project.

The other feature discovered by this testing was a cluster of whole and painted vessels, some of which contained portions of human cremations. Feature 58 consisted of 7 vessels: 1 loop-handled (handle missing) nonmicaceous plain ware jar; 1 nonmicaceous plain ware tab-handled jar, 1 nonmicaceous plain ware jar (incomplete), 3 Tanque Verde Red-on-Brown bowls (1 is a Black Paint Variety), and 1 Tanque Verde Red-on-Brown jar (Figs. 0.6, 0.7).

Feature 60

Feature 60 is discussed in the description of Feature 52.

Feature 61:   Pit

Feature 61 was recorded in the profile wall of an east-west machine trench through the center of Mound 1. The feature was located approximately 2 m west of the center of the mound, 25 cm to 30 cm below the surface of the mound. It consists of rocks, which are mostly fist-sized. Several of the rocks are mano fragments, while others are hammerstones. The feature appears to be prehistoric, but could be a collection of material deposited in the bottom of a pothunters hole. No diagnostic materials were present to facilitate temporal placement of the feature. It was not investigated further.

Feature 62:   House

Feature 62 was also excavated by a program not directly under the control of the Los Morteros Project. It was first recorded as Feature 40 during the flurry of testing on February 9, 1980. This testing revealed the edge of a house basin in a 2-m by 2-m test pit (N1438 E1073). Because another feature number was used during the subsequent excavation of a portion of the feature, the feature number originally assigned (40) has been voided.

At this time, there are no notes or analyses from the subsequent excavation in the possession of the project. The feature is a house (Tanque Verde phase?) located to the northwest of Feature 39, 30 m north of Mound 1 (in the area of N1430-1440 E1070-1080). It appeared to have burned, and the entryway may have faced to the west.

Feature 63:   Cremation Vessel

Feature 63 was assigned to an isolated urn cremation recovered from the backhoe bucket during the excavation of Trench 47, N1490 E955. The bone recovered from the vessel was analyzed as Cremation No. 2 by T. Michael Fink (see Appendix K).   The vessel is a Tanque Verde Red-on-brown loop-handled jar with a Tanque Verde Red-on-brown bowl cover sherd (IN 534, Figs. O.6 - O.7).   No further information is available about its context because of the manner in which it was discovered.   No obvious pit or other features were noticed when the trench was profiled.

Feature 66:   Pit, Well?

This feature was also recorded during the machine testing of the vegetation anomaly (Chapter 6) directed by Henry Wallace and James Holmlund.   (It is labeled Feature 51 in their notes, but was re-labeled here to fit into the master list.)   Originally thought to be a canal, Feature 66 instead seems to be a deep pit (Fig. 5.31).   Henry Wallace is hesitant to assign the feature a particular label or function without results from additional studies, such as pollen.   One possible interpretation of the feature is as a walk-in well, a type of feature noted in this general area in early historic times.

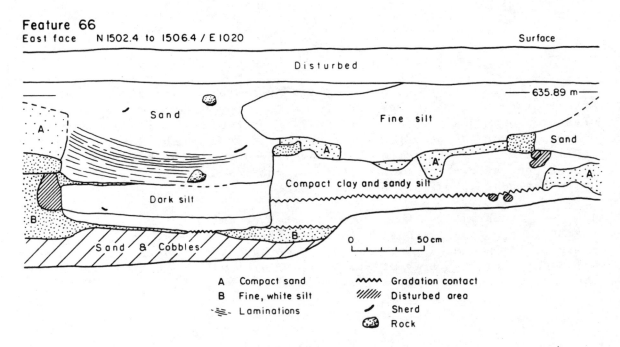

Figure 5.31.   Profile of Feature 66.

The feature, like many of the canal features, can be dated to the Tanque Verde phase. The bottom of the pit is approximately 1.25 m below present surface, the elevation at the top edge is 635.90 m, at the bottom, 634.94 m. Dimensions at the top of the feature, oval or roughly circular, are 1.5 m north-south by 1.3 m (minimum) east-west. The lower portion of the feature has dimensions of 1.25 m by 1.10 m. Feature 66 is located at N1492.6-1492.4 E1023.5-1025.

The fill of the pit contains several distinctive soil/sand mixes, as well as obvious laminations at certain levels. The upper fill contained many sherds (including Tanque Verde Red-on-brown), lithics, a whole mano, and fire-cracked rocks. Flakes, cores, a hammerstone, decorated and plain ware sherds, and several rocks were found in the lower fill. Many of these decorated sherds are also Tanque Verde Red-on-brown.

The Ball Court

The ball court at Los Morteros is located on the gravel terrace southwest of the core area of the site. It was noted at the time the caves on the slopes to the west were recorded (AZ AA:12:27), but has never been formally investigated.

The court is located at N 1000-1065 E 780-840. It is visible as a dark spot, caused by the dense creosote bush growth on its interior, on available aerial photographs taken from 1936 to 1980 (see Chapter 7 for a listing of these). An accurate but coarse map of the ballcourt is shown in Figure 5.32.

Mapping showed the dimensions to be roughly 60 m long by 25 m wide, with an orientation approximately 34.5 degrees west of true north. This relatively small size and general north-south orientation would lead to its classification as a "Casa Grande type" ball court, dating to the Sedentary and Classic periods (Kelly 1978: 5). This general dating is supported by the surface collections from this area of the terrace. Two clusters of unshaped, small- to medium-sized (basketball-sized or less) volcanic boulders occur in the court. One is approximately at the center, the other is off-center at the northern end of the court. Although it can be assumed that these rock clusters "belong" to the court, testing would be necessary to confirm this.

N 1060—

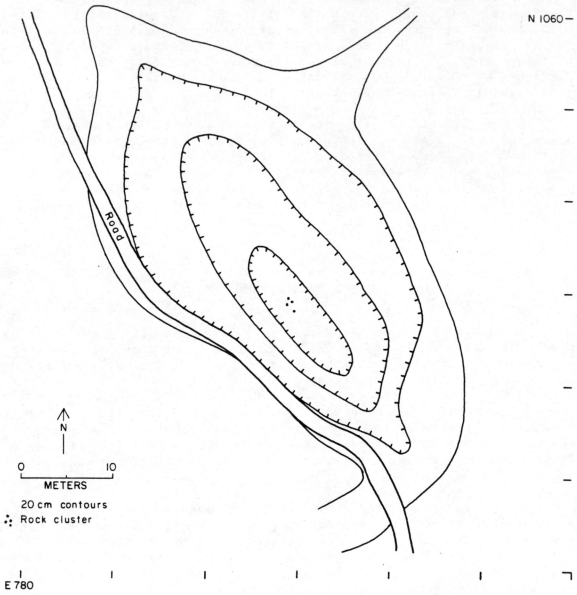

N

0   10
METERS

20 cm contours
Rock cluster

E 780

Figure 5.32. Plan map of the ball court.

Chapter 6

SPECIFIC TESTING ACTIVITIES

Richard C. Lange

In conjunction with the initial testing of Los Morteros, several specific activities were conducted. These involved a machine trenching test of the southern vegetation anomaly, directed by Henry Wallace and James Holmlund; excavations around the bedrock mortars, directed by me; and excavations in the hill-slope trincheras, directed by several persons. These activities are summarized here.

A Test of the Southern Vegetation Anomaly

In the area of Los Morteros north and east of the terrace, there are several recurrent patterns (lines and arcs of vegetation) that show up consistently on the earliest known aerial photographs of the site area. Some are thought to be shadows of subsurface canals, others could be related to village features, such as a compound.

There are three principal features, which we termed "vegetation anomalies." Two are horseshoe-shaped features, both opening to the south with one displaced slightly to the northwest of the most visible one; and a long linear feature that cuts through the southern horseshoe and runs into or alongside the northern one. The western arm of the southern anomaly was cut several times with backhoe trenches during the initial testing. Each time the arm was cut, it appeared that some sort of feature, usually a house basin, was found near the vegetation anomaly.

During the spring of 1981, a further test of the southern anomaly was directed by Wallace and Holmlund in conjunction with students from a University of Arizona Continuing Education class. The test consisted of two large machine trenches oriented north-south, and a smaller one oriented east-west (Fig. 6.1), excavated by either a 910 or 950 Caterpillar front-end loader. Use of the heavy equipment was arranged through Larry McIntyre, a resident in the La Puerta del Norte trailer park. The excavations were made in the northeastern "arm" of the anomaly in the area N1460-1530 E1020-1030. This is on the

148

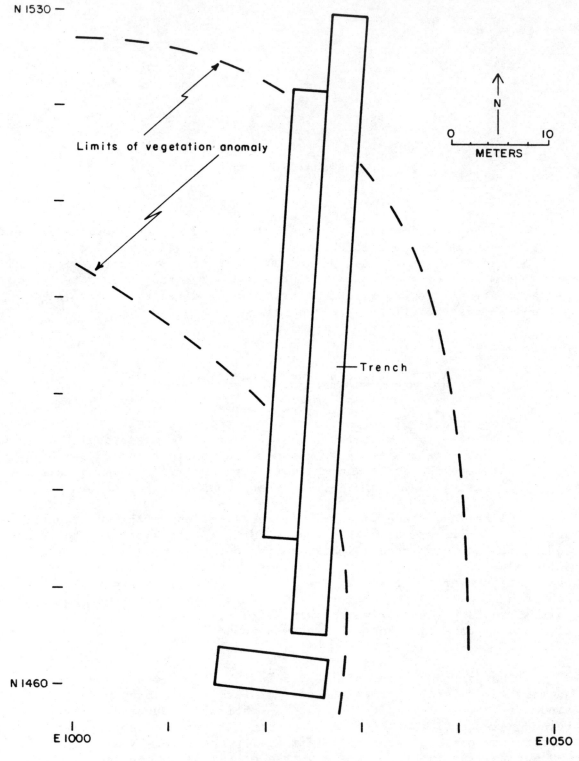

Figure 6.1. Machine trenches excavated in the northeastern area of the southern vegetation anomaly.

O'Daniels/ Waddell-Haskins property, Site Area 8 (see Fig. 1.2).
Portions of the trenches were excavated to over 2 m in depth.

Numerous features were identified in the floors of the trenches
and in the profile walls. Only those features that were tested or
excavated--Features 47, 48, and 66--were assigned numbers.
Descriptions of these features are provided in Chapter 5.

This investigation of the vegetation anomaly reveal did not one
feature or type of feature that was responsible for the anomaly. This
area of the site seems to contain a concentration of various types of
features and trash deposits. Further investigation, especially by wide
horizontal exposures, will be necessary to establish definitive
relationships between the anomaly and particular features.

Testing Near the Bedrock Mortars

In the fall of 1982, test excavations were made in the vicinity
of the bedrock mortars. These mortars, from which the site takes its
name, are located near the center of the site, in the Donated Parcel
(Site Area 2, Fig. 1.2). A persistent dark stain being eroded to the
west of the tall mortar boulder led to expectations that artifacts and
features related to the use of the mortars might be identified.

The bedrock mortars and petroglyphs of the Los Morteros area
have been thoroughly documented (Wallace and Holmlund 1983). The major
bedrock mortar boulders, designated MK-1 and MK-2 in Wallace and
Holmlund's study, are referred to as the taller and lower boulders,
respectively. Unfortunately, their map and our map were made to
different grid orientations and scales, and a map that combines the two
versions has not been prepared. We had left off mapping each individual
mortar knowing that Wallace and Holmlund had mapped the rock, hoping to
just overlay our outline of the newly excavated area and mortars over
theirs. The incongruence of our maps was not discovered until the Los
Morteros Project was out of the field. Figure 6.2 shows the limits of
our excavations and the extent of the bedrock in those units.

After clearing vegetation, a 5-m by 15-m area, divided into 5-m
by 5-m grids, was set out. This was located at N1200-1215 E960-965.
Two 2-m by 2-m units were used to test the dark stain. Very few
artifacts were found in association with the stain in these units,
located at N1198 E962 and N1196 E962, and there was little depth to the
stain (2 cm or less). A closer examination of the ashy material
determined that the stain may have been briquette dust from a barbecue
grill.

The other units were excavated immediately around the lower
mortar boulder. Comparison of a photograph taken in 1912 in conjunction
with Ellsworth Huntington's studies (1912: 399) revealed about 30 cm to
40 cm of soil build-up around the mortars since 1912. From the photo,

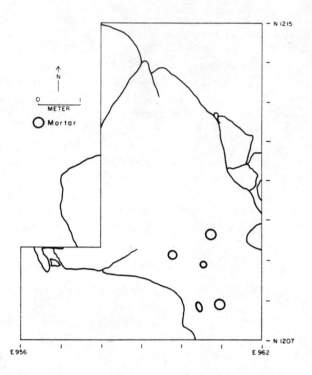

Figure 6.2. Plan map of the excavations near the bedrock mortars.

it appears that at least one mortar has been buried by the soil build-up. The photograph also shows saguaros on and below the terrace. Today, the saguaros are restricted to the slopes of the Tucson Mountains west of Silverbell Road.

Excavations located the buried mortar on the north face of the boulder, as well as five others on the southeast corner of the boulder. In a hollow on the southern face of the boulder, several rough rocks were found that could be blanks for pestles. In this same area, a metate, turned upside down, was recovered from N1209 E958(2). Otherwise, relatively little artifactual material was recovered and no other features were identified (Fig. 6.2). Ceramics that were recovered from the bedrock mortar area indicate that use of the mortars was probably not restricted to just one phase (Tables 6.1 and 6.2).

An intriguing possibility was raised by the testing. Depth below surface to the bedrock on the southeast corner of the lower boulder was remarkably shallow, and a small tip of bedrock is exposed between the two large boulders. Thus the lower and taller bedrock mortar boulders could be joined by a "bridge" of bedrock. Additional mortars could be present on this surface, making this an even more important work area at the site. Not all areas of bedrock are expected to have mortars, as the bedrock is often crumbly and not suitable for mortars at particular areas on the main boulders. This may be the

Table 6.1

CERAMICS FROM ALL LEVELS, N1196 AND N1198 E962, BEDROCK MORTARS AREA

Types	Counts
Tanque Verde Red-on-brown	3
Indeterminate Red-on-brown	3
Indeterminate Red-on-buff	5
Indeterminate painted	1
Plain ware (micaceous variety)	46
Plain ware (nonmicaceous variety)	62
Total	120

Table 6.2

CERAMICS FROM ALL LEVELS, N1207-1211 E956-960, BEDROCK MORTARS AREA

Types	Counts
Rillito-Rincon Red-on-brown	1
Rincon Red-on-brown	3
Cortaro-Tanque Verde Red-on-brown	1
Tanque Verde Red-on-brown	3
Indeterminate Red-on-brown	11
Sacaton Red-on-buff	1
Indeterminate Red-on-buff	1
Buff ware	1
Indeterminate brown ware	5
Indeterminate red ware	1
Plain (micaceous variety)	200
Plain (nonmicaceous variety)	244
Total	472

principal reason an outcrop 20 m to 30 m to the west and north of the bedrock mortars has no apparent mortars, grinding surfaces, or petroglyphs.

Investigations of the Trincheras

Part of the archaeological activity at Los Morteros was focused on an investigation of the trincheras (terrace, "fort") features located on the hill slopes west of the intersection of Linda Vista Boulevard and Silverbell Road. In an effort to understand these features, reference panels of butcher paper were placed at various points on the hill slope and an aerial photograph was taken. On the resulting aerial photograph, the features were located and identified. Each feature was measured and a surface collection made. Two small test trenches were excavated to recover pollen and soil samples.

Later, two terraces that were relatively low on the hillside were tested under the direction of Christian Downum and Denise Shay. Two houses (one definitely Tanque Verde phase in age, the other possibly earlier) were discovered and excavated during this testing. Samples for archaeomagnetic dating and a radiocarbon sample were recovered and analyzed from the hearth of each house. These results are presented in Appendix M and N. Susan Wells also directed testing on top of the trincheras hill in a cleared "plaza" area. Ceramics recovered from the trincheras indicate a predominantly Tanque Verde phase use of the hill slope. A summary of trincheras ceramics is included in Appendix B.

A detailed description of this work can be found in Fish, Fish, and Downum (1984) and in Downum (1986).

Chapter 7

DISCUSSION AND SUMMARY

Richard C. Lange

The testing done at Los Morteros (AZ AA:12:57) has met the initial research goals. It is evident that little disturbance or destruction has affected the site, and it is possible to recover a variety of valuable information.

Ceramic, lithic, and macrobotanical data have been integrated into the discussion in preceding chapters when possible. These data, along with ancillary descriptions of various aspects of the site and the results of special studies, are also presented in the appendixes to this report. Specifically, the appendixes include tabulations of trench and feature locations, pollen samples taken, analyses of human and animal remains, analysis of the botanical remains recovered, and descriptions of the principal soil components. Results from chronometric analyses, an experiment in phosphate testing, an analysis of paint pigments used on Tanque Verde Red-on-brown pottery, and a discussion of locations of manufacture of tools and projectile points are also included. These studies and tabulations show that a wide range of information is present at Los Morteros, and that valuable insights, of at least a preliminary nature, are available from this initial testing of the site.

The testing has revealed that the site is a spatially large village, or cluster of roughly contemporaneous smaller villages, predominantly dating to the late Colonial, Sedentary, and early Classic periods (Rillito, Rincon, and Tanque Verde phases). There is one principal core area at the site, defined by the higher density of surface artifacts (Chapter 3, Fig. 3.1), by the higher concentration of features discovered by subsurface testing (Chapter 5, Fig. 5.1), and by the greater occurrence of superposition of the features in this area. Most of the mounds also occur in this area, although the apparent distribution may be distorted by modern disturbances. This core area is approximately 350 m by 250 m in size, and occurs from N 1200 to 1550, E 850 to 1100 in our grid system. It lies northeast of the terrace area and probably includes the terrace area, as the bedrock mortars, several mounds, and the ball court are located there (Fig. 7.1). Although ball courts are not as rare in the Tucson Basin as once thought (Doyel 1984: 184), the presence of the ball court still accords Los Morteros a place as a major or central site in the settlement system.

154

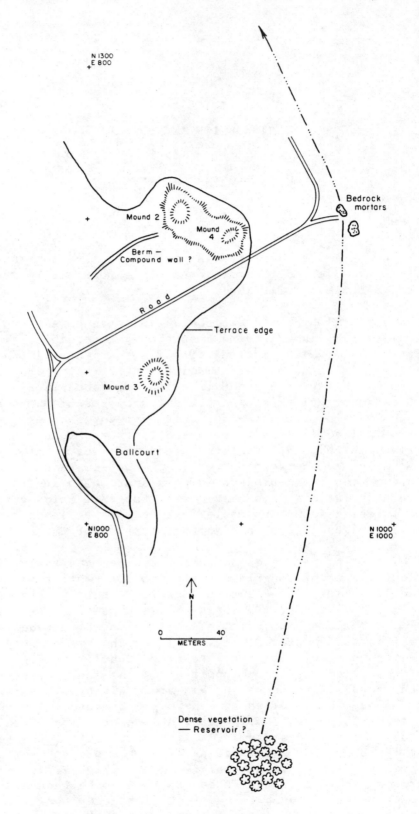

N 1300
E 800

Bedrock
mortars

Mound 2

Mound
4

Berm —
Compound wall ?

Road

Terrace edge

Mound 3

Ballcourt

N1000
E 800

N 1000
E 1000

N

0   40
METERS

Dense vegetation
— Reservoir ?

Figure 7.1. Map of the terrace area at Los Morteros.

There is one other feature on the terrace that is only tentatively defined at present. Roughly abutted to Mound 2, a dirt berm, filled with fire-cracked rock and sherds, arcs away to the west and southwest (Fig. 7.1). It encloses a flat area to the south that curiously is clear of sherds and large pebbles. The berm may be part of a compound wall. It is assumed to be a prehistoric feature, but needs to be investigated further before its temporal or cultural placement can be ascertained.

Also noted near Mound 2 on the terrace was a possible stone foundation of a house, but it has been badly disturbed by vandalism. Such houses were noted at Los Morteros in the early 1900s by Ellsworth Huntington (Huntington 1912). Only one other instance of above-ground architecture or stone foundations is presently visible--along the modern sewage canal running across the northern end of the site. The rare stone foundations at Los Morteros contrasts markedly with the Huntington Site (AZ AA:12:73), just north of Rillito Peak, or through the pass at the north end of the Tucson Mountains from Los Morteros. The occupation of the Huntington Site appears to go into the Tucson phase. At the Huntington site there is a block of contiguous above-ground rooms and more Gila Polychrome pottery than is found at Los Morteros.

The occupation of the Los Morteros site area seems to initially occur in the Rillito and Rincon phases, with the heavier occupation in the Rincon phase. Only sparse material is available from the preceding Colonial and Archaic periods, indicating some unintensive use of the site area in these times. A Cañada del Oro and Rillito phase site is located just south of Los Morteros. This is now known as Red Tail Village (AZ AA:12:149), and has been investigated by William D. Hohmann and the Arizona Archaeological and Historical Society, and by the Institute for American Research, in conjunction with development by the American Continental Corporation.

The Rillito and Rincon phase occupations occur north of Linda Vista Boulevard in the core area, and in the field south of Linda Vista. The occupation south of Linda Vista may have been a satellite settlement to the core area or just one of several small house clusters in the general vicinity. After the Rincon phase, a more serious nucleation into the core area seems to occur. The surface and subsurface collections reflect minimal occupation or no use in the south field during the Classic period (see Appendix B, Site Area 6). Subsequent alluviation has effectively protected the remains in the south field, despite a long period of mechanized agriculture.

The core area of Los Morteros continued to be occupied during the Tanque Verde phase, with the dominance of Tanque Verde Red-on-brown in the ceramic collections indicating an even more intensive occupation than had previously occurred. Even this occupation seems to have been effectively sealed by subsequent alluviation (see Chapter 6, discussion of the bedrock mortar area). Little plowing was done in the area north of Linda Vista: the area was regarded as being too sandy. Plowing may have disturbed several features, for example Feature 48, but most features seem to be largely intact. None of the trenching revealed features that had been disturbed by channel cutting in the floodplain. The alluviation pattern in the canals and the bowl that seemingly was buried near a gravel bar (Feature 20) may indicate active channels near the core area of the site.

The occupation of Los Morteros seems to end in the Tanque Verde phase; ceramic and architectural evidence is lacking for any Tucson phase component. Something curious about the architectural remains seems apparent given the dominance of Tanque Verde Red-on-brown pottery in the ceramic collection. Of all the houses that seem to date to the Tanque Verde phase (8 of the 17 total houses, see Table 5.1), only two-- Features 6 and 35--exhibit the heavy adobe/caliche foundations of the standing wall houses considered typical of the architecture of the phase (Kelly 1978: 7-8).

Of the features discovered during testing (66 were given numbers), 62 percent of the ones that are tentatively datable (45 fit this criteria) are dated to the Tanque Verde phase, and 31 percent are dated to the Rillito and Rincon phases. This lack of "typical" Tanque Verde phase architecture may indicate that this type of architecture is not in fact typical, or that the occupation of Los Morteros is so early in the phase that what became "typical" had not yet gelled.

A third alternative, scouring and destruction of features by flooding, is discounted at this time. With continual deposition, Tanque Verde phase features could be expected to be relatively higher than other features. A major flood could scour these features away, leaving no evidence of their presence. However, the proportion of Tanque Verde phase features is in line with the predominance of Tanque Verde Red-on-brown pottery in the ceramic assemblage. It would seem unlikely that a major portion of the evidence of the Tanque Verde occupation is missing, and that the site was later re-capped by alluvium, thus protecting the remaining features against recent flooding and agriculture. Further detailed study of the floodplain stratigraphy may help in resolving this issue.

The dating techniques attempted at Los Morteros--radiocarbon and archaeomagnetism--produced mixed results. On the negative side, multiple samples from a single feature produced different interpretations, and there is often disagreement between the archaeomagnetic and radiocarbon results (Fig. 7.2). One method does not give consistently earlier or later results than the other. On the positive side, the general date ranges from both techniques support the late Preclassic and early Classic period occupation of Los Morteros, and the contemporaneity of some features can be established (for example, Features 52 and 60). The most consistent anomaly in the dating seems to be with respect to the placement of the Tanque Verde phase. The archaeomagnetic dates for the Tanque Verde features fall into the A.D. 1000 or 1050 to 1200 period (Features 109 and 137 in the trincheras, and Features 8, 32, and, to some extent, 39). This indicates a potentially

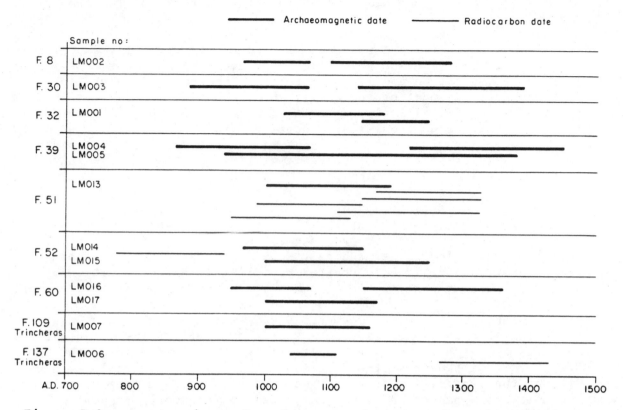

Figure 7.2. A comparison of archaeomagnetic and radiocarbon dates from Los Morteros.

earlier date for the Tanque Verde phase than the A.D. 1200 date that is traditionally accepted (see also Wallace and Holmlund 1984: 170 for similar indications).

The distribution and significance of features remain largely unknown in the three areas of the site--the donated parcel (Site Area 2), the trailer park (Site Area 10), and the vegetation anomalies. Also, no information was found indicating the location of a cremation floor or mound. Because no systematic trenching was done in the donated parcel (the terrace area), it is not certain what sorts of features may be there. The ball court, bedrock mortars, several mounds, and a possible compound wall are visible on the surface. There is also a potential reservoir in that area. It is expected that houses and other features also occur in the parcel.

Two volunteers, Joe and Kay Burke, canvassed the trailer park to ask about what residents may have found, to inspect yards for surface artifacts if permitted, and to note the locations of possible mounds. These contacts eventually led to the recovery of a burial from one yard (see Appendix J). Several mounds were noted and artifact distribution may indicate an extension of the core area into the western portion of

158

the trailer court. Actual distribution of artifacts and features
remains unknown.

The vegetation anomalies have also not been totally explained
(see Chapter 6). A number of different feature types occur in and near
the denser vegetation and lines of trees. The southern vegetation
pattern surrounds part of the core area of the site. This area is also
on a ridge that is slightly higher than other areas below the terrace.
There seems to be no consistent feature or group of features that can
currently explain the vegetation patterns. Only further investigation
exposing wide areas of the subsurface will reveal the relationships
among features and vegetation patterns.

Although three crematories were discovered (Features 32, 47, and
48), only two were located near each other (47 and 48). These two
features may be part of a larger cremation floor, but this is uncertain
at the moment. The large machine trenches excavated during testing of
the vegetation anomaly (see Chapter 6) failed to expose additional
crematories in this area. More could be located north of the trenches.

Three of the canal segments discovered are within the "higher"
elevation area inside the southern horseshoe. All of the water control
features at Los Morteros are essentially in the floodplain of the Santa
Cruz River, within or at the margins of the 100-year flood line.
Without the present day deep entrenchment of the Santa Cruz River, the
Los Morteros area may have been subjected to much more frequent
inundation than it is today.

Water and aspects of water management can be seen as central
factors in the occupation and development of Los Morteros. Along the
Santa Cruz River in the Tucson area, groundwater is close to the surface
in two areas; one near Black Mountain and Tumamoc Hill, the other
between Ina Road and the far north point of the Tucson Mountains. Two
factors may contribute to the higher water table at Los Morteros.
First, Los Morteros is hydrologically and geologically outside the
Tucson Basin, in what is known as the Cortaro Basin (Fogg 1978). These
basins are separated by a dike or large plug located near Ina Road that
lies well below the ground's surface. The floor of the Cortaro Basin is
higher than the floor of the Tucson Basin. Second, the Tucson Basin
narrows as it follows the course of the Santa Cruz out of the basin
proper. Both factors combine to force the water table higher around Los
Morteros. Walk-in wells were noted in the area in historic times, and
one prehistoric well may have been discovered by the testing (Feature
66; see Chapter 5).

Five features were identified as canals or possible canals. Why
are there canals in the floodplain; especially a floodplain where the
water table is high? Further study is necessary before this question
can be answered, including intensive trenching or areal exposures to
trace the canals and microstratigraphic studies of them. The following
interpretation, based on several related issues, may or may not be
supported.

The seeming lack of canals in the Tucson Basin has often been noted as (Doyel 1984: 153) or implied to be a major difference between the Tucson Basin and Salt-Gila Basin Hohokam. Although canals have been identified at several sites in the Tucson area, it is clear that none achieve the scale of those in the Salt-Gila Basin. A source for this difference between the Tucson and Salt-Gila basins may be due largely to physiographic differences in the basins and the major streams that water them.

With no quantified data to support the statements, it is nonetheless this author's impression that there are at least three major differences: (1) the floodplain of the Santa Cruz through the Tucson Basin is narrower and more limited in total acreage than similar lengths along the Salt and Gila rivers where the Hohokam lived, (2) the terraces above the floodplain are not as well developed and are also more limited in area for the Santa Cruz channel as compared to the Salt and Gila rivers in the Phoenix area, and (3) the stream flow is less, perhaps even much less, for the Santa Cruz in comparison to the Salt and Gila rivers (see also S. Fish, P. Fish, and Madsen 1985). Doyel (1984: 153) also notes: "the topography of the [Tucson] Basin does not lend itself to terrace agriculture by means of canals due to the predominance of heavy gravels, thin soil, and the lack of good locations for canal heads." These factors taken together help explain the limited use of canals in the Tucson Basin.

Without sufficient stream flow to push water into a canal system, little terrace land suitable for agriculture, and no good locations for heading canals, there was no reason, and largely no way, to conduct terrace agriculture along the Santa Cruz River. Terrace agriculture may have been essential to farming along the Salt and Gila rivers because violent flooding destroyed any attempts to do large-scale farming in the floodplain, destroying both crops and facilities such as canals. Without suitable terrace land, prehistoric Tucson Basin farmers used the bajada slopes—controlling the run-off and effectively harvesting water (Fish, Fish, Miksicek, and Madsen 1985)—and they used the floodplain. Less stream flow made this a safer proposition on the Santa Cruz. Canals could be used and if destroyed, were relatively easily rebuilt in the alluvial soils of the floodplain.

In an area with a high water table such as Los Morteros floodplain farming was even more inviting. Additional water brought in by canals may have been unnecessary or only needed in particular years. One possibility following from this thought is that the canals at Los Morteros were used more to collect and divert water through and around the site than to transport water into the site. There is some evidence that lends support to this.

Examining older aerial photographs (L479, 2/26/36; DHQ-2N-5 and DHQ-2N-8, 2/17/54; DHQ-2HH-102, 4/21/67; and CAS 2-6, 4/8/80—all on file at the Arizona State Museum), there is no indication of a major canal heading on the bends of the Santa Cruz to the southeast of Los Morteros. It is certainly possible that a canal head has been destroyed

by post-occupational scouring and changes of the river bed, but this is
seen as unlikely in light of the general stability and good preservation
of the rest of the site. In short, there is no indication that water
was transported from the main channel of the Santa Cruz to the Los
Morteros core area where the canal segments are found.

From the short visible segments and the alignments from one side
of a backhoe trench to another, the canals seem to be oriented north-
south. Looking again at the aerial photos (especially DHQ--2N-5) the
drainages from the east slopes of the Tucson Mountains, as far south as
Safford Peak, do not drain east directly into the Santa Cruz River.
Instead, they tend to drain north, combining into a major channel that
skirts the western edge of the floodplain, swirling out around the
terrace at Los Morteros, curving back to the west along the Tucsons, and
moving north to eventually empty into the Santa Cruz at Rillito Peak
(Fig. 7.1). Feature 33, a possible canal, may be an artificial
channeling or natural portion of this major drainage along the western
edge of the floodplain.

Four canals (Features 22, 19, 27 and 28) are located within the
arc of the southern vegetation anomaly. Based on limited evidence, all
of the canals seem to date to the Tanque Verde phase (see descriptions
in Chapter 5). The relationship of Feature 22 to the others is unclear,
but Features 19, 27, and 28 do appear to be related. Elevations of the
bottoms of the three canal segments show that a northward gradient from
19 into 27 and 28 is possible. As noted in Chapter 5, Feature 19 may
branch into Features 27 and 28.

Projecting the paths of these canals to the south, they lead
back to the area of the bedrock mortars and to the main drainage channel
as it skirts the terrace. The area along the property boundary near the
mortars is in this channel. It often holds water for days after a rain.
Following the drainage further south, there is a large clump of quite
large trees, directly in the path of the major drainage (just north of
Linda Vista Boulevard and in the southeast corner of the donated parcel,
Site Area 2). This is what is suspected to be a reservoir. It would
serve to capture runoff from a large slope area of the Tucson Mountains,
and hold it to be released into the major drainage or into one or more
of several canals that seem to pass through the core area of the site.

These canals may have had some combination of three specific
roles. To describe these roles, it is first necessary to add a brief
note about the nature of the canals. None of the canals discovered show
any sign of formal plastering or lining. Instead, in marked contrast,
the bottoms of the canals were excavated into porous strata of sand and
loose cobbles. Thus, the canals may have served more as drains to
remove surplus water from the site area, rather than as canals to
transport water. A related benefit would be a readily accessible water
supply throughout the core area of the site when the canals were
flowing. In periods or seasons of an extremely high water table the
canals could have been fed by infiltration, again providing a handy
water supply. Although the bottoms of the canals are below most

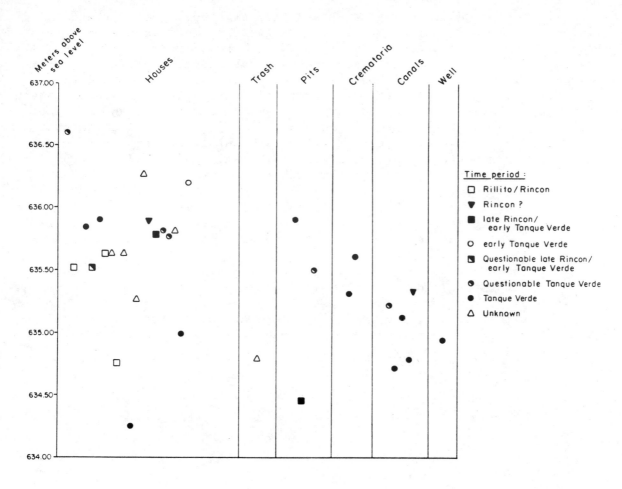

Figure 7.3. A comparison of feature floor elevations.

features, a few storage pits and houses are lower (Fig. 7.3) and could have been waterlogged if the water table could rise higher than the level of the canal bottoms. The concentration of features inside of the southern horseshoe of vegetation, on a slightly higher area, may be related to keeping the house floors above the water table.

These functions or benefits of the canals may have combined with another. The water may have been channeled north of the core of the site into an area of historically dense mesquite growth near Rillito Peak (only a small area presently remains along the west side of the gravel pit). The Cortaro area was named from the Spanish cortar (to cut) because of the need to clear dense thickets of mesquite in order to farm. Perhaps the prehistoric residents of Los Morteros were encouraging the thicket by irrigation in order to harvest a rich crop of mesquite beans. Bedrock mortars, like those from which the site takes its name, have been known to be used in processing mesquite and other hard beans (see Wallace and Holmlund 1983: 148-150).

Testing done to date at Los Morteros has provided a tantalizing
initial glimpse into the most intact large Hohokam village site
remaining in the Tucson Basin. Valuable information for studying a
variety of research problems appears to be abundantly available and
excellently preserved. Of particular interest is the potential to
answer questions related to settlement structure and to the Tucson Basin
chronology because of the relatively long-term occupation and the good
preservation of the features. The role of a site like Los Morteros in
the regional settlement system is being brought into focus by the
Northern Tucson Basin Survey (P. Fish, S. Fish, and J. Madsen 1985).
Research being done in association with this survey is also documenting
the diversity and intensity of agriculture conducted by the Hohokam in
this area of the Tucson Basin (S. Fish, P. Fish, Miksicek, and J. Madsen
1985). The possible Tanque Verde phase use of canals at Los Morteros is
an interesting addition to the strategies used to increase production.

Los Morteros has had a long and complex history, portions of
which are preserved in the archaeological remains that are buried there.
It is hoped that time and opportunity will permit the proper study of
these remains before urban growth and development destroys them as it
has so many other aspects of Tucson's past.

Appendix A

TRENCH DETAILS

Table A.1

TRENCH LOCATIONS AND FEATURES

Trench Number	Location (Grid Coordinates)		Orientation	Features
1	N 800	E1000	N	
2	N 700	E1000	N	
3	N 600	E1000	N	
4	N 500	E1000	N	
5	N 400	E1000	N	
6	N 315	E1000	N	
7	N 300	E1050	N	
8	N 400	E1050	N	
9	N 400	E1100	N	
10	N 300	E1100	N	
11	N 500	E1150	N	
12	N 500	E1200	N	
13	N 500	E1100	N	
14	N 600	E1050	N	
15	N 500	E1050	N	
16	N 600	E1100	N	1 through 3
17	N 700	E1050	N	
18	N 800	E1100	N	
19	N 700	E1150	N	
20	N 600	E1150	N	
21	N 600	E1200	N	
22	N 600	E1250	N	
23	N 600	E1125	N	
24	N 585	E1100	N	
25	N 515	E 950	N	
26	N 600	E 955	N	
27	N 700	E 950	N	
28	N 785	E 950	N	
29	N 615	E1110	N	
30	N 515	E1100	N	
31	N 485	E 925	N	
32	N 785	E1050	N	
33	N 785	E1100	N	
34	N 785	E1150	N	
35	N 615	E 900	N	
36	N1300	E 900	N	
37	N1300	E 850	N	4
38	N1400	E 932.5	N	5
39	N1400	E 900	N	
40	N1500	E 900	N	6 through 9
41	N1500	E 850	N	

165

Table A.1, continued

TRENCH LOCATIONS AND FEATURES

Trench Number	Location (Grid Coordinates)	Orientation	Features
42	N1600 E 850	N	
43	N1600 E 800	N	
44	N1400 E 995	N	
45	N1450 E 995	N	10
46	N1450 E 941	N	11
47	N1500 E 950	N	63
48	N1530 E 950	N	12
49	N1700 E 800	N	
50	N1700 E 850	N	
51	N1700 E 900	N	13,14
52	N1450 E 890.5	N	15,16
53	N1450 E 847	N	
54	N1750 E 995	N	
55	N1800 E 950	N	17
56	N1800 E 900	N	18
57	N1600 E 995	N	
58	N1500 E 995	N	19
59	VOID -- same as Trench 49		
60	VOID -- same as Trench 50		
61	VOID -- same as Trench 51		
62	N1700 E 950	N	20
63	N1700 E 995	N	
64	N1650 E 995	N	
65	N 750 E 850	N	
66	N 600 E 850	N	
67	N 500 E 900	N	21
68	N 400 E 900	N	
69	N 450 E 850	N	
70	N 400 E 850	N	
71	N 700 E 850	N	
72	N 650 E 850	N	43
73	N 600 E 900	N	
74	N 500 E 850	N	
75	N 500 E 875	N	
76	N 600 E 875	N	
77	N1500 E 900-1000	E	22 through 28
78	N1800 E 995	N	
79	N1825 E 938	N	
80	N1841 E 881	N	
81	N1849 E 868	N	29
82	N1800 E 850	N	

Table A.1, continued

TRENCH LOCATIONS AND FEATURES

Trench Number	Location (Grid Coordinates)		Orientation	Features
83	N1800	E 800	N	
84	N1400	E 890-950	E	30 through 33
85	N1300	E 995	N	
86	N1300	E 950	N	
87	N 650	E 925-1400	E	34
88	NOT ASSIGNED			
89	NOT ASSIGNED			
90	N1600	E 950	N	
91	N1600	E 900	N	
92	N1445	E 900-925	E	35,36,41
93	N1500	E 925	N	
94	N1485	E 920-930	E	42
95	N1520	E 940	N	37
96	N1550	E 960-975	E	38
97	N1602	E 865	E	
98	N1900	E 700	N	
99	N1900	E 750	N	
100	N1850	E 750	N	
101	N1850	E 700	N	
102	N1800	E 700	N	
103	N1800	E 750	N	
104	N1700	E 750	N	
105	N1700	E 700	N	
106	N1600	E 700	N	
107	N1600	E 750	N	
108	N1500	E 750	N	
109	N1500	E 700	N	
110	N1500	E 800	N	
111	N1400	E 800	N	
112	N1400	E 850	N	
113	N1400	E 750	N	
114	N1400	E 700	N	
115	N1650	E 835-865	E	
116	N1860	E 890-910	E	
117	N1870	E 990	N	

N = North-south.
E = East-west.

Appendix B

CERAMIC DATA

Table B.1

CERAMIC TYPE BY FORM FOR ALL LOS MORTEROS PROVENIENCES

Type	Vessel Form								
	Bowl Body	Bowl Rim	Jar Body	Jar Rim	Indet. Body	Indet. Rim	Handle	Figurine	Totals
TUCSON BASIN HOHOKAM TYPES									
Cañada del Oro Red-on-brown	1	0	3	1	0	0	0	0	5
Rillito Red-on-brown	52	35	51	5	0	0	0	0	143
Rillito Red-on-brown white slip	1	0	1	0	1	0	0	0	3
Rillito-Rincon Red-on-brown	209	106	216	6	43	2	0	0	582
Rillito-Rincon Red-on-brown white slip	3	6	20	0	3	0	0	0	32
Rincon Red-on-brown	278	163	512	23	46	1	0	0	1,023
Rincon Red-on-brown white slip	9	12	38	3	0	0	0	0	62
Rincon Red	155	49	12	0	16	1	0	0	233
Rincon Polychrome	9	1	2	0	0	0	0	0	12
Cortaro Red-on-brown	346	214	82	2	21	4	0	0	669
Tanque Verde-Cortaro Red-on-brown	207	126	242	7	64	7	0	0	653
Tanque Verde Red-on-brown	989	915	1,852	94	592	28	3	0	4,473

Table B.1, continued

CERAMIC TYPE BY FORM FOR ALL LOS MORTEROS PROVENIENCES

Type	Vessel Form								
	Bowl Body	Bowl Rim	Jar Body	Jar Rim	Indet. Body	Indet. Rim	Handle	Figurine	Totals
TUCSON BASIN HOHOKAM TYPES (cont.)									
Tanque Verde Red-on-brown white slip	28	25	51	2	9	2	0	0	117
Tanque Verde Black-on-brown	39	25	93	2	13	0	0	0	172
Tanque Verde Polychrome (Tanque Verde Polychrome A)	3	5	1	0	2	0	0	0	11
Saguaro Polychrome (Tanque Verde Polychrome B)	0	0	4	0	1	0	0	0	5
Indeterminate red-on-brown	1729	768	2,523	133	5,074	512	1	2	10,742
Indeterminate red-on-brown white slip	15	7	56	2	48	5	0	0	133
Indeterminate red ware	75	28	21	1	152	11	0	1	289
Tucson Basin indeterminate black paint - cf. Rincon/Tanque Verde	12	2	14	0	22	3	0	0	53
Indeterminate Polychrome (cf. Sahuarita Polychrome, red-on-brown variety)	0	0	1	0	0	0	0	0	1

Table B.1, continued

CERAMIC TYPE BY FORM FOR ALL LOS MORTEROS PROVENIENCES

Type	Bowl Body	Bowl Rim	Jar Body	Jar Rim	Indet. Body	Indet. Rim	Handle	Figurine	Totals
				Vessel Form					
TUCSON BASIN HOHOKAM TYPES (cont.)									
Plain ware – micaceous variety	2,251	889	8,932	899	30,958	724	4	3	44,660
Plain ware – nonmicaceous variety	1,791	536	6,627	644	31,688	1,151	5	3	42,445
GILA BASIN HOHOKAM INTRUSIVES									
Snaketown Red-on-buff	1	0	0	0	0	0	0	0	1
Santa Cruz Red-on-buff	12	18	19	0	2	0	0	0	51
Santa Cruz-Sacaton Red-on-buff	1	0	2	0	0	0	0	0	3
Sacaton Red-on-buff	109	87	191	25	45	0	0	1	459
Casa Grande Red-on-buff	1	0	7	1	2	0	0	0	12
Indeterminate Red-on-buff	232	239	379	12	705	31	1	0	1,599
Buff ware (no paint)	63	36	57	6	470	25	0	0	657
Gila Plain	1	5	4	2	4	0	0	0	16

Table B.1, continued

CERAMIC TYPE BY FORM FOR ALL LOS MORTEROS PROVENIENCES

Type	Vessel Form								Totals
	Bowl Body	Bowl Rim	Jar Body	Jar Rim	Indet. Body	Indet. Rim	Handle	Figurine	
EAST-CENTRAL ARIZONA INTRUSIVES									
San Carlos Red-on-brown	2	1	1	1	10	0	0	0	15
San Carlos Red	18	5	4	1	0	0	0	0	28
Indeterminate Brown ware	2	1	2	0	56	3	0	0	64
Gila Red	10	4	2	1	0	0	0	0	17
Gila Polychrome	0	1	0	0	0	0	0	0	1
White ware	2	2	2	0	1	0	0	0	7
Indeterminate Black/White	1	0	4	1	0	1	0	0	7
Indeterminate Corrugated	8	3	1	0	17	0	0	0	29
PAPAGUERIAN INTRUSIVES									
Sells Red	21	13	1	0	25	0	0	0	60

Table B.1, continued

CERAMIC TYPE BY FORM FOR ALL LOS MORTEROS PROVENIENCES

Type	Vessel Form								
	Bowl Body	Bowl Rim	Jar Body	Jar Rim	Indet. Body	Indet. Rim	Handle	Figurine	Totals
MISCELLANEOUS TYPES									
Wingfield Plain	0	0	14	1	34	4	0	0	53
Historic	1	0	1	0	2	0	0	0	4
Other	5	2	3	0	1	1	0	0	12
Totals	8,692	4,329	22,048	1,875	70,127	2,518	14	10	109,613
Column Percentages	7.93	3.95	20.11	1.71	63.98	2.30	0.01	0.01	100.00

Note: Indet. = Indeterminate

Table B.2

CERAMIC DATA, SITE AREA 2

Type	Number	Percent
Cañada del Oro Red-on-brown	1	0.0
Rillito Red-on-brown	47	0.2
Rillito-Rincon Red-on-brown	116	0.4
Rincon Red-on-brown	151	0.5
Cortaro Red-on-brown	15	0.1
Cortaro-Tanque Verde Red-on-brown	17	0.1
Tanque Verde Red-on-brown	454	1.5
Tucson Red-on-brown	5	0.0
Indeterminate Red-on-brown	2,020	6.8
Rincon Polychrome	4	0.0
Gila Polychrome	1	0.0
Indeterminate painted	10	0.0
White ware	2	0.0
Indeterminate Black-on-white	1	0.0
Indeterminate corrugated	5	0.0
Santa Cruz Red-on-buff	28	0.1
Santa Cruz-Sacaton Red-on-buff	3	0.0
Sacaton Red-on-buff	73	0.2
Casa Grande Red-on-buff	4	0.0
Indeterminate Red-on-buff	831	2.8
Buff ware	75	0.3
Rincon Red	84	0.3
San Carlos Red	4	0.0
Sells Red	11	0.0
Indeterminate red ware	48	0.2
Gila Plain	2	0.0
Plain ware, micaceous variety	11,351	38.0
Plain ware, nonmicaceous variety	14,506	48.5
Indeterminate brown ware	6	0.0
Historic	2	0.0
Other	4	0.0
Total	29,881	100.1

Table B.3

CERAMIC DATA, SITE AREA 3

Type	Number	Percent
Rillito Red-on-brown	1	1.1
Rillito-Rincon Red-on-brown	2	2.1
Rincon Red-on-brown	2	2.1
Indeterminate Red-on-brown	3	3.2
Indeterminate Red-on-buff	1	1.1
Plain ware, micaceous variety	46	48.4
Plain ware, nonmicaceous variety	40	42.1
Total	95	100.0

Table B.4

CERAMIC DATA, SITE AREA 4

Type	Number	Percent
Tanque Verde Red-on-brown	10	9.4
Indeterminate Red-on-brown	16	15.1
Plain ware, micaceous variety	36	34.0
Plain ware, nonmicaceous variety	44	41.5
Total	106	100.0

Table B.5

CERAMIC DATA, SITE AREA 5

Type	Number	Percent
Cañada del Oro Red-on-brown	3	0.0
Rillito Red-on-brown	48	0.2
Rillito-Rincon Red-on-brown	280	1.1
Rincon Red-on-brown	608	2.3
Cortaro Red-on-brown	107	0.4
Cortaro-Tanque Verde Red-on-brown	129	0.5
Tanque Verde Red-on-brown	1,414	5.4
Tucson Red-on-brown	2	0.0
Indeterminate Red-on-brown	3,232	12.3
San Carlos Red-on-brown	2	0.0
Rincon polychrome	3	0.0
Indeterminate painted	13	0.0
Indeterminate polychrome	1	0.0
White ware	2	0.0
Indeterminate Black-on-white	3	0.0
Indeterminate corrugated	5	0.0
Santa Cruz Red-on-buff	10	0.0
Sacaton Red-on-buff	157	0.6
Casa Grande Red-on-buff	1	0.0
Indeterminate Red-on-buff	394	1.5
Buff ware	281	1.1
Rincon Red	85	0.3
Gila Red	11	0.0
San Carlos Red	13	0.0
Sells Red	27	0.0
Indeterminate red ware	87	0.3
Gila Plain	3	0.0
Wingfield Plain	37	0.1
Plain ware, micaceous variety	11,350	3.1
Plain ware, nonmicaceous variety	8,001	30.4
Indeterminate brown ware	39	0.1
Historic	1	0.0
Other	2	0.0
Total	26,351	99.7

Table B.6

CERAMIC DATA, SITE AREA 6

Type	Number	Percent
Rillito Red-on-brown	14	0.3
Rillito-Rincon Red-on-brown	85	2.1
Rincon Red-on-brown	22	0.5
Cortaro Red-on-brown	27	0.7
Cortaro-Tanque Verde Red-on-brown	1	0.0
Tanque Verde Red-on-brown	9	0.2
Indeterminate Red-on-brown	434	10.7
Rincon Polychrome	1	0.0
Indeterminate painted	8	0.2
Santa Cruz Red-on-buff	3	0.1
Sacaton Red-on-buff	11	0.3
Indeterminate Red-on-buff	57	1.4
Buff ware	40	1.0
Rincon Red	9	0.2
Indeterminate red ware	20	0.5
Plain ware, micaceous variety	2,454	60.5
Plain ware, nonmicaceous variety	860	21.2
Indeterminate brown ware	1	0.0
Other	1	0.0
Total	4,057	100.0

Table B.7

CERAMIC DATA, SITE AREA 8

Type	Number	Percent
Rillito Red-on-brown	35	0.1
Rillito-Rincon Red-on-brown	131	0.3
Rincon Red-on-brown	296	0.7
Cortaro Red-on-brown	519	1.3
Cortaro-Tanque Verde Red-on-brown	505	1.3
Tanque Verde Red-on-brown	2,632	6.6
Tucson Red-on-Brown	5	0.0
Indeterminate Red-on-brown	4,910	12.3
San Carlos Red-on-brown	13	0.0
Rincon Polychrome	4	0.0
Indeterminate painted	22	0.1
White ware	3	0.0
Indeterminate Black-on-white	3	0.0
Indeterminate corrugated	19	0.0
Snaketown Red-on-buff	1	0.0
Santa Cruz Red-on-buff	10	0.0
Sacaton Red-on-buff	218	0.5
Casa Grande Red-on-buff	7	0.0
Indeterminate Red-on-buff	311	0.8
Buff ware	254	0.6
Rincon Red	55	0.1
Gila Red	6	0.0
San Carlos Red	11	0.0
Sells Red	22	0.1
Indeterminate red ware	114	0.3
Gila Plain	6	0.0
Wingfield Plain	15	0.0
Plain ware, micaceous variety	14,657	36.6
Plain ware, nonmicaceous variety	15,216	38.0
Historic	1	0.0
Other	4	0.0
Total	40,005	100.0

Table B.8

CERAMIC DATA, SITE AREA 10

Type	Number	Percent
Tanque Verde Red-on-brown	1	14.3
Plain ware, micaceous variety	5	71.4
Plain ware, nonmicaceous variety	1	14.3
Total	7	100.0

Table B.9

CERAMIC DATA, SITE AREA 11

Type	Number	Percent
Cañada del Oro Red-on-brown	1	0.0
Rillito Red-on-brown	1	0.0
Rincon Red-on-brown	6	0.1
Cortaro Red-on-brown	1	0.0
Cortaro-Tanque Verde Red-on-brown	1	0.0
Tanque Verde Red-on-brown	257	3.1
Indeterminate Red-on-brown	241	2.9
Indeterminate Red-on-buff	5	0.1
Buff ware	6	0.1
Indeterminate red ware	16	0.2
Gila Plain	21	0.3
Wingfield Plain	1	0.0
Plain ware, micaceous variety	4,302	1.8
Plain ware, nonmicaceous variety	3,431	41.3
Indeterminate brown ware	17	0.2
Total	8,307	100.0

Table B.10

TYPES, VARIETIES, AND REFERENCES BY COLOR SCHEME AND CHRONOLOGICAL PERIOD

Period	Type and Variety	References
RED-ON-WHITE (red paint, white-slipped)		
Colonial Period	Cañada del Oro Red-on-brown, white-slipped variety	Deaver (1984: 286, 292; 1988: 149; 1989a)
	Rillito Red-on-brown, white-slipped variety	Deaver (1984: 298; 1988: 151; 1989a)
		Doelle and Wallace (1986: 17)
		Whittlesey (1986, Table 6.15)
		Beckwith (1987: 223)
Sedentary Period	Rincon Red-on-brown, white-slipped variety	Huckell (1978: 126, 129)
		Deaver and Tagg (1984: 20)
		Greenleaf (1975: 48, 50)
		Ervin (1982: 25-37)
		Wallace (1985a: 104, 116; 1986c: 27, 37, 55; 1986a: 151)
		Whittlesey (1986, Table 6.15)
		Doyel (1977: 31, 36, 84, 87)
		Huntington (1982: 110)
		Simpson and Wells (1983: 64; 1984: 108)
		Doelle and Wallace (1986: 25, 27, 29)
		Deaver (1984: 316; 1989c)
		Beckwith (1987: 221)
Classic Period	Tanque Verde Red-on-brown, white-slipped variety	Simpson and Wells (1984: 108)
		Doelle and Wallace (1986: 32)
		DiPeso (1956: 318-319)
		Zahniser (1965: 63-64; 1966: 143)

Table B.10, continued

TYPES, VARIETIES, AND REFERENCES BY COLOR SCHEME AND CHRONOLOGICAL PERIOD

Period	Type and Variety	References
RED-ON-WHITE (continued)		
Classic Period	Tanque Verde Red-on-brown, white-slipped variety	Whittlesey (1986, Table 6.15) Beckwith (1987: 209) Scantling (1940: 28) Grebinger and Adams (1974: 230)
	Ramanote Red-on-brown, white-slipped variety	DiPeso (1956: 323)
RED-ON-BLACK (red paint, smudged)		
Colonial Period	Rillito Red-on-brown, smudged variety	Frick (1954: 53) Wallace (1985: 97)
Sedentary Period	Rincon Red-on-brown, smudged variety	Huckell (1978: 129) Deaver and Tagg (1984: 20) Greenleaf (1975: 62-64) Kelly (1978: 38) Wallace (1985a: 99, 104, 113; 1986a: 153; 1986c: 27, 37, 55) Doyel (1977: 30) Huntington (1982: 110) Doelle and Wallace (1986: 25, 27) Deaver (1984: 316; 1989c) Whittlesey (1986, Table 6.15) Beckwith (1987: 221)

Table B.10, continued

TYPES, VARIETIES, AND REFERENCES BY COLOR SCHEME AND CHRONOLOGICAL PERIOD

Period	Type and Variety	References
RED-ON-BLACK (continued)		
Classic Period	Tanque Verde Red-on-brown, smudged variety	Kelly (1978: 48, 57)
		Doelle and Wallace (1986: 32)
		Whittlesey (1987, Table 9.2)
		Beckwith (1987: 209)
		Grebinger and Adams (1974: 230)
		Zahniser (1965: 63-64; 1966: 142-143)
		Gable (1931: 49)
		Fraps (1935: 4)
		Hawley (1930: 525)
		DiPeso (1956: 319)
		Danson (1957: 221)
	Ramanote Red-on-brown, smudged variety	DiPeso (1956: 323)
BLACK-ON-BROWN (black paint)		
Sedentary Period	Rincon Black-on-brown	Deaver and Tagg (1984: 20)
		Huntington (1982: 110)
		Simpson and Wells (1983: 64; 1984: 108)
		Doelle and Wallace (1986: 27, 29)
		Deaver (1984: 322-326; 1989c)
		Wallace (1986a: 151; 1986c: 37)
		Whittlesey (1986, Table 6.15)
		Ervin (1982: 25-37)

181

Table B.10, continued

TYPES, VARIETIES, AND REFERENCES BY COLOR SCHEME AND CHRONOLOGICAL PERIOD

Period	Type and Variety	References
BLACK-ON-BROWN (continued)		
Sedentary Period	Sahuarita Polychrome, black-on-brown variety	Deaver (1984: 328-329) Deaver and Tagg (1984: 20) Ervin (1982: 41) Wallace (1986a, Table 6.17; 1986c: 87)
Classic Period	Tanque Verde Black-on-brown	Simpson and Wells (1984: 108) Doelle and Wallace (1986: 32) Whittlesey (1986, Table 6.15; 1987, Table 9.2) Deaver (1982) Beckwith (1987: 209)
BLACK-ON-WHITE (black paint, white-slipped)		
Sedentary Period	Rincon Black-on-brown, white-slipped variety	Deaver and Tagg (1984: 20) Ervin (1982: 25-32, 37) Wallace (1986a: 146; 1986c: 37) Doelle and Wallace (1986: 29) Deaver (1984: 324) Whittlesey (1986, Table 6.15) Huntington (1982: 110)
	Rincon Polychrome	Wallace (1986a, Table 5.17; 1986c: 37)

Table B.10, continued

TYPES, VARIETIES, AND REFERENCES BY COLOR SCHEME AND CHRONOLOGICAL PERIOD

Period	Type and Variety	References

BLACK-ON-WHITE (continued)

Classic Period	Tanque Verde Black-on-brown, white-slipped variety	Deaver (1982)
		Whittlesey (1986, Table 6.15)
		Beckwith (1987: 209)
		Slawson (1988: 141)

BLACK-ON-WHITE-ON-RED (black and white paints, red-slipped)

Sedentary Period	Rincon Polychrome	Kelly (1978: 77)
		DiPeso (1956: 351)
		Deaver and Tagg (1984: 20)
		Greenleaf (1975: 67-73)
		Ervin (1982: 37-41)
		Wallace (1986a: Table 6.17; 1986c: 84)
		Huntington (1982: 114)
		Simpson and Wells (1983: 54)
		Doelle and Wallace (1986: 33)
		Deaver (1984: 326)
		Bradley (1980: 28)

RED-ON-BROWN (exterior red paint, interior red-slipped)

| Sedentary Period | Sahuarita Polychrome, red-on-brown variety | Deaver (1984: 328-329) |
| | | Deaver and Tagg (1984: 20) |

184

Table B.10, continued

TYPES, VARIETIES, AND REFERENCES BY COLOR SCHEME AND CHRONOLOGICAL PERIOD

Period	Type and Variety	References
RED-ON-BROWN (exterior red paint, interior red-slipped)		
Sedentary Period	Sahuarita Polychrome, red-on-brown variety	Wallace (1985a: 128; 1986c: 87) Huntington (1982: 114) Frick (1954: 64)
Classic Period	Unknown Type	Beckwith (1987: 209-210)
BLACK-ON-RED (black paint, red-slipped)		
Sedentary Period	Rincon Polychrome, variant	Deaver and Tagg (1984: 20-21) Wallace (1986a, Table 6.17; 1986c: 84) Huckell (1978: 22)
Classic Period	Unknown Type	Gabel (1931: 50)
	Tucson Black-on-red	Franklin (1980: 83-104)
BLACK-AND-WHITE-ON-RED (black and white paints, red-slipped)		
Sedentary Period	Rincon Polychrome, variant	Greenleaf (1975: 67-73) Wallace (1986c: 84)
Classic Period	Unknown Type	Beckwith (1987: 209)

Table B.10, continued

TYPES, VARIETIES, AND REFERENCES BY COLOR SCHEME AND CHRONOLOGICAL PERIOD

Period	Type and Variety	References
BLACK-AND-WHITE-ON-RED (continued)		
Classic Period	Tucson Polychrome	Gabel (1931: 52-53)
		Danson (1957: 226-229)
RED-AND-BLACK-ON-BROWN (red and black paints)		
Sedentary Period	Rio Rico Polychrome	Doyel (1977: 36-41, 60, 84; 1988)
		Ervin (1982: 41)
		Frick (1954: 63)
		DiPeso (1956: 334)
		Deaver (1984: 326-327)
	Sahuarita Polychrome	Deaver (1984: 328-329)
		Wallace (1986c: 87)
Classic Period	Tanque Verde Polychrome	Doelle and Wallace (1986: 34)
		Hayden (1957: 223)
		Deaver (1982)
		Beckwith (1987: 210)
RED-AND-BLACK-ON-WHITE (red and black paints, white-slipped)		
Sedentary Period	Rincon Polychrome, variant	Doelle and Wallace (1986: 34)

Table B.10, continued

TYPES, VARIETIES, AND REFERENCES BY COLOR SCHEME AND CHRONOLOGICAL PERIOD

Period	Type and Variety	References
RED-AND-BLACK-ON-WHITE (continued)		
Classic Period	Tanque Verde Polychrome	DiPeso (1956: 319)
RED-AND-WHITE-ON-BROWN (red and white paints)		
Classic Period	Saguaro Polychrome	Zahniser (1970: 109)
		Beckwith (1987: 210)
		Deaver (1982)
WHITE-ON-BROWN (white paint)		
Classic Period	Unknown type	Beckwith (1987: 209)
WHITE-ON-RED (white paint, red-slipped)		
Classic Period	Sells White-on-red	DiPeso (1956: 309)
		Scantling (1940: 32)
WHITE-AND-RED-ON-RED (white and red paints, red-slipped)		
Classic Period	Sells Polychrome	DiPeso (1956: 309)

Appendix C

LITHIC DATA

Table C.1

LITHIC DATA, SITE AREA 5 (N = 437)

| | Category | | | | | | | |
Material Type	Misc. Ground Stone	Mano	Mano (frag.)	Metate (frag.)	Tool	Projectile Point	Cores/ Hammerstone	Debitage
andesite	2	1	3		4		4	31
basalt	6		1	11			10	33
chalcedony								1
chert					1	1	2	32
diorite						1		1
gneiss		1		1	1		1	
granite			11		1	1	1	2
jasper								8
limestone							2	1
silicified limestone							1	14
quartz	5	2	4					5
quartzite	6	2	5		3		15	90
rhyolite					7	1	17	80
sandstone	1	1						
other	1	1						2

Table C.2

LITHIC DATA, SITE AREA 6, (N = 128)

Material Type	Misc. Ground Stone	Mano (frag.)	Metate (frag.)	Tool	Projectile Point	Cores/ Hammerstone	Debitage
andesite		1				2	10
basalt	5	7	8			3	3
chalcedony						1	
chert					1	1	11
gneiss	1						
granite	1				1		
silicified limestone				5			4
quartzite	2			4	2	6	15
rhyolite	4			3	6	3	15
sandstone	1			1			
silicified tuff							1
slate						1	
other					2		

Category

Table C.3

LITHIC DATA, SITE AREA 8 (N = 611)

Raw Material Type	Misc. Ground Stone	Mano	Mano (frag.)	Metate (frag.)	Tool	Cores/ Hammerstone	Debitage
				Category			
andesite		1		2		6	90
basalt	3		4	2	3	3	122
chalcedony							7
chert					1	2	29
diorite				1	1		
gneiss		1					
granite		1		5	5	5	1
jasper							16
limestone		1					
silicified limestone						26	
quartz			3	3		3	3
quartzite			2	1			12
rhyolite	4		1	1	3	15	193
sandstone							1
schist						2	2
silicified tuff	1						
slate			1			1	
other						2	19

Table C.4

LITHIC DATA, SITE AREA 11 (N = 3)

| Material Type | Category | |
	Cores/ Hammerstones	Debitage
andesite		1
basalt	1	
quartz		1

Appendix D

FEATURE DATA

Table D.1

SUMMARY DATA FOR FEATURES

Feature Number	Grid Location	Type	Floor Elevation (m)	Date
F.1	N 600 E1100	pit		
F.2	N 600 E1100	pit		Rillito/Rincon
F.3	N 600 E1100	house		Rillito/Rincon
F.4	N1300 E 850	house	636.61	Tanque Verde ?
F.5	N1390 E 930	houses (2)	635.52	Rillito/Rincon
F.6	N1490 E 900	house	635.84	Tanque Verde
F.7	N1495 E 900	house	635.52	early Tanque Verde or late Rincon
F.8	N1490 E 900	pit	635.90	Tanque Verde
F.9	N1490 E 900	house ?		
F.10	N1445 E 995	house	635.90	
F.11	N1445 E 940	house	635.63	Rillito/Rincon
F.12	N1520 E 950	house	635.63	
F.13	N1695 E 900	pit	634.46	late Rincon or early Tanque Verde
F.14	N1691 E 900	cremation	634.96	Tanque Verde
F.15	N1439 E 890	house	634.76	Rillito/Rincon
F.16	N1448 E 890	house ?	635.63	
F.17	N1800 E 950.5	horno	633.50	
F.18	N1797 E 900	house	634.25	Tanque Verde
F.19	N1490 E 995	canal ?	635.22	Tanque Verde?
F.20	N1690 E 950	iso. vessel	639.90	TV/Cortaro
F.21	N 480 E 900	house/trash		early Rincon
F.22	N1500 E 901	canal	634.72	Tanque Verde?
F.23	N1500 E 910	pit	635.15	Tanque Verde
F.24	---------- NOT RELOCATED DURING PROFILING --------------------			
F.25	N1500 E 925	house	635.27	
F.26	N1500 E 941	house	635.27	
F.27	N1500 E 986	canal	635.12	Tanque Verde
F.28	N1500 E 982	canal	634.77	Tanque Verde
F.29	N1832 E 867	horno		Tanque Verde?
F.30	N1400 E 946	house	635.90	Rincon
F.31	N1400 E 936	house	635.78	late Rincon or early Tanque Verde
F.32	N1401 E 922	crematory	635.61	Tanque Verde
F.33	N1400 E 892	canal ?	635.33	Preclassic?
F.34	N 650 E1377	house		Preclassic?
F.35	N1445 E 915	house	635.82	early Tanque Verde
F.36	N1445 E 920	house	635.77	Tanque Verde
F.37	N1515 E 940	house	635.81	
F.38	N1545 E 965	house	634.99	Tanque Verde

Table D.1, continued

SUMMARY DATA FOR FEATURES

Feature Number	Grid Location	Type	Floor Elevation (m)	Date
F.39	N1425 E1073	house	636.20	early Tanque Verde
F.40	------------------- SEE FEATURE 62 -----------------------			
F.41	N1445 E 915	pit	635.75	Tanque Verde
F.42	N1485 E 925	house ?	635.49	
F.43	N 650 E 850	house ?		
F.44	N1413 E1080	sherd pile		
F.45	in F. 39	pit		Tanque Verde
F.46	N1447 E1073	pit		
F.47	N1522 E1022	crematory		Tanque Verde
F.48	N1518 E1027	crematory		Tanque Verde
F.49	------------------- NOT ASSIGNED -----------------------			
F.50	N1354 E1082	house		Rincon
F.51	N1200 E1030	house		Rincon
F.52	N1360 E 934	horno		Rincon
F.53	Mound 7	house		
F.54	Mound 7	pit		
F.55	Mound 7	house		
F.56	Mound 7	house		
F.57	Mound 7	house		
F.58	Mound 7	cremations (4)		Tanque Verde
F.59	Mound 7	house		
F.60	N1355 E 934	horno		Rincon
F.61	Mound 1	pit		
F.62	N1438 E1073	house		Tanque Verde
F.63	N1490 E 950	cremation		Tanque Verde
F.64	N1279 E1031	house		
F.65	N1279 E1029	house		

Appendix E

SYNOPSIS OF SOIL PROFILES

James P. Holmlund

With a few exceptions, these profiles represent very generalized views of the more micro-stratigraphically complex layers found in the north section of Los Morteros. Unfortunately, time considerations, precluded more detailed mapping of these profiles; they are presented here to give an overall view of the soil components that may be found in this area. More detailed macro- and micro-stratigraphic studies, coupled with the detailed examination of the many aerial photographs of the area, could lead to an understanding of the role of the Santa Cruz River in the cultural development and use of this site. In addition, studies might determine the flood impact and cycles and river movement-- from a braided, meandering perennial stream on the west side to its current position as an entrenched seasonal river on the east side.

In general, we found a disturbed layer from the surface to a depth of about 35 cm. This depth varies from 20 cm to 45 cm or so. The grayish-brown color is probably due to agriculture (the plowzone) or the high amount of organic material in this layer. This is frequently underlain by a somewhat unconsolidated clay-sand or sand gravel layer, which is usually thin. Then there is a characteristic clayey silt layer (which may vary in percentage of clay, sand and silt), characterized by its fine texture, blocky, angular fracture and hardness (which may be due to a high calcareous content) and usually tan color. This level is frequently divided into several layers, which may represent differences in hardness, color, grain size, or constituent and thus should be thought of as a group or family of layers. It occasionally has lenses of loam or sand-gravel contained within it. Thickness is between 0.5 and 1.25 m. Below this is usually one or two of the three distinct layers consisting of the brown loamy clay layer, the reddish, or dark (weathered?), caliche layer (usually containing gravel and sand) or the unsorted sand, gravel, pebble, and cobble layer--a very characteristic layer--containing large cobbles (well smoothed and rounded and of heterogeneous lithology). The "cobble" layer indicates a high energy environment and may represent former river channels as the surface of this cobble layer is very irregular throughout the trenches. Study of this layer would probably lead to a much better understanding of the reason for the location of cultural features at this site, particularly near the terrace area.

Other Layers

A. Lenses or Thin Layers

1. dark brown-black clayey loam: grainy texture;
   thickness .05m-.20m (example: Trenches 111 and 112).
2. dark, generally well sorted, sand, or silt or gravel or
   pebble lenses and layers: loose to consolidated:
   thickness from .05m to .5m (Trenches 42, 82, 83, 99,
   109, and, 114.

B. Bottom of Trench Layers (Thicknesses Unknown)

1. brown loamy-clay: grainy consolidated texture;
   thickness from >.25m to >.60m (Trenches 83, 104, and
   105)
2. dark unconsolidated sand-gravel-pebble-cobble layer.
   characteristic layer when encountered near bottom of
   trench; unsorted large cobbles with mixed-in sand,
   gravel, and pebbles; thickness probably >.25m (Trenches
   47, 63, 93, and 114?)
3. reddish-reddish-brown caliche clay: contains some sand
   and gravel (cobbles?), fairly well compacted; thickness
   >.5m (Trenches 36, 101, 102, 103, 113, and 114?)
4. unconsolidated fine sand and silt. This example (Trench
   49) may represent a thick layer of A-2 (above), which
   frequently overlays the characteristic tan clayey silt
   layer. If true this would represent a deep dip in the
   surface of the clayey-silt layer. Thickness here >1.0m
   (see Trenches 42, 56, 82, 99, 113 and 114).

Characteristic Layers

Disturbed Layer

This layer ranges from a brownish-gray clayey silt (or silty
clay) to a sandy-clayey silt to a sandy silt. It occasionally contains
some gravel. Characteristic features include its grayish-brown color,
angular, blocky fracture but fine grain size, and the numerous rootlets
found in this soil. These characteristics are necessarily the result of
historic plowing in the area, and the depth of this layer generally
conforms to this type of disturbance (about 35 cm) although a few
trenches (see Trenches 44, 112, 113, 114) are deeper.

Tan Clayey-Silt Layer

This layer ranges from a gray clay to a tan silt with many grades in between (brown to tan clayey silt, gray to tan silty clay, gray to brown sandy-silty clay or sandy silt). This layer should probably be considered a family of layers because in some cases (Trenches 50,90,98,100) there may be distinctions between the relative percentage of constituents, color, or compactness and several layers are shown. But generally speaking this family of layers is quite distinct in characteristics from the rest of the usually finer layers that may overlay it or the layers that may underlay it. Characteristic features of this layer include the fine texture, angular blocky fracture, and relative hardness. Occasional lenses or layers of sand, gravel, or loam may appear either overlying or within this layer. The precipitation of salts after drying of the soil was apparent through all layers. Thickness varied from <.5m to >1.25m and in many trenches represented the bottom layer.

Appendix F

THE UTILITY OF PHOSPHATE TESTING AT LOS MORTEROS

Susan J. Wells

Phosphate testing has become popular in American archaeology in recent years. Relative amounts of phosphate present in soil samples can be used to define and interpret archaeological sites. The procedure is not new. Arrhenius (1963) began examining the phosphate content of soils at archaeological sites in Sweden in 1926. The enrichment of soil phosphates by humans has been recognized since at least the mid-nineteenth century (Woods 1975).

The presence of high levels of phosphorous, in the form of phosphate compounds, has been positively linked to past human occupation or activity. Most organic residues that collect in houses, burials, activity areas and trash concentrations decompose and then leach out of the soil. This is not the case with phosphates. Barring erosion or other major soil disturbances phosphate compounds seldom move more than a few centimeters horizontally or vertically over archaeological time spans (Eidt 1973). For this reason, soil samples from undisturbed archaeological deposits can be tested to determine relative levels of phosphate present. The test results can then be used to define the areal extent of a site (Baker 1975; Dietz 1957; Eidt 1973, 1977; Overstreet 1974; Shirk 1979; Sjoberg 1976; Woods 1975) to help define features (Arrhenius 1963, Cruxent 1962, Solecki 1951), and possibly even to define the temporal extent of a site's occupation (Eidt 1977).

This appendix focuses on the utility of phosphate testing as a method of intra-site analysis at Los Morteros, AZ AA:12:57 (ASM). I was assisted by the staff and students of the University of Arizona undergraduate field class under the direction of Paul R. Fish and Richard C. Lange in the fall semester of 1980.

A variation of the qualitative spot test outlined by Eidt (1973) was used to determine relative levels of phosphate in soil samples systematically collected at Los Morteros. The test results were examined along with artifact counts and information concerning known cultural features at the site. It was hoped that positive correlations of phosphate readings, artifact counts, and feature information would establish the usefulness of phosphate testing for predicting the location of features or activity areas within the site boundaries. Statistical Package for the Social Sciences (SPSS)(Nie and others 1975) computer programs were used to calculate Student's t, Persons's r and the non-parametric, rank order correlation coefficients-Spearman's rho and Kendall's tau--to evaluate the strength of these correlations.

Qualitative Versus Quantitative Tests for Phosphate

Accurate quantitative tests of the phosphate present in soil samples require expertise and laboratory equipment beyond the reach of most archaeological projects. The expense of sending large numbers of samples to a soils laboratory is prohibitive in most cases. Furthermore, most laboratories are not prepared to help interpret the results archaeologically (Woods 1975).

The relative levels of phosphate in soil samples collected in and around a site can be sufficient for archaeological purposes. Absolute quantitative values will vary enormously from site to site because of local soil chemistry. A qualitative test that allows one to determine that Sample A has more phosphate than Sample B and that sample B has more than Sample C may provide enough information to identify a site, determine size boundaries or define features within a site. The qualitative spot test developed by Gundlach (1961) and modified by Eidt (1973, 1977) is such a test. An actual comparison of samples tested by a soils laboratory and by the author will be discussed in the analysis section below.

Eidt streamlined the testing procedure so that an archaeologist can test soil samples with a minimum amount of equipment. By following a cookbook procedure and using an arbitrary, visual scale the archaeologist can assess relative levels of phosphate. The spot test is discussed briefly in this paper, but those interested in a complete, step-by-step explanation of the procedure and the chemistry involved are asked to refer to Eidt (1973, 1977), Shirk (1979), and Woods (1975).

Sampling at Los Morteros

The Los Morteros soil samples were collected from the north-central portion of the site. This part of the site is bounded by private land and the Tucson Mountains to the west, agricultural fields and a gravel pit to the north, a trailer park to the east, and agricultural fields to the south. The site continues east into the trailer park and to the south and possibly even to the north of the tested parcel of land. A crew of two or three functioned efficiently in the collection process. The 50-m by 50-m grid system used at the site to control surface collection and excavation was adopted for the phosphate study. By using the same grid system, surface artifact counts could be compared with phosphate test results and subsurface artifact counts made during the study.

The sampling was done on two levels. To get an overall picture of the site, samples were taken from the northwest corner of each 50-m by 50-m unit that fell in the area designated by the grid coordinates N1300 to N1800 and E750 to E1050. Seventy-five of the 77 units in this area were sampled. On a smaller scale, samples were collected at 10 m intervals within the 50-m by 50-m unit N1500 E950 for a total of 25 sample units. In addition, soil samples collected from two pit houses, Feature 30 and Feature 39, were tested for phosphate.

A posthole measuring approximately 30 cm in diameter was dug one meter south and one meter east of each designated grid corner. The hole was dug to a depth of 60 cm whenever possible. In many cases a hard calcium carbonate (caliche) layer was encountered which prohibited digging deeper than approximately 30 cm. Based on the profiles drawn during the backhoe trench testing in this part of the site, it seemed safe to assume that prehistoric cultural remains were not likely to be found below the caliche layer. In the case of the more closely spaced sampling in N1500 E950, the 25 holes were dug to a uniform depth of 60 cm. A shovel was used to dig the postholes, because the soil was so dry and silty that it simply fell out of the auger. A posthole-digging tool was also unsuccessful for the same reason.

Three soil samples were gathered from each posthole. Samples were taken at each of three evenly spaced depths. The spacing was determined by the depth of the hole. For example, if the hole was 60 cm deep samples were taken at 20 cm, 40 cm, and 60 cm intervals. If the hole was only 30 cm deep, the samples came from 10 cm, 20 cm, and 30 cm. Based on problems that arose later with the analysis of the phosphate data, it appears that it would have been better to collect soil samples at standard depths regardless of the depth of the hole. Missing data can be easier to deal with than a large number of values for a crucial analytical variable. To deal with this problem, phosphate values were examined at the measured depth below surface and also examined at the relative depth below surface (that is, top, middle, or bottom).

Soil samples were taken from the bottom up to lessen the chance of contamination. Before the soil was removed, the exposed surface was scraped clean with a spoon or trowel. Each soil sample was placed in a new, sealable plastic bag. Each bag was labeled with the north and east coordinates and the depth.

After the soil samples had been collected, the soil removed from the posthole was screened through one-quarter-inch mesh. All artifacts, both ceramic and lithic, were collected and placed in labeled paper bags.

Although the spot test for phosphate was developed for use in the field, all samples, and artifacts were brought back to the Arizona State Museum, University of Arizona, for analysis. The soil samples were tested for phosphate. The total number of artifacts recovered from each posthole was recorded.

Qualitative Phosphate Testing of the Los Morteros Samples

The spot test procedure described by Eidt (1973) was used on the Los Morteros samples, but consultation with personnel at the Soils, Water, and Plant Tissue Testing Laboratory, at the University of Arizona College of Agriculture led me to believe that there would be problems using this procedure, and indeed there were. Soils in the Tucson Basin are naturally high in phosphate. According to Gelderman (1972: 14), the Gila Loam on which the site lies is moderately alkaline (pH 7.9-8.4) and generally calcareous. The correlation between calcareous soils and soils naturally high in phosphate has been noted by Woods (1975). The resolution of this problem involved modification of Eidt's procedure. The changes made in the procedure will be presented after the Eidt spot test has been described.

Spot Test Procedure

The procedure used to test for phosphate is reasonably straightforward and simple. Two solutions are prepared. Solution A contains 30 ml of 5N (N = normal) hydrochloric acid and 5 gm of ammonium molybdate dissolved in 100 ml of cold, distilled water.

When (Solution A) is applied to the soil, the hydrochloric acid releases the bound phosphate compounds and converts them (in) to phosphoric acid. The phosphoric acid then reacts with the molybdate compound and forms phosphor molybdate (Shirk 1979:19).

Solution B is made by mixing one gram of ascorbic acid in 200 milliliters of distilled water. This solution acts as the reducing agent (Eidt 1973). When Solution B is added to the soil already treated with Solution A the phosphor molybdate is reduced to molybdenum blue compounds (Shirk 1979: 19). The amount of molybdenum blue can be assessed visually and is assigned a value that represents the relative amount of phosphate present in the soil sample.

To test the samples, a small amount of soil is placed on a piece of clean, ash-free filter paper. The filter paper is suspended on a tripod stand or ring stand. Following Eidt's procedure, two drops of Solution A are applied to the soil. After 30 seconds, two drops of Solution B are added. After two minutes, the results should be evident. It should be mentioned that at the beginning of each laboratory session an empty piece of filter paper should be subjected to the testing procedure to ensure that there had been no contamination of the solutions, the filter paper, or the equipment.

If any molybdenum blue compounds have been formed, a blue ring will appear on the filter paper. The test is a form of ring chromatography (Eidt 1977:1329). Eidt (1973) has described how to use a visual scale to evaluate the test results. The scale takes a number of things into account, including the time of appearance of the blue color, the length of the rays emanating from the sample, the percent closure of the ring of color, and the intensity of the blue color. He suggests reading the filter paper two minutes after the addition of Solution B and says that at 10 minutes all the filter papers will look alike unless treated in a bath of sodium citrate at the two-minute mark (Eidt 1977:1329).

Variation in the Testing Procedure

The procedure as outlined was used by Shirk (1979) and Woods (1975) with success, but I was not so lucky with the Los Morteros samples. As already mentioned, the soils of the Tucson Basin are naturally high in phosphate. Following Eidt's procedure produced uniform results with my samples. That is to say, each sample tested left a dark blue ring on the filter paper after two minutes had elapsed. It was impossible to detect any differences between samples. A graduate student in the University of Arizona Chemistry Department suggested that I alter the procedure by (1) cutting the amount of Solution B, the reducing agent, in half (one drop, not two) and by (2) reading the results after only 30 seconds, not two minutes. These suggestions were adopted and allowed me to detect differences between samples being tested.

Assigning Values to the Samples

An afternoon spent testing soil samples was sufficient to allow me to develop a feeling for visual differences in the test results. Values from one to five were assigned based on the intensity of the molybdenum blue color. The values assigned were noted directly on each filter paper along with the sample identification information. No sodium citrate bath was used to fix the results permanently on the filter paper. I recommend adding this step to the test. Being able to look back at the papers and compare them with one another would be enormously useful in terms of consistency of values assigned.

After spending more time testing samples I felt I could detect subtle differences in the test results, so I began to assign half values such as 2.5 or 3.5 as well as integer values. Later in the analysis all values were doubled so the scale used actually had values from 1 to 10. This did not alter the test results, since I was dealing with rank order variables: doubling the values did not change the relative position of the values along the scale.

A color chart was developed during the course of the analysis to aid in the consistency of values assigned. The chart consists of a strip of color chips that show the full range of test results. Colors range from stark white to shades of pale blue, medium blue, and very dark blue. It was not difficult to mix a color that matched the molybdenum blue and then dilute it to get the correct progression of dark to light. The color chart is permanent, unlike the color chart mentioned by Baker (1975), which was made of molybdenum blue stained filter papers. Since all tested filter papers eventually look alike unless fixed with sodium citrate, Baker's color chart had a very short use life.

Analysis of the Los Morteros Data

A variety of statistical analyses were performed using the Los Morteros phosphate data. The Student's t-test was used to see if the differences between the mean phosphate values at different depths below surface were significant. The Pearson correlation coefficient was calculated to determine if the surface and subsurface artifact counts for each grid unit co-varied. Phosphate values and artifact counts were paired so that the Spearman's rho and Kendall's tau coefficients could be calculated. The phosphate values of samples taken from two pit houses were examined. Finally, six soil samples, which were quantitatively tested for phosphate by the University of Arizona soils laboratory, were also tested by the author using the Eidt spot test. The test results are compared graphically.

Comparison of Mean Phosphate Readings

The Student's t-test was employed to determine if significant differences existed between the means of phosphate readings taken at different depths. Three samples had been taken at evenly spaced intervals in each posthole. The samples were not taken at uniform depths. For this reason the data were examined in two ways using the t-test. First, phosphate readings were grouped into 10-cm levels and compared (Table F.1); then, the readings were classed as top, middle or bottom readings, regardless of actual depth (Table F.2).

Using the 21 samples classed by measured depth, there were only two cases when the difference in sample means was significant at the 0.1 level (see Table F.1). These were the difference in means between the test results at P30 (phosphate at 30 cm to 39 cm below surface) and P50 (phosphate at 50 cm to 59 cm below surface) and the difference between the means at P50 and PAVE (average phosphate reading for each unit sampled). Three values could not be calculated. The other 16 values were not significantly different from one another. These results are difficult to interpret but overall it appears that there are no outstanding patterned differences.

Table F.1

STUDENT'S T-TEST: COMPARISON OF MEANS OF PHOSPHATE READINGS AT
MEASURED DEPTHS

Pairs of Phosphate Readings A with B	No. of Cases	Mean of A	Mean of B	Difference in Means	T-Test Value	Degrees of Freedom	2-Tail Probability
P10 P20	24	7.6667	7.1250	0.5417	1.88	23	0.073
P10 P30	24	7.6250	6.8750	0.7500	1.58	23	0.128
P10 P40	14	7.2143	6.8571	0.3571	0.59	13	0.567
P10 P50	2	9.0000	7.0000	2.0000	1.00	1	0.500
P10 P60	0	--	--	--	--	-	---
P10 PAVE	32	7.5938	10.2656	-2.6719	-.86	31	0.398
P20 P30	23	7.4348	6.9565	0.4783	1.44	22	0.164
P20 P40	41	8.0976	8.4390	-.3415	-.64	40	0.529
P20 P50	8	7.3750	6.1250	1.2500	1.85	7	0.106
P20 P60	34	8.3824	8.0882	0.2941	0.83	33	0.413
P20 PAVE	64	7.8594	8.7437	-.8844	-.53	63	0.595
P30 P40	7	7.2857	6.8571	0.4286	0.49	6	0.639
P30 P50	8	7.2500	6.3750	-.8750	2.50	7	0.041
P30 P60	1	6.0	6.0	--	--	-	--
P30 PAVE	32	6.9688	10.2531	-3.2844	-1.06	31	0.297
P40 P50	0	--	--	--	--	-	--
P40 P60	32	8.8125	8.0625	0.7500	1.13	31	.266
P40 PAVE	46	8.2609	7.1543	1.1065	0.91	45	.366
P50 P60	2	6.000	8.5000	-2.5000	-5.00	1	0.126
P50 PAVE	10	6.3000	7.4500	-0.8500	-3.93	9	0.003
P60 PAVE	34	8.0294	7.1706	0.8588	0.81	33	0.423

P10 = Phosphate reading at 10-19 cm below surface (others follow suit).
PAVE = Average phosphate reading for each unit sampled.

It is easier to interpret the results when the relative location, top, middle or bottom, of each phosphate sample was used to calculate Student's t (see Table F.2). The only case in which there was a significant difference in the sample means was when the top phosphate reading (PTOP) was paired with the bottom phosphate reading (PBOT). The

Table F.2

STUDENT'S T-TEST: COMPARISON OF MEANS OF PHOSPHATE READINGS AT
RELATIVE DEPTHS

Pairs of Phosphate Readings A with B	No. of Cases	Mean of A	Mean of B	Difference in Means	T-Test Value	Degrees of Freedom	2-Tail Probability
PTOP PBOT	73	7.9863	6.7808	1.2055	2.21	72	0.031
PTOP PMID	74	7.9595	7.8243	0.1351	0.41	73	0.682
PTOP PAVE	73	7.9863	8.5233	-.5370	-.37	72	0.713
PBOT PMID	73	6.7808	7.8493	-1.0685	-1.36	72	0.178
PBOT PAVE	72	6.7639	8.5583	-1.7944	-1.30	71	0.197
PMID PAVE	73	7.8493	8.5233	-.6740	-.43	72	0.668

PTOP = Top phosphate reading for sampled unit.
PMID = Middle phosphate reading for sampled unit.
PBOT = Bottom phosphate reading for sampled unit.
PAVE = Average phosphate reading for each sampled unit.

t value is 2.21, which has a 0.031 level of significance. Generally speaking, the top sample is from the most disturbed level of the test hole. The average depth of modern disturbance (plow zone) on the site is 27.8 cm below surface. The average depth of the top sample is 16.5 cm, which means that most top soil samples were taken from well within this disturbed zone. The average depth of middle samples is 32.8 cm, implying that most are below the disturbed level, while the average depth of the bottom samples is 48.3 cm, well below the disturbed zone in most cases.

The fact that the mean of the top readings is significantly higher than the mean of the bottom readings may be related to the disturbance already mentioned. It is logical to expect that the greatest differences in phosphate readings will be seen between the most widely separated samples.

Surface and Subsurface Artifact Counts

One stage of the research at Los Morteros involved the systematic surface collection of artifacts. Collections were made using the 50-m by 50-m grid system. Decorated sherds and diagnostic artifacts were collected from each 50-m by 50-m unit. All artifacts were collected from each 5-m by 5-m unit in the northwest corner of each 50-m by 50-m grid (see Fig. F.1). The artifacts collected from each 5-m by 5-m unit were bagged separately from the diagnostics collected elsewhere in the unit. Each posthole was placed one meter south and one meter east of the northwest grid corner.

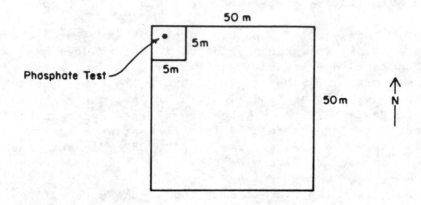

Figure F.1. Los Morteros grid and sample unit locations.

The sherd counts from each 5-m by 5-m unit were tabulated and used by William L. Deaver to produce a contour map of sherd density for the surface of the site (see Fig. 3.2).

The artifact counts from the postholes dug during the collection of soil samples for the study were tabulated. Rather than compare the surface and subsurface artifact counts by drawing a second contour map, the Pearson product moment correlation coefficient (Pearson's r) was calculated using SPSS subprogram PEARSON CORR (Nie and others 1975:280-287). The surface sherd counts from the 5-m by 5-m units were paired with the subsurface artifact counts from the posthole in the same 50-m by 50-m unit. In cases of missing data, the pair was deleted from the calculation. With 72 cases included in the calculation, the correlation coefficient was equal to 0.5715, which was significant at the 0.001 level. This is a very high level of correlation, there being only one chance in a thousand that this linear relationship is due to chance.

A significant correlation coefficient indicates that two variables tend to vary together, either positively or negatively (Roscoe

210

1975:93). The strong correlation between the surface and subsurface
artifact counts is particularly interesting if one considers the
differences in scale between the two. The surface artifact counts
represent a 25 square meter surface area that has been heavily
disturbed. The subsurface counts are from a hole of variable depth with
a maximum volume of 0.042 cubic meters. Disturbance is found in less
than half the hole's volume in most cases.

Phosphate Readings and Known Site Data

The values assigned to the soil samples tested for phosphate are
rank order variables: "linear relationships do not exist between ranks
and accurate quantitative comparisons cannot be made" (Woods 1975:23).

A sample assigned a value of 6 does not have twice the amount of
phosphate as a sample assigned a value of 3, but it does have more
phosphate than samples assigned lower values. To deal with ordinal
scales, one may use nonparametric statistics. To determine degree of
correlation one uses either Kendall's tau or Spearman's rho instead of
Pearson's. In Tables F.3 and F.4 the Kendall and Spearman coefficients
are presented. They are calculated in different ways but the results
are quite similar. The SPSS program NONPAR CORR (Nie and others
1975:288-292) was used to determine these coefficients.

The data from the overall sampling of the site will be discussed
first. The phosphate readings were paired with surface and subsurface
artifact counts. The phosphate data were again classed in two different
ways--using the measured depth below surface and then using the relative
level below surface, top, middle, or bottom. When the phosphate
readings at measured depths were compared with surface artifact counts
there were no significant Kendall or Spearman values. When phosphate
values at measured depths were paired with subsurface artifact counts
the Kendall and Spearman coefficients were significant at levels better
than 0.1 for P10, P20, P30, P40 and PAVE and at levels only slightly
higher than 0.1 for P50 and P60 (Table F.3).

Phosphate readings at relative levels below surface were paired
with surface artifact counts. The result was that there were no significant correlations (Table F.2). But when the same phosphate values
were paired with subsurface artifact counts, all Kendall and Spearman
coefficients were significant at the 0.1 level Table F.4).

The fact that significant levels of correlation occur between
most of the phosphate readings and the subsurface artifact counts speaks
well for the results of the phosphate testing. If the level of
phosphate present is actually related to cultural enrichment of the
soil, it makes sense that there are better correlations with the
subsurface artifact counts than with surface artifact counts,
particularly if the surface has been disturbed.

TABLE F.3

Kendall's Tau and Spearman's Rho for Phosphate Readings Paired with
Surface and Subsurface Artifact Counts

Phosphate Readings at Measured Levels
Paired with Surface Artifacts Counts

Phosphate at	n	Kendall's Tau	Level of Significance	Spearman's Rho	Level of Significance
P10	32	-.0348	.401	-.0381	.418
P20	63	.1009	.147	.1325	.151
P30	32	.0464	.369	.0593	.374
P40	45	.0245	.414	.0385	.401
P50	10	-.1711	.278	-.2288	.263
P60	3	-.0235	.431	-.0253	.445
PAVE	72	-.0197	.408	-.0247	.419

Phosphate Readings at Measured Levels
Paired with Subsurface Artifact Counts

P10	31	.2900	.029	.3521	.027
P20	64	.3098	.001	.3840	.001
P30	31	.3649	.009	.4406	.007
P40	47	.1528	.086	.1937	.097
P50	10	.3703	.112	.4370	.104
P60	35	.1393	.146	.1771	.155
PAVE	73	.2265	.005	.3175	.004

Phosphate at Relative Levels with Surface Counts

PTOP	72	.0144	.437	.0288	.406
PMID	72	.0072	.468	.0084	.473
PBOT	71	.0108	.452	.0153	.450

Phosphate at Relative Levels with Surface Counts

PTOP	73	.2483	.004	.3113	.004
PMID	73	.2457	.005	.3127	.004
PBOT	72	.1350	.072	.1737	.073

P10 = Phosphate at 10-19 cm below surface, P20 = 20-29 cm etc.
PAVE = Average phosphate reading for each unit tested.
PTOP = Top phosphate reading.
PMID = Middle phosphate reading.
PBOT = Bottom phosphate reading.

TABLE F.4

Kendall's Tau and Spearman's Rho for Phosphate Readings and for Subsurface Artifact Counts from N1500-E950

Phosphate Readings Paired with Each Other

Phosphate Pairs		Kendall's Tau	Level of Significance	Spearman's RHO	Level of Significance
P20	P40	.2566	.070	.3105	.066
P40	P60	.3818	.012	.4248	.018
P20	P60	.0724	.336	.1103	.300

Phosphate Readings Paired with Subsurfae Artifact Counts

Pairs		Kendall's Tau	Level of Significance	Spearman's Rho	Level of Significance
P20	ART	.0275	.432	.0502	.406
P40	ART	.2676	.046	.3494	.044
P60	ART	.4493	.002	.5371	.003

P20 = Phosphate reading at 20 cm below surface; P40 = 40 cm below surface, etc.

ART = Subsurface artifact counts.

Note: Sample size is 25 units; samples from 20 cm, 40 cm, 60 cm below surface.

In the smaller scale sampling unit, the 25 postholes dug in the single 50-m by 50-m unit, there was fairly good correlation of the phosphate levels with each other and with subsurface artifact counts. No surface counts were available for these smaller units.

The Kendall and Spearman coefficients for the pairs P20 with P40 and P40 with P60 were both significant at the 0.1 level (Table F.4).

The pair P20 with P60 was not significant but one would expect that the top and bottom samples would be the most divergent pair.

The Kendall and Spearman coefficients for the pairs P40 with subsurface artifact counts and P60 with subsurface artifact counts were significant at the 0.05 level (Table F.4). However, the coefficient for the pair P20 with subsurface artifacts was not significant at the 0.1 or even the 0.2 level. This may be due to an unusual amount of disturbance in the first 20 cm below the surface.

An attempt to use information concerning the location of backhoe trenches and known features at Los Morteros was not successful. Changes in computer commands selected for three sets of conditions: (1) the presence of a backhoe trench and the presence of a feature both in the same 50-m by 50-m unit, (2) the presence of a backhoe trench but no known feature in a 50-m by 50-m unit and (3) the cases of no backhoe trench and no known feature in a 50-m by 50-m unit. The lack of correlation seen overall made me question the assumption that the location of a feature in a backhoe trench would necessarily mean that a feature would be penetrated by the adjacent posthole. The assumption was determined to be false given a minimum distance of 1 m between any posthole and backhoe trench and a maximum distance of 20 m between a posthole and its adjacent backhoe trench.

Phosphate Samples from Features

Soil samples were collected from the profiles of two features at Los Morteros. Features 30 and 39 are Hohokam pit houses that were excavated by the field school. The phosphate data for the features are contained in Tables F. 5 and F.6. Figures F.2 and F.3 are drawings of the profiles that are labeled with the phosphate reading at its position in the feature.

Soil samples were taken from the north profile wall of Feature 30. Five sets of samples, spaced one meter apart horizontally, were taken from 10 cm above the floor, at the floor level, and from 10 cm and 40 cm below the floor (Table F.5). Examination of the profile drawing (Fig. F.2) shows that most samples taken from the house fill, the floor, and just below the floor have reasonably high phosphate values of 8, 9, and 10. Exceptions to this are a value of 6 at N1402-E929.2 at the floor level and at the east end of the feature at N1402-E931.2 with moderate values of 5, 6 and 7. Further information about the pit house may explain these phosphate readings. The samples taken at 40 cm below floor level have more moderate values of 5, 6 and 7. The high value for the sample at N1402-E930.2 is due to a pit or posthole that extends below the floor.

Four sets of soil samples spaced about one meter apart were collected from the south profile wall of Feature 39. The samples are from measured levels above, below and on the pit house floor. The

Table F.5

PHOSPHATE VALUES FOR SOIL SAMPLES FROM FEATURE 30, PIT HOUSE, PROFILE

	N1402 E 927.2	E 928.2	E 929.2	E 930.2	E 931.2
10 cm above floor	9	9	8	8	6
floor level	9	9	6	10	5
10 cm below floor	9	8	8	10	7
40 cm below floor	5	6	7	10	-

Table F.6

PHOSPHATE VALUES FOR SOIL SAMPLES FROM FEATURE 39, PIT HOUSE, PROFILE

	N1427.25 E1075	E1074	E1073	E1072.5	E1072
40 cm above floor	-	-	10	-	-
10 cm above floor	10	10	10	-	10
floor level	7	10	7	-	7
10 cm below floor	4	6	8	-	8
40 cm below floor	4	6	6	-	8
pit				10,9,8,8,10,8 ave=8.83	

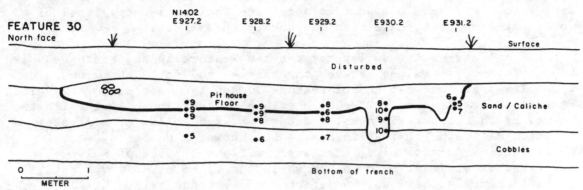

Figure F.2. Feature 30 profile and location of phosphate samples taken.

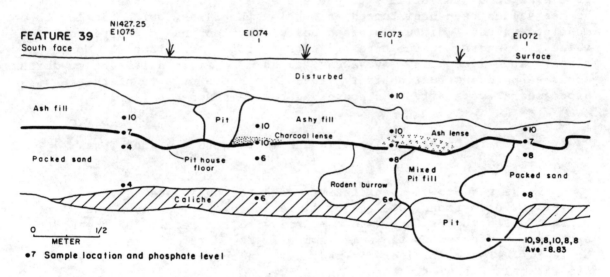

Figure F.3. Feature 39 profile and location of phosphate samples taken.

phosphate values are presented in Table F.6. As with Feature 30, the samples tested from the house fill and at the floor level had high phosphate values of 7, 8, and 10. At 10 cm and 40 cm below the floor there are two different things happening. At the east end of the feature the samples at N1427.25-E1075 and E1074 are low and moderate with readings of 4 and 6. Moving west into a highly disturbed area the values are moderate to high values of 6, 8, and 10. Readings in the disturbed area may indicate if the soil comes from cultural or non-cultural context.

A deep pit extends almost 70 cm below the floor level. A soil sample was collected from the bottom of the pit. Soil from this feature was tested six different times. The results were all high, 10, 9, 8,

10, 8, and 8, with an average value of 8.83. This multiple testing of soil from one sample was done to determine the consistency level of my work: it appears to have been reasonably consistent.

An interesting difference between Feature 30 and Feature 39 is the difference in values between the samples collected at 10 cm below floor level at the west end of Feature 30 and the east end of 39. The Feature 30 samples retain the high values of the floor level while the values of the Feature 39 samples drop from high to low or moderate values. Although the real reason is not known, a number of possibilities come to mind. Perhaps the floor surface of F.39 was plastered or at least hard-packed while the floor of F.30 was not. Or perhaps there is previously undetected disturbance below the floor of F. 30. In any event, something about the two houses is different in a way that can be detected by phosphate testing.

The results of the phosphate testing of the pit house soil are a good example of the utility of phosphate testing. The house fill had higher values than undisturbed soil below the floor, which had low to moderate values. Disturbed areas below the floor had moderate to high values, depending on the type and extent of the disturbance. More closely spaced sampling may have revealed more small differences, which could help reconstruct activity areas in a house or some of the processes at work after the house had been abandoned.

Comparison of Quantitative Lab Tests with the Spot Test

The results of quantitative tests for phosphate performed by the University of Arizona, College of Agriculture, Soils, Water and Plant Tissue Testing Laboratory were compared with the results of the Eidt spot test performed on the same samples. The data are presented in Table F.7. The comparison was made using a chart rather than by statistical manipulation (see Figure F.4).

The tests by the laboratory were performed in May of 1980. Two different phosphate tests were done. One test was for available phosphate. It involved a carbon dioxide extraction and cost $3.00 per sample at 1980 prices. The other tested for total phosphate using a perchloric acid digestion and cost $5.00 per sample at 1980 prices. The cost of performing both tests on six soil samples was more than double the cost of the testing equipment and supplies purchased for this study. More than 500 actual tests were performed for this small investment. Of course, the costs did not include labor since this was a graduate student project.

Upon examining Figure F.4 it appeared that the results of the two laboratory tests differed somewhat. The laboratory test results were then compared with the phosphate values determined by using the Los Morteros modification of the Eidt spot test. It appears that there is a reasonably good correspondence between the results of the spot test and

TABLE F.7

Comparison of Spot Test Results with Laboratory Test Results

Sample No.	ASM Field No.	Available PO₄-P (ppm)	Total PO₄-P (ppm)	Spot Test Results
1	1127	1.00	1840	4
2	1126	1.65	1600	7
3	1238	5.75	1480	8
4	1153	2.50	1840	10
5	1239	5.75	1600	10
6	1242	6.25	2360	10

Laboratory tests were performed by the Soils, Water, and Plant Tissue Testing Laboratory in the Department of Soils, Water, and Engineering, College of Agriculture, University of Arizona, Tucson, Arizona.

the test for available phosphate. On the graph, the values for both rise overall except for Sample 3 which drops slightly in the available phosphate test. The total phosphate curve falls and rises twice. It is clear that the spot test results are actually closer to the overall results of the available phosphate test than the laboratory tests are to each other. The overall similarity of the two curves suggests that the spot test is reasonably reliable.

Based on my limited knowledge of chemistry it does not appear that either of the lab procedures mentioned above is the same as the sequential fractionization process Eidt (1977) used to distinguish natural phosphate from culturally deposited phosphate. The test he describes would probably provide the most useful information from an archaeological point of view. But, as he has already been argued, such quantitative analysis is unnecessary for most archaeological applications of phosphate testing.

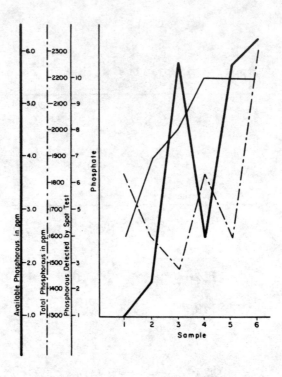

Figure F.4. Comparison of spot test results with laboratory tested results.

Concluding Remarks

The results of the analyses performed on the phosphate data indicate that phosphate testing can be useful for intra-site analysis at Los Morteros. The spot test was successfully modified so that the soil at the site which is naturally high in phosphate could be tested. The comparison of the qualitative spot test results with quantitative laboratory results suggests that the technique used is fairly reliable. Given the high cost of outside laboratory testing, the spot test appears to be sufficient to deal with most archaeological applications of phosphate testing.

The high degree of correlation between phosphate readings and subsurface artifact counts (significant at the .001 level) contrasts with the lack of correlation between phosphate readings and surface artifact counts. In terms of intra-site analysis, this raises two rather important issues. The first is the matter of the scale at which phosphate analysis is useful. The phosphate data are probably a good indication of what one will find in and immediately adjacent to the posthole. The horizontal and vertical distances between the samples from Features 30 and 39 are not large but the phosphate readings can be considerably different from one another when separated by only 10 cm. Therefore, the phosphate data cannot readily be applied to an area that is meters away such as the area adjacent to the posthole that was surface collected. The phosphate test results may provide a good, fine-grained picture but the close correlation of surface and subsurface artifact counts suggests that at Los Morteros the subsurface artifact count may provide more robust data that can be used to draw an overall picture of the site.

The second issue grows out of the first. It seems that soil samples with high phosphate values come from postholes with large numbers of artifacts. If one digs a posthole and finds lots of artifacts, why is a phosphate test necessary? To answer this question we must determine what kind of information we want from our testing of the site. Do we want to know if there are any cultural deposits? Or, do we want to know if a feature of some sort is present? To answer the first question, an artifact count might suffice. To answer the second question, phosphate testing might be useful if, through further work at Los Morteros, we could find correlations between phosphate readings and specific types of features.

Los Morteros is a site with many surface and subsurface artifacts. Backhoe testing and limited excavation have confirmed the overall picture of the site developed from surface artifact density maps. Other types of sites, particularly those with a paucity of artifacts, may find phosphate testing useful to determine site boundaries or to locate features. The utility of phosphate testing within features was illustrated by the samples tested from Features 30 and 39. This may be the area with the most potential for future phosphate analysis at Los Morteros.

Overall, the results of the various analyses have been very positive. I must admit that I am surprised to have so many positive things to say because until I actually examined the statistics and drew the figures I was sure that this project had been doomed to fail. Even after modifying the spot test procedure, I was concerned because the soils being tested were naturally high in phosphate. This fact led me to believe that it was possible that the variation seen between samples was the result of natural variability in the levels of phosphate present. My fears were magnified by the fact that the spot test cannot distinguish between organic and inorganic forms of phosphate (Eidt 1977). However, the high degree of correlation of phosphate readings and subsurface artifact counts and the results of the samples tested from the pit houses indicated that my fears had been unfounded.

Another problem was anticipated. I had not gathered any soil samples outside of the site boundaries and therefore had no noncultural background phosphate levels. Collecting samples off-site was difficult since the land around the site was either privately owned and off limits or was under cultivation. However, the internal consistency of the data provided almost the full range of phosphate values so that off-site data were not necessary.

It appears, then, that phosphate analysis can be a useful analytical tool at Los Morteros. Because of the apparent reliability of surface and subsurface artifact counts, phosphate testing may not be the best technique for developing an overall picture of the site. Its usefulness for this type of analysis at sites other than Los Morteros is not being questioned here. Rather, it is being suggested that if further phosphate testing is done at Los Morteros, it should be used to aid in the interpretation of features with an eye toward discerning correlations between phosphate levels, types of features, and locations of features.

Appendix G

FAUNAL MATERIALS

Laverne Conway

By gleaning from backdirt and using one-quarter-inch mesh
screen, 155 specimens of bone were recovered during the testing at the
Los Morteros site. Of this number, 62 pieces (40 percent) were
identifiable to at least the ordinal level. Two bone awls were present
in the collection.

It must be emphasized that these remains constitute an extremely
small sample from the site, which limits the conclusions that can be
made. This analysis should be viewed as a partial attempt to understand
the site's fauna, one that does not include results of stratigraphic or
areal analysis and other information essential to a final faunal report.

The focus of this study is to present background data that will
eventually be useful in a more complete study. The systematics section
includes, for each taxon represented at the site, (1) its present
distribution, (2) a brief biographical sketch, (3) its representation in
this assemblage, (4) ethnographic data pertaining to its use and, (5)
its occurrence in other archaeological contexts. In the analysis
section, possible implications are discussed. Finally, a selection of
topics regarding prehistoric animal use that warrant consideration in
future studies from the site is presented.

Methods

Each lot of bagged bone was examined and a tally of its contents
was recorded on index cards. Identifiable and unidentifiable bones were
counted and described. A bone was considered identifiable it it was
whole or if an articular surface or other morphological feature that
could aid in its identification was present. All bones in this genre
were identified to the lowest possible taxon. Information recorded
included element, butchering marks, dentition, epiphyseal closure, and
evidence of burning. No attempt was made to age individuals represented
by the bones. In general, the assignment of a species identification
was very conservatively made. Categories of large mammal, medium-to-
large mammal, medium mammal, small mammal, and mammal were used. The
large mammal category incorporated remains of animals in the deer-size
range, the medium mammal category was for dog-to bobcat-size range, and
the small mammal was for rodent sized remains. The mammal category
primarily included those bones, such as ribs and vertebrae, which have a
wide variation in size within the body of an individual and thus could
not be assigned a more exact identification.

222

Post-identification procedures were limited by the small size of the sample. Calculations that were considered appropriate were a listing of species identified from the remains (see Table G.1), the total number of fragments for each of these species (Table G.2), and the minimum number of individuals (MNI) represented (also in Table G.2).

Table G.1

TAXONOMIC LIST OF ANIMAL SPECIES PRESENT AT LOS MORTEROS

Reptilia

Phrynosoma solare   Regal Horned Lizard

Aves

Lophortyx gambelii   Gambel's Quail

Mammalia

Lepus californicus   Black-tailed Jackrabbit
Lepus alleni   Antelope Jackrabbit
Lepus sp.   Jackrabbit
Sylvilagus sp.   Cottontail
Ammospermophilus harrisii-small   Harris' Antelope Squirrel-
Spermophilus   small Ground Squirrel
Spermophilus sp.   Ground Squirrel
Peromyscus sp.   Mouse
Canis sp.   Dog/Coyote
Taxidea taxus   Badger
?Lynx rufus   Bobcat
Odocoileus virginianus couesi   Coues' White-tailed Deer
Odocoileus sp.   Deer
Bos taurus   Cattle
Equus caballus   Horse

Table G.2

FREQUENCIES OF IDENTIFIED SPECIES

Fauna	Number of elements	Percent	MNI	Percent
Phyrnosoma solare	1	1.61	1	5.56
Lophortyx gambelii	1	1.61	1	5.56
Lepus californicus	24	38.70	3	16.67
Lepus alleni	5	8.06	1	5.56
Lepus sp.	17	27.42	1	5.56
Sylvilagus sp.	2	3.23	1	5.56
Ammospermophilus harrisii- small Spermophilus sp.	1	1.61	1	5.56
Spermophilus sp.	1	1.61	1	5.56
Peromyscus sp.	2	3.23	1	5.56
Canis sp.	2	3.23	1	5.56
Taxidea taxus	1	1.61	1	5.56
?Lynx rufus	1	1.61	1	5.56
Odocoileus virginianus couesi	1	1.61	1	5.56
Odocoileus sp.	1	1.61	1	5.56
Bos taurus	1	1.61	1	5.56
Equus caballus	1	1.61	1	5.56
Totals	62	99.97	18	100.07

MNI = Minimum number of individuals.

Systematics

Phyrnosoma solare: Regal Horned Lizard

        This lizard occurs in both the Lower and Upper Sonoran Life
Zones of Arizona, from the southern portion of the central plateau south
into northern Sinaloa, Mexico. It frequents arid regions, both on the
plains and in the mountains, often where there is mesquite or saguaro.
The adults of this species are 3" to 4.5" in snout-vent length; the tail
is about one-half of the head-body measurement (Stebbins 1954: 263).

        The frill from the base of a skull was recovered at Los
Morteros, which consisted of 4 closely set occipital horns, rather than
2 horns, as with other horned lizards (Stebbins 1954: 263).

Ethnographic references include lizards as part of the Papago diet. Audubon (1906: 148-150) characterized the Papago as living on turtles and what game they could get. He states that they "kill them (lizards) with a light wand, giving them a dextrous tap on the head."

Remains of P. solare also were identified from a room floor in the Escalante Ruins (Sparling 1974: 227,230,231).

Lophortyx gambelii: Gambel's Quail

This is a common quail, found in drier habitats than the California quail, which it resembles (Robbins and others 1966: 88). It is an abundant resident in all areas where mesquite occurs (Monson and Phillips 1964: 192).

A single proximal fragment of a humerus was recovered from the site.

Gambel's quail was the most important food bird of the Papago. The birds were trapped in very rough cages of split giant cactus ribs (Castetter and Underhill 1935: 43). According to Castetter and Underhill (1935: 43), the Papago did not use the eggs of these birds, but according to Castetter and Bell (1942: 69), quail eggs were the only bird eggs utilized by the Pima. DiPeso (1956: 446) states that the Gambel's quail was considered an important Ootam food item that was hunted at night with flares.

Gambel's quail remains have been reported from the Escalante Ruins (Sparling 1974: 222), Ventana Cave (Haury 1950: 52), Snaketown (Haury 1976: 375), and the Quijotoa Valley (White 1978: 238).

Lepus sp.: Jackrabbit

Lepus californicus, the black-tailed jackrabbit, has a pan-Arizona distribution (Lowe 1964: 251). In southern Arizona, their range overlaps with that of Sylvilagus sp., the desert cottontail. According to Collins Cochran, a general comparison of the habitats of these two genera of leporids reveals that Lepus sp. prefers more open areas, while Sylvilagus sp. appears to need more cover. The length of L. californicus is 18 to 26 inches, while its weight is 4 to 8 pounds (Gilbert 1973: 61).

L. californicus was represented in this collection by 24 elements including scapulae, humeri, radii, ulnae, metapodials, pelvises, tibiae, calcanei, phalanges, and an astragalus.

These small game animals were of considerable importance in prehistoric economies. The Papago considered jackrabbit meat inferior to and not as sweet as that of Sylvilagus sp., but it was of considerable value because it was both plentiful and available at all seasons. One early reference characterizes the Papago as living on seeds, grass, rabbits, rats, and wild fruits (Castetter and Bell 1942: 66).

The Papago differed from their neighbors in their rabbit hunting techniques; rather than trapping or clubbing them, they shot them with a bow and arrow of creosote bush wood with a wooden tip hardened in fire (Castetter and Underhill 1935: 42). Except for a communal drive made before the spring drinking ceremony, rabbits were customarily shot by boys, although men did shoot them when they encountered them (Castetter and Bell 1942: 66). As White (1978 :252) notes, the discovery of a hunting net made from human hair and recovered from a cave in the Baboquivari Mountains is limited archaeological evidence that rabbit drives in which large numbers of animals are taken in a brief time period were practiced in the Papagueria.

L. californicus remains have been recorded at numerous sites in southern Arizona, including Ramanote Cave and San Cayetano Village in the San Pedro River Valley (DiPeso 1956: Fig. 79); Valshni Village (Withers 1941: 34); the Quijotoa Valley (White 1978: 228); Ventana Cave (Haury 1950: 151) in the Papaguería, and at sites in the middle Santa Cruz River Valley (Olsen 1977: 179, 180).

Lepus alleni, the antelope jackrabbit, is restricted in range to the central one-third of southern Arizona (Cockrum 1960: 68). Its average weight is from 2.7 to 5.9 kilograms, making it larger than L. californicus. These white-sided jackrabbits range for the most part in semiarid zones supporting a fairly dense ground vegetation, particularly mesquite grassland and thorn forest. Only in western Sonora does it occur in true desert, and even there it frequents brushy watercourses, rather than the bare desert plains (Leopold 1972). Arnold (1940), in his study of the vertebrate animals of the mesquite forest along the Santa Cruz River, found L. alleni more frequently in the bosque than L. californicus.

L. alleni was represented in the collection by five elements, including a radius, ulna, and two metatarsals. Skeletal elements of L. alleni were differentiated from those of L. californicus by their greater size. In several instances, bones intermediate in size between L. alleni and L. californicus were placed in the Lepus sp. taxon.

Remains of L. alleni were recovered at Ramanote Cave and San Cayetano Village (DiPeso 1956: Fig. 65), Valshni Village (Withers 1941: 304), Ventana Cave (Haury 1950: 151), and in the Quijotoa Valley (White 1978: 232).

Sylvilagus sp.: Cottontail

Sylvilagus audubonii, the desert cottontail, is common throughout the state at elevations below 6,000 feet (Cockrum 1964: 252).

As previously mentioned, the cottontail's habitat differs slightly from the jackrabbit's within their overlapping ranges. The head and body length ranges from about 250 to 450 mm. and the tail is 25 mm. long. The weight varies from about 400 to 2,300 grams. These animals occupy burrows made by other animals or they inhabit almost any available shelter. They often will not break from cover, even when closely approached. This trait probably has aided their survival in areas cultivated and thickly populated by man (Walker 1975: 660).

Material examined consisted of two elements, the shaft fragments of a tibia and femur. These remains were distinguished from those of _Lepus_ sp. by their small size. Although they compared favorably to _Sylvilagus audubonii_, it is possible that they pertain to _S. nuttali_ (Nuttal's cottontail) or _S. floridanus_ (eastern cottontail). Therefore, these bones were classified as _Sylvilagus_ sp.

Sylvilagus sp. remains were recovered at Valshni Village (Withers 1941: 34), Escalante Ruins (Sparling 1974: 216, 228, and 237), Ramanote Cave and San Cayetano Village (DiPeso 1956: Fig. 65 and 70), Punta de Agua (Greenleaf 1975: 106), Ventana Cave (Haury 1950: 153). Snaketown (Haury 1976: 370), the middle Santa Cruz River Valley (Olsen 1977: 179 and 181), and the Quijotoa Valley (White 1978: 233).

Ammospermophilus harrisii: Harris' Antelope Ground Squirrel

The range of the five _Ammospermophilus_ species covers the arid sparsely vegetated plains and lower mountain slopes of the southwestern United States (Walker 1975: 710). _A. harrisii_ occurs from the western central portion to the southern central portion of Arizona (Hall and Kelson 1959: 331).

These are true ground squirrels that live in burrows that they dig and possess few traits of either the tree squirrels (_Sciurus_ sp.) or chipmunks (_Tamias_ and _Eutamias_). The length of the body and head is 140 to 155 millimeters and the length of the tail is 55 to 95 millimeters. Adults weigh 112 to 142 grams. These squirrels are diurnal and are active throughout the year, except in the higher and cold parts of their range, where they become inactive during cold weather, but never truly hibernate. They feed on seeds, fruits, plant stems and roots, some insects, and carrion. When irrigation is practiced, these animals become a nuisance by destroying crops (Walker 1959: 710).

A single tibia in the _Ammospermophilus harrisii_-small _Spermophilus_ sp. size range was recovered from Los Morteros.

Ethnographic use of these animals as food items has already been mentioned.

Ammospermophilus harrisii also was noted from the Punta de Agua site (Greenleaf 1975: 106).

<u>Spermophilus</u> sp.: Ground Squirrel

     Three species of this genus occur in the Tucson Basin. These
are <u>S</u>. <u>spilosoma</u> (spotted ground squirrel), <u>S</u>. <u>variegatus</u> (rock
squirrel), and <u>S</u>. <u>tereticaudus</u> (round-tailed ground squirrel) (Hall and
Kelson 1959: 335-363). These animals prefer a habitat of arid grassy
lands or rocky areas. Their head and body length is 154 to 406
millimeters, and length of tail is 38 to 254 millimeters. The range of
weights for adults is 85 to 1000 grams. Ground squirrels are short
legged and adapted to a life on the ground; they dig their own burrows
or live near logs and rocks as shelter for their nests and food stores.
They are active by day, searching for seeds, nuts, roots, bulbs, some
plant stems, leaves, mice, insects, birds, and eggs. They live in loose
colonies and in large numbers if food is adequate (Walker 1975: 720).

     A single mandible fragment retaining one cheek tooth was
recovered from the site. This specimen was a small species of ground
squirrel, either <u>S</u>. <u>spilosoma</u> or <u>S</u>. <u>tereticaudus</u>.

     As already mentioned, ground squirrels were hunted as a food
item by the Papago.

     <u>Spermophilus</u> sp. remains were recovered at San Cayetano Village
(DiPeso 1956: Fig. 65), Snaketown (Haury 1976: 368), Ventana Cave (Haury
1950: 153), and in the Quijotoa Valley (White 1978: 228).

<u>Peromyscus</u> sp.: Mouse

     Five species of <u>Peromyscus</u> sp. are likely to be living in the
area of the site. These include <u>P</u>. <u>eremicus</u> (cactus mouse), <u>P</u>. <u>Merriam</u>
(Merriam's mouse), <u>P</u>. <u>maniculatus</u> (deer mouse), <u>P</u>. <u>leucopus</u> (white-
footed mouse), and <u>P</u>. <u>boylii</u> (brush mouse) (Hall and Kelson 1959: 613-
658). These rodents can be found in almost every habitat within their
range, where they are usually the most abundant of all mammals (Walker
1975: 776).

     Material examined included an immature femur and an immature
tibia recovered from the screening of cremation number 3. These
probably represent intrusions into the crematory. Assignment to the
species level could not be made on the basis of these elements.

     Castetter and Underhill state that pocket mice (<u>Perognathus</u>
sp.), which are approximately equivalent in size, were too small to be
used commonly as food, but were eaten in "the hungry time" (1935: 42).

     <u>Peromyscus</u> sp. also has been reported from the Escalante Ruins
(Sparling 1974: 223 and 234).

<u>Canis</u> sp.: Dog or Coyote

The members of the family Canidae have a body length of 340 to 1,300 millimeters and the tail is 110 to 540 millimeters in length. <u>Canis</u> <u>latrans</u>, the coyote, has a statewide distribution (Walker 1975: 1148).

Two specimens were assigned to this taxon, including a calcaneum and a distal phalanx. These two elements were too large to pertain to any of the foxes, and in size they compared most favorably with <u>Canis</u> <u>latrans</u>; however, neither of these elements are diagnostic in distinguishing between <u>C</u>. <u>familiaris</u> (domesticated dog) and <u>C</u>. <u>latrans</u>. Therefore, assignment to <u>Canis</u> sp. was considered appropriate.

Castetter and Bell (1942: 57) found that the dog was the only domesticated animal of the Pima and Papago Indians. "Dogs were used to guard the houses, rarely for hunting. The breed was a small white one, in build like a coyote . . . but with softer fur and only half the size. Coyotes were kept as pets if captured young" (Castetter and Underhill 1935: 43).

<u>C</u>. <u>familiaris</u> was noted at Ramanote Cave and San Cayetano Village (DiPeso 1956: Fig. 65 and 70), the Escalante Ruin group (Sparling 1974: 126, 223, and 239), Hodges Ruin (Kelly 1978: 122), Snaketown (Haury 1976: 368), and in the Quijotoa Valley (White 1978: 236). <u>C</u>. <u>latrans</u> was identified from Valshni Village (Withers 1941: 304), the middle Santa Cruz River Valley (Olsen 1978: 180), the Quijotoa Valley (White 1978: 235), Snaketown (Haury 1965: 156), and Ventana Cave (Haury 1950: 151).

<u>Taxidea</u> <u>taxus</u>: Badger

This species occurs statewide, from elevations of 120 to 7,000 feet. Its length is from 26 to 35 inches and weight is 13 to 30 pounds. Its habitat is open country where ground squirrels and other burrowing animals abound (Gilbert 1973: 65). The badger is a regular consumer of rodents, lizards, and snakes, and is likely to be seen anywhere a diet of this sort can be obtained (Greene and Mathews 1976: 369).

This species was represented by a single shaft fragment of an unfused radius.

Badger was negligibly present in the faunal assemblages at Snaketown (Haury 1976: 368), at Ramanote Cave and San Cayetano Village (DiPeso 1956: Fig. 65), Ventana Cave (Haury 1950: 151), and in the Quijotoa Valley (White 1978: 236).

<u>Lynx</u> <u>rufus</u>: Bobcat

The occurrence of this cat is statewide (Cockrum 1960: 247-248) and its habitats within this range are varied. Length of this animal is from 22.5 to 50 inches, and weight is 10 to 40 pounds. Although their meat is edible, it is doubtful that they were a very important prehistoric food item (Walker 1975: 1,271). The pelts may have been utilized.

A weathered phalanx that tentatively represents this species was recovered.

L. rufus was also noted at Valshni Village (Withers 1941: 3-4).

Odocoileus sp.: Deer

Both the mule deer (O. hemionus) and the white-tailed deer (O. virginianus) are reported from the Tucson Basin (Cockrum 1960: 252). The distribution of O. hemionus in Arizona is statewide at elevations of 250 to 9,000 feet, but this distribution is not uniform (Cockrum 1960: 259). The length of O. hemionus is 55 to 75 inches in length and weight is from 125 to 475 pounds. This species lives most of the year in small groups--females with their fawns, yearlings tending to form stable social units of two to six animals, and the males running together in bands of like size. Some deer of either sex live entirely alone. Each deer or band of deer has a specified home range within which it lives. These ranges vary in size, depending on availability of cover, food, and water. Home ranges may shift annually. The deer eat a wide variety of plants including ironwood, paloverde, fruits and fleshy leaves of cacti, mesquite, and catclaw beans (Leopold 1972: 50).

O. virginianus couesi is a smaller subspecies of O. virginianus. O. virginianus occurs in southern Arizona from 1,200 to 9,000 feet in elevation (Lowe 1964: 259). The ranges of O. virginianus and O. hemionus do not overlap greatly, with the greatest incidence of this occurring around the 4,500 feet elevation. Some researchers believe that O. virginianus was once at lower elevations and attribute the restriction of its range to higher elevations to either more successful competition by the mule deer or the increased presence of man. In Mexico, O. virginianus can still be found at lower elevations. Collins Cochran has stated that this lends support to the theory that its present distribution in Arizona may be restricted.

Dense brushland is this species' favorite habitat, including thickets of mesquite and acacia. Leopold (1972: 50) suggests that this predilection for thick cover is one of the factors that protects white-tails from extermination. In contrast, mule deer, antelope, and bighorn sheep like open spaces and withstand heavy hunting very poorly.

Deer remains were represented in this collection by two elements. The weathered tip of an antler tine was assigned to the genus Odocoileus, with no determination of species. A split metacarpal that was shaped into an awl was classified as O. virginianus couesi on the basis of its small size.

Castetter and Bell (1942: 64-65) state that O. hemionus, mule deer, was formerly more abundant in the Pimeria Alta, was hunted through most of the year and was of considerable value as a source of food and clothing for both the Papago and the Pima. Its importance to the Papago is indicated by the fact that it is the game animal around which some of their ceremonies centered. O. virginianus couesi was more rarely hunted by both Pima and Papago. In reference to the Papago, Castetter and Bell (1942: 58) state that

> Among animals their reliance was upon deer, in
> diminishing order, rabbits, antelope, mountain sheep,
> rats and larvae. A family group formerly had no more
> than one to two hunters, each killing about twelve to
> fifteen deer per year. Many families had no hunter,
> so the kill was distributed among the entire economic
> unit with which they were affiliated, ranging usually
> from two to ten families.

Deer bones of one or both species have been reported from most local archaeological sites. Remains of Odocoileus sp. were reported at the Punta de Agua site (Greenleaf 1975: 106), Valshni Village (Withers 1941: 3-4), San Cayetano village and Ramanote Cave (DiPeso 1956: Fig. 65 and 70), the middle Santa Cruz River Valley (Olsen 1977: 179-181) and at Snaketown (Haury 1976: 371). O. hemionus bones have been found at Ventana Cave (Haury 1950: 153), Hodges Ruin (Kelly 1978: 122), Escalante Ruins (Sparling 1974: 216, 219, and 231), San Cayetano Village (DiPeso 1956: Fig. 65), Valshni Village (Withers 1941: 304), the middle Santa Cruz River Valley (Olsen 1978: 179), and at Snaketown (Greene and Mathews 1976: 371).

Bos taurus: Cattle, and Equus caballus: Horse

At the beginning of the eighteenth century, Father Kino distributed horses, cattle, sheep, and goats to all his missions and to villages where he hoped to establish missions. When the Jesuits were expelled from the New World, most of these animals went wild. The cattle were killed by the natives for their meat and especially their hides, which were used by the Papago to make shields and sandals. Foals were caught and raised by the Pimas (Castetter and Bell 1935: 43-44).

A fragment of tooth enamel represents B. taurus in this collection. The most that can be inferred, is that it is historic in nature. A burned epiphysis of an E. caballus femur was also noted. This also represents historic activity at the site.

Bone Awls

Two bone awl fragments were included in this collection. The first of these was a right proximal half of an <u>Odocoileus virginianus couesi</u> metacarpal that had been split longitudinally and shaped, probably into a fine-pointed awl, although this cannot be stated with certainty because the tip is missing. Modification of the articular area was not made; thus this specimen can be placed into Kidder's Type 1 classification (1932: 211). The fragment measured 93 millimeters in length, 19 millimeters in width, and 18 millimeters in thickness. The second fragment was a fine-pointed awl, consisting of a broken tip that was shaped from a bone splinter. The fragment measured 29 millimeters in length, 7 millimeters in width, and 3 millimeters in thickness. This artifact can be classified as a Type II awl in Kidder's typology (Kidder 1932: 213).

Awls are among the commonest of bone artifacts from sites in southern Arizona. At Valshni Village, worked bone was almost exclusively awls, and was of both types noted above (Withers 1941: 69). At the Punta de Agua sites, the six bone artifacts excavated were each fragments of bone awls manufactured from split metapodials of deer or mountain sheep (Greenleaf 1975: 98). At the Hodges Ruin, 56 bone awls were excavated. The earliest types were splinter awls and awls with unmodified articular ends associated with the Cañada del Oro phase. Those with modified articular condyles occurred in the Rincon, Rillito, and Tanque Verde phases, with splinter awls also present in the latter. Kelly notes that, in general, bone was not a popular item of grave furniture in the Tucson area. Many of the bone awls were found on house floors and in trash (Kelly 1978: 121-122). Both of the specimens from Los Morteros were recovered from the backdirt produced by a backhoe.

It is generally agreed that fine-pointed awls are used primarily in basket weaving and secondarily as a tool in making skin clothing and other objects that demand the perforating of materials (Olsen 1979: 355).

Butchered Bone

A single bone with evidence of butchering was noted. This consisted of the shaft portion of a medium- to large-sized mammal that was hand-sawn transversely on one end with a metal saw. The marks produced by each thrust of the saw were only roughly parallel to each other; this distinguished the marks from those produced by an automatic saw, which would have been more uniformly parallel.

This fragment was recovered from the site's surface and represents undetermined historic activity at the site.

General Comments

The bone in this collection was in an excellent state of preservation. No pathology or carnivore gnawing was noted, and in general, rodent gnawing was negligible.

Analysis

Paleoecological Interpretations

All species recovered from the site still live in the area today, so little can be said regarding environmental change. As already stated, Odocoileus virginianus couesi may have occurred more commonly at lower elevations than it does today. Probably the most significant changes in local distribution and abundance of species are a result of recent man-induced alterations of the Santa Cruz River and its riparian zone. For example, the mesquite bosques once common along the river are no longer extant, and this change in vegetation implies a change in faunal populations. In addition, if agricultural fields and canals were prehistorically maintained at the site, fauna may have been attracted or repelled by these manipulations of the landscape.

Cultural Interpretations

With the exception of the historic fauna, Bos taurus and Equus caballus) all of the fauna listed in Table G.1 could have been food sources for the Hohokam. It is also true however, that all of these species could be intrusive into the deposits, especially those that are burrowers. An examination of the frequencies of the identified fauna in Table G.2 reveals that the leporids, with a combined MNI of three, are the most common animal represented. Their relative abundance in the collection enhances the likelihood that these species were utilized as food; however, the small sample size precludes any definite statements. In addition, a total of 32 (20.65 percent) of the bones from the site were burned. These are tabulated in Table G.3. Although consistent patterns of burned bone can imply use as a food animal, such information is not obtainable from this small collection.

The relative importance of each species in the prehistoric economy also is difficult to address, given the present collection. Individual frequencies are likely to change significantly in future analyses of the site's fauna, because, with the exception of Trench 1 in Mound 1, trash mounds were purposefully avoided during testing. Thus those areas of the site that may be richest in faunal remains have not been adequately sampled. If rabbits dominate the assemblage, in future work care must be taken in interpreting this abundance. At Snaketown, Greene and Mathews (1976) demonstrated that the priority of rabbits was lost when weight per individual was considered. They found that for every mule deer, it takes 33 jackrabbits to furnish an equal amount of usable meat (Greene and Mathews 1976: 369-370). A determination of MNI can help assess which species were most important and is considered a supplementary method to simple element counts. Once MNI have been ascertained, meat weights represented can be calculated, which further defines the relative importance of each species in the prehistoric

Table G.3

BURNED BONE

Fauna	No. of elements
Lepus californicus	8
Lepus sp.	1
Equus caballus	1
Medium-to-large mammal	2
Mammal	20
Total	32

economy. Although I have calculated the MNI for taxa in this collection, I cannot state the relative importance of each species, or pursue other calculations, based on such preliminary figures.

Conclusions

Due to the small size of the analyzed sample, no firm conclusions can be derived from this preliminary report on the Los Morteros fauna. Some observations and topics for future analysis can be presented.

Site Catchment

The site is located in close proximity to a variety of ecological zones with their associated faunas. Montane resources were to be found in the Tucson, Tortolita, and Santa Catalina mountains, and the other ranges forming the boundaries of the Tucson Basin. Riparian resources were available along the Santa Cruz River and its drainages. If the site's catchment is determined to be fairly limited, this may reflect the local abundance and availability of fauna or the food preferences developed by an agrarian-based economy.

Methods of Hunting, Butchering, and Cooking

Although hunting techniques are difficult to assess from faunal remains, methods of butchering and cooking are sometimes possible to reconstruct. The degree and quality of fragmentation and burning should be noted, as an aid in such studies. White (1978) attempted to reconstruct the butchery and cooking of rabbits in his study of the faunal remains from the Quijotoa Valley. Data from Los Morteros could help determine the validity or applicability of his conclusions.

Relative Importance of Game in the Diet

Bone generally has been scarce in Tucson Basin archaeological contexts. At Snaketown, Haury found that a scant meat supply was indicated by the amount of bone recovered relative to the volume of dirt sampled. He could not readily explain this, but suggested that this resulted from either a low local animal population or a preference for grown or gathered vegetal products (Haury 1976: 114). Although most of the present collection was from backhoe backdirt, Trench 1 in Mound 1 had approximately 46.8 cubic meters of earth that was screened. A total of 38 bones was extracted, which yields an extremely low concentration index of .81 per cubic meter of midden. This is less than 1 bone recovered for each cubic meter of earth. It remains to be determined if this low figure will prevail in other areas of the site, and possibly, if this concentration changed through time. Such concentration indices for bone can aid in determining differing areal uses of a site. Any fluctuation in the reliance upon game could be related to fluctuations in the human population, preferences or availability of game, or procurement capabilities.

Conclusions from this sample are difficult to make because of its size. It is hoped that screened samples will be taken from a variety of features and areas of the site. Serial screening, for recovery of small sized rodents, amphibians, and fish, should be considered in future sampling plans. This will enable us to add to our understanding of the range of faunas and subsistence strategies utilized by the prehistoric inhabitants of the site. The biocultural history of the site will be incomplete without such an assessment.

Acknowledgments

I thank Paul Fish for giving me the opportunity to analyze the Los Morteros faunal material; Stanley Olsen and Richard Lange for editorial comments; and especially Sandra Olsen for her critical review of a rough draft of this report. All errors are the responsibility of this author.

Appendix H

POLLEN SAMPLES

This appendix lists pollen samples recovered during the initial
backhoe testing. Additional samples were taken from many of the other
features during subsequent work at the site, but no full listing of
these has been compiled.

Table H.1

POLLEN SAMPLES TAKEN

Sample Number	Inventory Number	Feature Number	Location
100		17	pit
101		7	upper floor
102		7	upper floor
103		7	upper floor
104		7	lower floor
105		7	lower floor
106		7	fill between floors
107		6	house floor
108		6	house floor
109		15	house floor
110		15	bottom of large pit
111		31	floor
112		30	bottom of pit
113		30	floor
114		30	pit in floor
115		33	side of canal
116		5	lowest floor
117		5	upper floor
118		5	another upper floor
119		5	lower floor
120		4	floor
121		22	canal bottom
122		23	pit bottom
123		25	floor
124		26	floor
125		27	canal bottom
126		28	canal bottom
127		36	house floor
128		36	pit bottom
129		41	pit bottom
130		35	house floor
131		16	house floor?
132		18	house floor
	314		in small bowl located at N585-599 E1125-26
	315	8	floor
	316	3	floor
	547	32	from vessel
	606	32	fill
	806	17	fill, near bottom
	848	32	bottom of pit

Appendix I

MACROBOTANICAL REMAINS

Assembled by

Charles H. Miksicek

Table I.1

PLANT REMAINS RECOVERED BY FLOTATION

Feature Number	Inventory Number	Context	Sample Weight (in grams)	Maize Cupules	Maize Kernels	Trianthema	Mesquite Seeds	Mesquite Leaves	Amaranth	Bursage	Yucca Fiber	Grass Stems	Other Remains
39	4110	N1427 E1074 Level 2	3.5									+	
39	4112	N1428 E1074 Level 3	5.7	1									Globemallow-1
39	4116	N1427 E1072 10 cm above floor	1.2			1			1				
47/48	5167	N1500 E1020 From soil 2B	3.7	3					15			+	Polanasia-1
47/48	5168	N1500 E1020 SE	5.6			1							
47/48	6275	SW 90-100cm	531.3			1							
47/48	6276	N1500 E1020 SE Sample 4	2.0									+	

Table I.1, continued

PLANT REMAINS RECOVERED BY FLOTATION

Feature Number	Inventory Number	Context	Sample Weight (in grams)	Maize Cupules	Maize Kernels	Trianthema	Mesquite Seeds	Mesquite Leaves	Amaranth	Bursage	Yucca Fiber	Grass Stems	Other Remains
47/48	6278	N1500 E1020 SE From profile-soil 4	5.8				1					+	
50	5512	N1355.2 E1080 Level 2	9.2										Globemallow-1
50	5508	N1355.2 E1080 Fill from hearth Level 3	1.9										
51	5889	SW side-intramural Level 3	14.9	1	1	1	1					+	Argemone spp.-1
51	6309	N1283.5 E1033 Firepit Sample 2	2.8									+	
51	6369	Unit 9 intramural 50-65 cm BD	1.3										

Table I.1, continued

PLANT REMAINS RECOVERED BY FLOTATION

Feature Number	Inventory Number	Context	Sample Weight (in grams)	Maize Cupules	Maize Kernels	Trianthema	Mesquite Seeds	Mesquite Leaves	Amaranth	Bursage	Yucca Fiber	Grass Stems	Other Remains
52	6224	N1360 E935 1.52–1.77 m BD	253.6									++	
52	6225	N1360 E935 1.27–1.52 m BD	9.5									+	
52	6305	N1360 E935 1.77–2.02 m BD	105.8									++	Little Barley-1
52	6343	N1362 E937 0–10 cm BGS	11.2		1		1	3		2			
52	6351	N1362 E937 10–20 cm BD	4.2									+	
52	6352	N1367.80 E935.70 20–30 cm BGS	3.7						1				

Table I.1, continued

PLANT REMAINS RECOVERED BY FLOTATION

Feature Number	Inventory Number	Context	Sample Weight (in grams)	Maize Cupules	Maize Kernels	Trianthema	Mesquite Seeds	Mesquite Leaves	Amaranth	Bursage	Yucca Fiber	Grass Stems	Other Remains
52	6354	N1367.80 E935.70 0-10 cm BGS	7.2									+	
52	6359	53-63 cm BD	2.0							+			
60	6338	N1356 E934 E1/2	21.3								1	+	
60	6340	N1356 E934 SW1/4 1.15-1.25 m BD	4.7										
60	6341	N1358 E934 E1/2 1.75-1.85 m BD	25.3			1					1	+	Escholtzia-2
60	6342	N1356 E934 SW1/4 1.55-1.65 m BD	16.8								1		
60	6344	N1358 E934 E1/2 1.85-1.95 m BD	30.2									+	

242

Table I.1, continued

PLANT REMAINS RECOVERED BY FLOTATION

Feature Number	Inventory Number	Context	Sample Weight (in grams)	Maize Cupules	Maize Kernels	Trianthema	Mesquite Seeds	Mesquite Leaves	Amaranth	Bursage	Yucca Fiber	Grass Stems	Other Remains
60	6345	N1356 E934 SW1/4 1.45-1.55 m BD	15.3									+	
60	6350	N1356 E934 1.65-1.75 m BD	10.8									++	Prickly Pear-1
Md.7	5504	N1367.25 E1059.65 Below metate	5.5									++	
Md.7	6046	N1367.25 E1059.65 Below metate	21.1										
Md.7	6347	N1346 E1066 40-60 cm BD	2.7	1					1				Physalis-1
Md.9	5936	N1373 E1078 0-10 cm BD	7.6	1								+	Tansy mustard-1

Table I.1, continued

PLANT REMAINS RECOVERED BY FLOTATION

Feature Number	Inventory Number	Context	Sample Weight (in grams)	Maize Cupules	Maize Kernels	Trianthema	Mesquite Seeds	Mesquite Leaves	Amaranth	Bursage	Yucca Fiber	Grass Stems	Other Remains
Md.9	5942	N1373 E1078 30-40 cm BD	3.2	2								+	
Md.9	5944	N1373 E1078 40-50 cm BD	1.9		1								
Md.9	5952	N1373 E1082 30-40 cm BD	3.2	1					1				

BD = Below datum
Md.= Mound
BGS= Below ground surface

243

Table I.2

CHARCOAL RECOVERED BY FLOTATION

Feature Number	Inventory Number	Context	Willow	Cottonwood	Desert Willow	Saltbush	Blue Palo Verde	Mesquite	Baccharis	Foothills Palo Verde	Ocotillo	Saguaro	Brittle bush	Creosotebush	Ironwood	Yucca	Other
			Riparian			Halophyte	Ephemeral Streams			Desert							
4	1232	37						4									
13	1231	51			1	3											
15	1233	52					1	2		6							
18	1234	56					2	2									
26	1235	77					2	8		3							
32	546	84				5	2		8	6	2					1	
39	1219	0°N				1		2									
39	1221	0°N								4					4		
39	2827	Profile trench					3	3		1							Juniper-1

Table I.2, continued

CHARCOAL RECOVERED BY FLOTATION

Feature Number	Inventory Number	Context	Riparian			Halo-phyte	Ephemeral Streams			Desert							Other
			Willow	Cottonwood	Desert Willow	Saltbush	Blue Palo Verde	Mesquite	Baccharis	Foothills Palo Verde	Ocotillo	Saguaro	Brittle bush	Creosotebush	Ironwood	Yucca	
39	4109	N1428 E1074 Level 2			1		4			1						1	
39	4110	N1427 E1074 Level 2			1		1									1	
39	4112	N1428 E1074 Level 3			2		6	7									
39	4113	N1427 E1075 Level 2			2			5									
39	4115	N1427 E1073 10 cm above floor					3									1	
39	4116	N1427 E1073 10 cm above floor					7										Yucca leaves-2

Table I.2, continued

CHARCOAL RECOVERED BY FLOTATION

Feature Number	Inventory Number	Context	Riparian			Halo-phyte	Ephemeral Streams			Desert								Other
			Willow	Cottonwood	Desert Willow	Saltbush	Blue Palo Verde	Mesquite	Baccharis	Foothills Palo Verde	Ocotillo	Saguaro	Brittle bush	Creosotebush	Ironwood	Yucca	
47		SW 70-80 cm 8.6g			4		5	11									Hawaiia sp.-2
39	4116	N1427 E1073 10 cm above floor						7									Yucca leaves-2
47		SW 70-80 cm 8.6g			4		5	11									Hawaiia sp.-2
47		SW 80-90 cm 44.7			3			17									Hawaiia sp.-1
47		NW 70-80 cm 9.2						16							1		Maize kernel-1 Succinea -1 Pupilid-2
47		70-80 cm 20.7						20									Hydrobiid-1 Pupilid-2
47		NW 80-90 cm 78.8			1			19									Hawaiia sp.-1

Table I.2, continued

CHARCOAL RECOVERED BY FLOTATION

Feature Number	Inventory Number	Context	Riparian			Halophyte	Ephemeral Streams			Desert							Other
			Willow	Cottonwood	Desert Willow	Saltbush	Blue Palo Verde	Mesquite	Baccharis	Foothills Palo Verde	Ocotillo	Saguaro	Brittle bush	Creosotebush	Ironwood	Yucca	
47/48	5167	N1500 E1020 From soil 2B					3	4									
47/48	5168	N1510 E1020 SE					4	6									
47/48	6276	N1500 E1020 SE Sample 4					1			2							
47/48	6277	N1500 E1020 SE Sample 5				6	1	3									
47/48	6278	N1500 E1020 SE From soil 4					1	3		1				1			Juniper-3 Maize stems-1
48		NE Corner 50-60 cm BS					4	8		2					1		

Table I.2, continued

CHARCOAL RECOVERED BY FLOTATION

Feature Number	Inventory Number	Context	Riparian			Halo-phyte	Ephemeral Streams			Desert							Other
			Willow	Cottonwood	Desert Willow	Saltbush	Blue Palo Verde	Mesquite	Baccharis	Foothills Palo Verde	Ocotillo	Saguaro	Brittle bush	Creosotebush	Ironwood	Yucca	
48		NE 90–100 cm BS			3	10	6	23		2					1		
48		SW 70–80 cm BS					5	10									Catclaw Acacia–3
48	6275	SW 90–100 cm BS		2	6	13	4	16	1	1				1			Whitethorn Acacia–4
50	5508	N1355.2 E1080 Level 3															Maize stalk–50+
50	5512	N1355.2 E1080 Level 2					1										Juniper–6 Pinyon–16 Maize stalk–3 Desert Hackberry–6

Table I.2, continued

CHARCOAL RECOVERED BY FLOTATION

Feature Number	Inventory Number	Context	Riparian			Halo-phyte	Ephemeral Streams			Desert							Other
			Willow	Cottonwood	Desert Willow	Saltbush	Blue Palo Verde	Mesquite	Baccharis	Foothills Palo Verde	Ocotillo	Saguaro	Brittle bush	Creosotebush	Ironwood	Yucca	
50	5999	Floor pit south of hearth								4							Juniper-4
50	6310	N1356.5 E1080 13-30 cm BD			1					5							
51	5889	SW side Intramural Level 3			3		8			2							Desert Hack-berry-1
51	5890	N1281.5 E1031												1			
51	5891	NW side Intramural Level 3	2	2													Maize stalk-1

Table I.2, continued

CHARCOAL RECOVERED BY FLOTATION

Feature Number	Inventory Number	Context	Riparian			Halophyte	Ephemeral Streams				Desert						Other
			Willow	Cottonwood	Desert Willow	Saltbush	Blue Palo Verde	Mesquite	Baccharis	Foothills Palo Verde	Ocotillo	Saguaro	Brittle bush	Creosotebush	Ironwood	Yucca	
51	5892	N1281.5 E1031 0-45 cm BD															Maize stalk-1
51	5898	N1280.5 E1031.3 Level 3		10					4		1						
51	6307	N1283.5 E1033 Firepit, Sample 1								1							
51	6309	N1283.5 E1033 Firepit, Sample 2					5			1							
51	6346	N1281.5 E1081 45 cm BD-floor			10												
51	6368	Unit 9 extramural 50-65 cm BD					1										

Table I.2, continued

CHARCOAL RECOVERED BY FLOTATION

Feature Number	Inventory Number	Context	Willow	Cottonwood	Desert Willow	Saltbush	Blue Palo Verde	Mesquite	Baccharis	Foothills Palo Verde	Ocotillo	Saguaro	Brittle bush	Creosotebush	Ironwood	Yucca	Other
		Riparian				**Halo-phyte**	**Ephemeral Streams**			**Desert**							**Other**
51	6369	Unit 9 intramural 50-65 cm BD					1			1							
52	6224	N1360 E935 1.52-1.77 m BD			3		16	1									
52	6225	N1360 E935 1.27-1.52 m BD			1		8	1		2	1						Whitethorn Acacia -1
52	6305	N1360 E935 1.77-2.02 m BD					30	2									
52	6343	N1362 E937 0-10 cm BD					1									2	
52	6348	N1362 E937 20-30 cm BD					2			1							

Table I.2, continued

CHARCOAL RECOVERED BY FLOTATION

Feature Number	Inventory Number	Context	Riparian Willow	Cottonwood	Desert Willow	Halo-phyte Saltbush	Ephemeral Streams Blue Palo Verde	Mesquite	Baccharis	Desert Foothills Palo Verde	Ocotillo	Saguaro	Brittle bush	Creosotebush	Ironwood	Yucca	Other
52	6349	N1360 E936.85 Level 1 Inside horno			3		1			1							
52	6351	N1362 E937 10-20 cm BD					2			1							
52	6358	N1367.8 E935.7 30-40 cm BD								2						1	
52	6359	53-63 cm BD					5										
60	6338	N1356 E934 SW 1/4 1.35-1.45 m BD		1			15	4		1						1	
60	6339	N1356 E934 SW 1/4 1.25-1.35 m BD			1		14	5									

Table I.2, continued

CHARCOAL RECOVERED BY FLOTATION

Feature Number	Inventory Number	Context	Riparian Willow	Cottonwood	Desert Willow	Halo-phyte Saltbush	Ephemeral Streams Blue Palo Verde	Mesquite	Baccharis	Desert Foothills Palo Verde	Ocotillo	Saguaro	Brittle bush	Creosotebush	Ironwood	Yucca	Other
60	6340	N1356 E934 SW 1/4 1.15-1.25 m BD					5	1									
60	6341	N1358 E934 E 1/2 1.75-1.85 m BD		1			13	4		2							
60	6342	N1356 E934 SW 1/4 1.55-1.65 m BD					13	7									
60	6344	N1358 E934 E 1/2 1.85-1.95 m BD	1	4		3	12										
60	6345	N1356 E934 SW 1/4 1.45-1.55 m BD					5	5									
60	6350	N1356 E934 SW 1/4 1.65-1.75 m BD					8	4									

254

Table I.2, continued

CHARCOAL RECOVERED BY FLOTATION

Feature Number	Inventory Number	Context	Riparian Willow	Cottonwood	Desert Willow	Halo-phyte Saltbush	Ephemeral Streams Blue Palo Verde	Mesquite	Baccharis	Desert Foothills Palo Verde	Ocotillo	Saguaro	Brittle bush	Creosotebush	Ironwood	Other Yucca
60	6353	N1356 E934 SW 1/4 1.05–1.15 m BD					5			2						1
60	6355	N1358 E935 NE 1/4 1.25–1.35 m BD					6			1						
60	6356	N1358 E935 NE 1/4 NE1/4 Level 1					6									
Md.1	1217	0°N						4								
Md.7	5504	N1367.25 E1059.65 Below metate		1								10				
Md.7	6046	N1367.25 E1059.65 Below metate							1			20+				

Table I.2, continued

CHARCOAL RECOVERED BY FLOTATION

Feature Number	Inventory Number	Context	Riparian			Halo-phyte	Ephemeral Streams			Desert							Other
			Willow	Cottonwood	Desert Willow	Saltbush	Blue Palo Verde	Mesquite	Baccharis	Foothills Palo Verde	Ocotillo	Saguaro	Brittle bush	Creosotebush	Ironwood	Yucca	
Md.7	6347	N1364 E1066 40–60 cm BD			3					1		2					
Md.9	5938	N1373 E1078 10–20 cm BD									1			1			
Md.9	5942	N1373 E1078 30–40 cm BD								2							
Md.9	5944	N1373 E1078 40–50 cm BD								1							
Md.9	5948	N1373 E1082 20–30 cm BD					1										
Md.9	5950	N1373 E1082 10–20 cm BD					1										

Table I.2, continued

CHARCOAL RECOVERED BY FLOTATION

Feature Number	Inventory Number	Context	Riparian			Halo-phyte	Ephemeral Streams			Desert							Other
			Willow	Cottonwood	Desert Willow	Saltbush	Blue Palo Verde	Mesquite	Baccharis	Foothills Palo Verde	Ocotillo	Saguaro	Brittle bush	Creosotebush	Ironwood	Yucca	
Md.9	5952	N1373 E1082 30-40 cm BD					4								1		
Md.9	5953	N1373 E1082 0-10 cm BD			1												
Md.9	6366	N1373 E1082 40-50 cm BD					6										
Trincheras																	
88			4														
88	-	Entire feature?			4												
88	6302	Dark burned layer			2												Unidentified seed

Table I.2, continued

CHARCOAL RECOVERED BY FLOTATION

Feature Number	Inventory Number	Context	Riparian			Halo-phyte	Ephemeral Streams				Desert							Other
			Willow	Cottonwood	Desert Willow	Saltbush	Blue Palo Verde	Mesquite	Baccharis	Foothills Palo Verde	Ocotillo	Saguaro	Brittle bush	Creosotebush	Ironwood	Yucca	
109		Vessel Fill		2													
109	4475	30-40 cm BGS															
109	4524	SW Qund 2.55W .95S 20-35 cm BGS Bag 1 of 2					2		2	2							
109	4524	Bag 2 of 2			1		3	3	2	2							
109	4546	NE 1/4-Hearthfill 31 cm BGS			1					2							

Table I.2, continued

CHARCOAL RECOVERED BY FLOTATION

Feature Number	Inventory Number	Context	Riparian			Halo-phyte	Ephemeral Streams			Desert							Other
			Willow	Cottonwood	Desert Willow	Saltbush	Blue Palo Verde	Mesquite	Baccharis	Foothills Palo Verde	Ocotillo	Saguaro	Brittle bush	Creosotebush	Ironwood	Yucca	
109	5515	NE Quad--adjacent to hearth 10 cm above floor to floor								2							
109	5664	NE Quad 10 cm above floor to floor			2			1									
109	5671	SW Quad 15-30 cm BGS			8					3							
109	6279	SW Quad			1					3						2	
109	6280	NE Quad 24-34 cm BGS			3		1			3							Grass stems-2

Table I.2, continued

CHARCOAL RECOVERED BY FLOTATION

Feature Number	Inventory Number	Context	Riparian			Halophyte	Ephemeral Streams			Desert							Other
			Willow	Cottonwood	Desert Willow	Saltbush	Blue Palo Verde	Mesquite	Baccharis	Foothills Palo Verde	Ocotillo	Saguaro	Brittle bush	Creosotebush	Ironwood	Yucca	
117	5663	.25M2 30-40 cm BGS			4		2			1							
137		Vessel Fill		2													
137		51-75 cm NE	11						1								
137		68-71 cm SE	10		1	1											
137		70-75 cm SE	4		1	1	1										
137		70-80 cm NE	14														
137		69-76 cm NE	5		3	2											
137	2879	Feature 1	6														

Table I.2, continued

CHARCOAL RECOVERED BY FLOTATION

Feature Number	Inventory Number	Context	Riparian			Halo-phyte	Ephemeral Streams			Desert							Other
			Willow	Cottonwood	Desert Willow	Saltbush	Blue Palo Verde	Mesquite	Baccharis	Foothills Palo Verde	Ocotillo	Saguaro	Brittle bush	Creosotebush	Ironwood	Yucca	
137	2880	SS Feat.1	5		5												
137	2883	Feature 1			14					1							Whitethorn Acacia-2
137	5666	NE Quad 2.40W 1.25N 65-70 cm BGS			8		1	2									
137	5667	SW Quad 50-60 cm BGS			6												
137	5668	NW Quad 55-65 cm BGS			4												
137	5669	SE Quad 1.95W .22S 54-59 cm BS					1			2	1						

Table I.2, continued

CHARCOAL RECOVERED BY FLOTATION

Feature Number	Inventory Number	Context	Riparian			Halo-phyte	Ephemeral Streams			Foothills Palo Verde	Desert						Other
			Willow	Cottonwood	Desert Willow	Saltbush	Blue Palo Verde	Mesquite	Baccharis		Ocotillo	Saguaro	Brittle bush	Creosotebush	Ironwood	Yucca	
137	5670	NE Quad 2.30N 1.10E 60-65 cm BGS			9		5				1						
137	6303	NE Quad Fill from hearth floor								4							
137	6430	50-60 cm BGS			11												
137	6431	NE Quad 1.10N 1.87 64-70 cm BGS			11			1		1							Whitethorn Acacia-1
137	6432	SE Quad			10		2										
137	6434	NE Quad			5		5										

Table I.2, continued

CHARCOAL RECOVERED BY FLOTATION

			Riparian			Halophyte	Ephemeral Streams			Desert							Other
Feature Number	Inventory Number	Context	Willow	Cottonwood	Desert Willow	Saltbush	Blue Palo Verde	Mesquite	Baccharis	Foothills Palo Verde	Ocotillo	Saguaro	Brittle bush	Creosotebush	Ironwood	Yucca	
137	6435	NE Quad			14	1											
137	6436	NW Quad			4	2			1								

BS = Below surface
BD = Below datum
BGS = Below ground surface

262

Table I.3

CARBONIZED SEEDS RECOVERED BY FLOTATION

Feature Number	Inventory Number	Feature	Sample Weight (in grams)	Cotton seeds	Maize kernels	Maize cupules	Trianthema	Pigweed	Saguaro	Prickly pear	Hedgehog cactus	Hackberry	Grass stems	Grass rhizomes	Bursage	Groundcherry
37	1232	Trench Fill	5.4					2			1	1				
51	1231	Rock Filled Pit	1.2		1	1										
52	1233	Bell Shaped Pit	18.0		1	1		1					4		2	
56	1234	House Floor	2.5			4										
77	1235	House Floor	31.9			1									9	1
84	546	Cremation	48.9	4	7			10				8		1		
92	1236	House Floor	4.2						1				3			
Mound 1																
0°N	1217	Exterior Pit Fill	3.2			2			1							
0°N	1218	Lower House Fill	1.2				1									

Table I.3, continued

CARBONIZED SEEDS RECOVERED BY FLOTATION

Feature Number	Inventory Number	Feature	Sample Weight (in grams)	Cotton seeds	Maize kernels	Maize cupules	Trianthema	Pigweed	Saguaro	Prickly pear	Hedgehog cactus	Hackberry	Grass stems	Grass rhizomes	Bursage	Groundcherry
0°N	1219	Upper House Floor	5.0		1	2										
0°N	1220	Ash Pit	7.7		1				3					1		
0°N	1221	Below House Floor	1.3													
0°N	1238	Fill	3.7		1					1						

Table I.4

MISCELLANEOUS MATERIALS RECOVERED FROM FLOTATION

Feature Number	Inventory Number	Context	Mollusca								Other
			Gastrocopta	Hawaiia	Vertigo	Succinea	Hydrobiid	Pupilid	Sonorella	Bulimus-like	
39	2827	Profile trench A Subfloor pit	2	9	2	1	2		1		
39	4109	N1428 E1074 Level 2	1	1	1						
39	4113	N1427 E1075 Level 2			1						
39	4116	N1427 E1072 10 cm above floor					1				
47/48	5167	N1500 E1020 SE Quad – S side of canal From soil 2B		1							
47/48	5168	N1500 E1020	2		2		2				
47/48	6276	N1500 E1020 Sample 4					1				
47/48	6277	N1500 E1020 Sample 5			2	1	1				
47/48	6278	N1500 E1020 From soil 4		1	2						
48	–	NE Quad 50–60 cm BS		1				1			
48	–	SW 70–80 cm BS	3	2	5		3		2		
48	–	NE 90–100 cm BS		2	1	1					
48	6275	SW 90–100 cm BS		2							

Table I.4, continued

MISCELLANEOUS MATERIALS RECOVERED FROM FLOTATION

Feature Number	Inventory Number	Context	Gastrocopta	Hawaiia	Vertigo	Succinea	Hydrobiid	Pupilid	Sonorella	Bulimus-like	Other
						Mollusca					Other
50	5512	N1355.2 E1080 Level 2	1	1							
50	6310	N1356.5 E1080 13-30 cm BD								1	
51	5889	SW Side Intramural Level 3	1								Bone fragments-3
51	5891	NW Side Intramural Level 3					1		1		Bone fragments-+
51	5898	N128-.5 E1031.3 Level 3	1								
51	6346	N1281.5 E1031 45 cm BD to floor	1								Bone fragments-1
51	6369	Unit 9 Intramural 50-65 cm BD		1	1						
52	6224	N1360 E935									Charred rodent fecal material-+
52	6305	N1360 E935 1.77-2.02 m BD			1						
52	6351	N1362 E937 10-20 cm BD			1						
52	6359	53-63 cm BD				3					

Table I.4, continued

MISCELLANEOUS MATERIALS RECOVERED FROM FLOTATION

Feature Number	Inventory Number	Context	Mollusca								Other
			Gastrocopta	Hawaiia	Vertigo	Succinea	Hydrobiid	Pupilid	Sonorella	Bulimus-like	
52	6360	N1367.8 E935.7 10-20 cm BGS	1								
60	6339	N1356 E934 SW1/4 1.25-1.35 m BD		1							
60	6341	N1358 E934 E1/2 1.75-1.85 m BD	1								
60	6342	N1356 E934 SW1/4 1.55-1.65 m BD	1								Charred rodent fecal material -+
60	6355	N1358 E935 NE1/4 1.25-1.35 m BD					1				
60	6356	N1358 E935 NE1/4 Level 1		1							
Md.7	5504	N1367.25 E1059.65 Below metate			1						
Md.7	6046	Same as 5504		1	2						
Md.7	6347	N1364 E1066 40-60 cm BD			1		1		1		Bone fragments -+
Md.9	5941	N1373 E1078 20-30 cm BD				1					
Md.9	5942	N1373 E1078 30-40 cm BD			2						

Table I.4, continued

MISCELLANEOUS MATERIALS RECOVERED FROM FLOTATION

Feature Number	Inventory Number	Context	Gastrocopta	Hawaiia	Vertigo	Succinea	Hydrobiid	Pupilid	Sonorella	Bulimus-like	Other
					Mollusca						
Md.9	5944	N1373 E1078 40-50 cm BD	1	1			1				
Md.9	5950	N1373 E1082 10-20 cm BD			1						
Md.9	6366	N1373 E1082	1	1	1		1		1		
109	5515	NE Quad Adjacent hearth 10 cm above floor to floor									Charred rodent fecal material material-+
109	5664	NE Quad 10 cm above floor to floor		1							
117	5663	30-40 cm BS	19					1			
137	2879	SS Feat.1 NE Quad	1								
137	2883	SS Feat.1					2				
137	5667	SW Quad	1								Bone fragments-+
137	5668	NW Quad 55-65 cm BGS				1					
137	6303	NE Quad Fill from hearth floor				1					
137	6430	50-60 cm BGS	1	1							

BS = Below surface
BGS = Below ground surface
BD = Below datum

Table I.5

SPECIES IDENTIFICATIONS FROM CHARCOAL SAMPLES AT LOS MORTEROS

Feature Number	Inventory Number	Provenience	Specimen Description	Number or Amount
	224	Trench 75	*Larrea divaricata* (creosote bush) charcoal	1
			Cercidium microphyllum (littleleaf palo verde) charcoal	1
21	291	Trench 67	*Olneya tesota* (ironwood) charcoal	1
			Berberis haematocarpa (bayberry) charcoal	4
32[a]	265	Trench 84	*Zea mays* (maize) kernels	72.2 gm
			Gossypium hirsutum var. *punctatum* (Hopi cotton) seeds	1
32	549	Trench 84	*Cercidium floridum* (blue palo verde) charcoal	1
			Prosopis sp. (mesquite) charcoal	15
			Atriplex canescens (fourwing saltbush) charcoal	4
32	550	Trench 84 Crematory Level 1 10 cm	mesquite charcoal	6
			saltbush charcoal	1
32	552	Trench 84 Crematory Level 4	mesquite charcoal	2
			saltbush charcoal	1
32	612	Trench 84	mesquite charcoal	6
32	613	Trench 84 Crematory Upper Level	mesquite charcoal	6
			ironwood charcoal	1
32	615	Trench 84 Level 3, Below Crematory Rim, 20-30 cm	mesquite charcoal	14
			saltbush charcoal	2
32	1269	Trench 84 Crematory floor	mesquite timber	
32	1272(a)	Trench 84 Crematory floor	Hopi cotton seeds	4
			Cucurbita pepo (squash) seeds	5
			Cucurbita sp. (squash) rind fragments	4
			maize kernels	3
32	1272(b)		squash seeds	13
			rind fragment	1
			mesquite sections	3
			Hopi cotton seeds	33
32	1270[b]	Trench 84	Charcoal	7.807 kg (9 bags)
			blue palo verde	(15%) 10
			littleleaf palo verde	(3%) 2

Table I.5, continued

SPECIES IDENTIFICATIONS FROM CHARCOAL SAMPLES AT LOS MORTEROS

Feature Number	Inventory Number	Provenience	Specimen Description	Number or Amount	
32	1270 (cont.)		mesquite	(29%)	20
			saltbush	(28%)	19
			ocotillo	(4%)	3
			ironwood	(13%)	9
			Populus fremontii (cottonwood)	(1%)	1
			Carnegiea gigantea (saguaro)	(4%)	3
			Acacia constricta (whitethorn)	(1%)	1
			maize kernels		427
			maize cupules		22
			Hopi cotton seeds		8
			squash seeds		10
			squash rind		3
36	853	Trench 92 Floor pit	blue palo verde charcoal		1
39	2118	N1426 E1073 Level 1	Chilopsis linearis (desert willow)		1
39	2526	no level	ironwood		1
39	2530	Trench Profile	blue palo verde		1
39	3236	N1425 E1074 No level	blue palo verde		1
39	4329	N1427 E1072 No level	blue palo verde		1
39	4418	Fill above subfloor pit	desert willow		1
			whitethorn acacia		1
39	4425	Posthole 2	blue palo verde		3
50	5289	N1356 E1080 Level 1	Pinus sp. (pinyon)		1
50	5424	Level 1	pinyon		5
50	5437	Backhoe trench	Fouquieria splendens (ocotillo)		1
			Pinus edulis		4
			desert willow		1
50	5650	Sample #7	pinyon		1
50	5651	Sample #6	desert willow		1
50	5653	Sample #8 N1354 E1080	Juniperus sp. (juniper)		1
50	5654	Sample #2	juniper		1
50	5659	N1358 E1078 No level	Celtis reticulata (hackberry) seeds		1
50	5824	N1356.2E1084-1085 East end - No level	blue palo verde		1

Table I.5, continued

SPECIES IDENTIFICATIONS FROM CHARCOAL SAMPLES AT LOS MORTEROS

Feature Number	Inventory Number	Provenience	Specimen Description	Number or Amount
50	5996	Sample #4	pinyon	1
50	5997	Sample #1	littleleaf palo verde	1
50	6480	N1354 E1052 40 cm BS	juniper	1
51	5453	Backhoe trench	desert willow	1
51	6074	N1283.5 E1031 45 cm BD to floor	desert willow	1
51	6374	N1283.5 E1033 Unit 8 Level 2	blue palo verde desert willow	2 3
51	6438	Floor contact	desert willow	1
52	6216	N1360 E935 (4) 1.27-1.52 m BD	blue palo verde	1
52	6220	N1360 E935 1.52-1.77 m BD	blue palo verde	1
52	6449	N1362 E938 No level	blue palo verde	1
60	6217	N1360 E935 (4) 1.27-1.52 m BD	blue palo verde	1
60	6394	N1356 E934 Levels 3-10	blue palo verde	1
60	6403	N1356 E934 No level	blue palo verde	1
60	6404	N1358 E934 Level 2	blue palo verde	1
60	6441	N1356 E934 (4) Levels 1-3	blue palo verde	1
60	6444	N1358 E934 Levels 3-10	blue palo verde	1
Md.1	1011	1 W 0-20 cm	mesquite charcoal Monocot flowering stalk (possible agave)	1 1
Md.1	1024	1 W 30-40 cm	Lycium sp. (wolfberry) charcoal ocotillo charcoal mesquite charcoal	1 1 1
Md.1	1086	1W 60-70 cm	mesquite charcoal	1
Md.1	1091	1 W 50-60 cm	mesquite charcoal littleleaf palo verde charcoal Acer negundo (boxelder) charcoal	1 1 1

Table I.5, continued

SPECIES IDENTIFICATIONS FROM CHARCOAL SAMPLES AT LOS MORTEROS

Feature Number	Inventory Number	Provenience	Specimen Description	Number or Amount
Md.6	5236	N1314 E1062 55-65 cm BD	maize kernels fused together	3
Md.7	6179	N1368 E1064 45 cm BD	desert willow	1

BD = Below datum

NOTES: a. See Table I.6 for description of _Zea mays_ kernels.
b. A grab sample of 68 pieces of charcoal was analyzed from FN 1270, which included both large and small fragments so it should be fairly representative. The percentages given represent the number of fragments of a given species out of all fragments identified. By weight, mesquite probably represented 80 to 90 percent of the total sample. Mesquite, palo verde, and ironwood were the major fuels for the cremation. Saltbush and the other woods were probably used as kindling.

Table I.6

DESCRIPTION OF <u>ZEA</u> <u>MAYS</u> KERNELS FROM FEATURE 32 (72.2 gm)

Type and %	Row Number	Kernel Width (mm)	Kernel Thickness (mm)	Kernel Height (mm)
Onaveño-23	10.3	6.9	4.8	7.3
Mais Blando-64	10.4	7.5	4.7	8.1
Harinoso de Ocho-14	8.0	8.7	5.3	8.4

Average Measurements for 13 <u>Zea</u> <u>mays</u> Cob Fragments

row number	cupule width	cupule length	cob diameter	rachis diameter
11.3	7.3	4.0	16.5	14.5

Two cob fragments were eight-row tiller ears, a little smaller than the rest of the collection. One cob, (row number 12, cupule width 6.0mm, cupule length 4.5), had an ash stick stuck in its shank end. This cob looked much more like Chapalote maize than any of the other cobs and may have been a ceremonial or seed ear.

Appendix J

ANALYSIS OF A HUMAN SKELETON (BURIAL 1) FROM LOS MORTEROS

Richard J. Harrington

A partial human skeleton from the prehistoric site of Los Morteros (AZ AA:12:57) was submitted to the Human Identification Laboratory on November 30, 1981, for analysis. The skeleton was recovered from the backyard of a resident of the trailer court. The remains were examined to determine probable sex, age, and race of the individual and to assess any discernible lesions or other antemortem (pre-death) skeletal modifications.

Recovered were the skull, lower jaw, 23 teeth, all of the long bones, most of the short bones and ribs, the scapulae, and a few vertebrae. Conspicuous among the missing bones were those of the pelvis and most of the vertebrae (a more detailed inventory is on file at the Human Identification Laboratory). Most of the bones are fragile, fragmented, and moderately eroded. The ends of all the long and short bones are missing (presumably disintegrated), and several bones, such as the vertebrae and scapulae, are represented only by the more resilient portions of those bones. The bones of the pelvis, the sternum, vertebral bodies, and hand and foot bones are relatively delicate, so their absence is most likely accounted for by postmortem (after death) destruction.

Features of the skull, lower jaw, and long bones indicate that the individual was a female (see Bass 1971 or Krogman 1962 for discussions of sex difference in the human skeleton). Age was more difficult to determine due to the lack of diagnostic bones (notably the pubic bones). The degree of tooth wear suggests an age range of 25 to 35 years (Brothwell 1963:67-70). Tooth wear is not an especially reliable indicator of age, so the assessment of 25 to 35 years is tentative. Probable race is likewise difficult to determine. The remains include shovel-shaped incisors, a trait considered diagnostic of "Mongoloid" ancestry (Dahlberg 1963:155-156). American Indian populations, prehistoric and present, typically show this trait.

Portions of the top of the skull are abnormally thick as a result of hypertrophy (excessive development) of the diploic bone (the bony tissue between the inner and outer surfaces). The fragmentary and eroded state of the cranium makes it difficult to determine the extent of involvement, but it appears that only parts of the frontal and parietal bones are affected. The inner surface of the skull appears normal and the outer surface is extremely thin but otherwise free of lesions. No other bones of the body appear to be affected, but several bones are missing, and many others are damaged. Perhaps the most common cause of hypertrophy of the skull is iron deficiency anemia (Saul

1972:38, Steinbock 1976: 230-234). Most of the other disorders that lead to diploic hypertrophy can be ruled out because they induce the formation of other lesions as well. This diagnosis of iron deficiency anemia should be considered tentative until a more intensive and exhaustive examination is performed. The examination may be impeded by the poor state of preservation of the bone.

If the burial is a case of porotic hyperostosis resulting from some form of anemia, then it would seem that some healing has occurred. Active porotic hyperostosis is characterized by a spongy appearance of the outer surface (that is, the outer surface has thinned to the point that the diploe is exposed), but the outer table of the skull is thin but intact. The possibility that this is a case of hyperostosis of the nonporotic variety cannot yet be excluded.

The individual's oral health appears to have been good. At least two molars were missing prior to death (and several teeth are unaccounted for) but the remaining teeth are free of cavities and calculus (plaque) formations, and there is no evidence of malocclusion, abscesses, impactions, or crowding. The teeth are moderately worn: the cusps on most of the molars are nearly flattened, and most of the teeth have exposed dentin.

No other lesions or abnormalities could be discerned. The skull was examined for possible artificial deformation, but the combined effects of the diploic hypertrophy and the postmortem damage renders any assessment difficult, if not impossible.

Appendix K

THE CREMATED HUMAN REMAINS FROM LOS MORTEROS

T. Michael Fink

The following are the results of the analysis of five cremation deposits recovered from the Hohokam site of Los Morteros (AZ AA:12:57) and submitted to the Human Identification Laboratory, Arizona State Museum, for examination. The cremated osseous material represents the partial remains of six individuals--five adults (one male, one male?, one female?, two sex indeterminate) and one immature. Also submitted for analysis were 13 miscellaneous deposits of calcined human bone. The results obtained from these latter examinations will also be presented in this report.

Sex determinations are based on the morphological characteristics of the skeleton as discussed by Bass (1971), Krogman (1962) and Stewart (1979). Estimations concerning age at death are generally based on the cortical thickness of the cranium and long bones as well as cranial suture closure (Krogman 1962: 81).

Data pertaining to nonmetric traits were recorded as outlined by Birkby (1973). This information will not be included with this report; it is on file in the Human Identification Laboratory, Arizona State Museum.

Because of their calcined state, the osseous remains from Los Morteros have been partially stabilized, so treatment with a chemical preservative (for example, Gelva) was deemed unnecessary.

Descriptions

Cremation No. 1: Trench 51, N 1690 E900 Feature 14, Individual "A"

Sex: Unknown

Age: Adult (age indeterminate)

Cranium: Present are identifiable fragments of the frontal, parietals, occipital (including base and condyles), sphenoid, and mandible (including both condyles).

Dentition: One root fragment representing the lower left first premolar is present. The maxillary dentition has not been preserved.

Postcranium: Identifiable elements present are fragments of the thoracic vertebrae, left humerus, radii, ribs, tibiae and miscellaneous hand and foot elements.

Pathologies: No overt bony pathologies are observable.

Notes: Differential burning is exhibited on the parietal bones of the cranium. Some fragments show signs of complete incineration while others are only charred with carbonization taking place. One fragment shows no sign of having been altered by the cremation fire.

Cremation No. 1, Individual "B"

Sex: Unknown

Age: Immature (age indeterminate)

Cranium: No remains are present.

Dentition: No remains are present.

Postcranium: Present are three fragments: one rib and two miscellaneous vertebrae.

Pathologies: None were observed.

Bone Weight: The total weight of Cremation No. 1, including both individuals "A" and "B," is 499.5 gm.

Cremation No. 2: Trench 47 in Tanque Verde Red-on-brown Handled Jar N1500 E 958, Feature 63

Sex: Unknown

Age: Adult (age indeterminate)

Cranium: No remains are present.

Dentition: No fragments of the dentition are preserved.

Postcranium: Present are fragments of the cervical and thoracic vertebrae, innominates, right femur, and left calcaneus.

Pathologies: No bony pathologies are present.

Bone Weight: 37.0 gm

Cremation No. 3:   Trench 84, Feature 32, N 1400   E 920, Tanque Verde
                   Phase

   <u>Sex</u>: Male

   <u>Age</u>: Adult (age indeterminate)

   <u>Cranium</u>: The identifiable fragments present include the
   parietals, temporals, nasals, maxillae, frontal and occipital.
   Also present are portions of the left side of the mandible.

   <u>Dentition</u>: Nine tooth or root fragments are present. One
   represents a molar (location unknown), and the others appear to be
   single rooted teeth. Although portions of the maxillae and
   mandible are present, the tooth sockets are not preserved.

   <u>Postcranium</u>: Fragments present and most readily identifiable
   include the first cervical vertebra, miscellaneous vertebrae,
   innominates, left humerus and radius, ulnae, and scapulae, left
   clavicle, ribs, femora, right patella, tibiae, and various hand
   and foot elements.

   <u>Pathologies</u>: No evidence of bony disease is observable.

   <u>Bone Weight</u>: 625.0 gm

   <u>Notes</u>: Evidence of differential burning is present in these
   remains. The cranium exhibits complete incineration while most of
   the postcranial material shows signs of incomplete incineration or
   charring. Of the postcranial system, only the right half of the
   first cervical vertebra, various rib fragments, and portions of
   the left humerus and right ulna are completely incinerated (see
   Fig. K.1).

Cremation No. 4:   Mound 2, in Micaceous Plainware Jar with Cover Sherds

   <u>Sex</u>: Female

   <u>Age</u>: Adult (age indeterminate)

   <u>Cranium</u>: Present are fragments of the parietals, temporals,
   maxillae, mandible, frontal, occipital (including base and
   condyles), and sphenoid.

   <u>Dentition</u>: One root fragment is present and represents the upper
   right first premolar; it exhibits a bifid root. Three of the ten
   preserved mandibular sockets exhibit evidence of partial bony
   resorption due to antemortem tooth loss. One other shows signs of
   complete resorption.

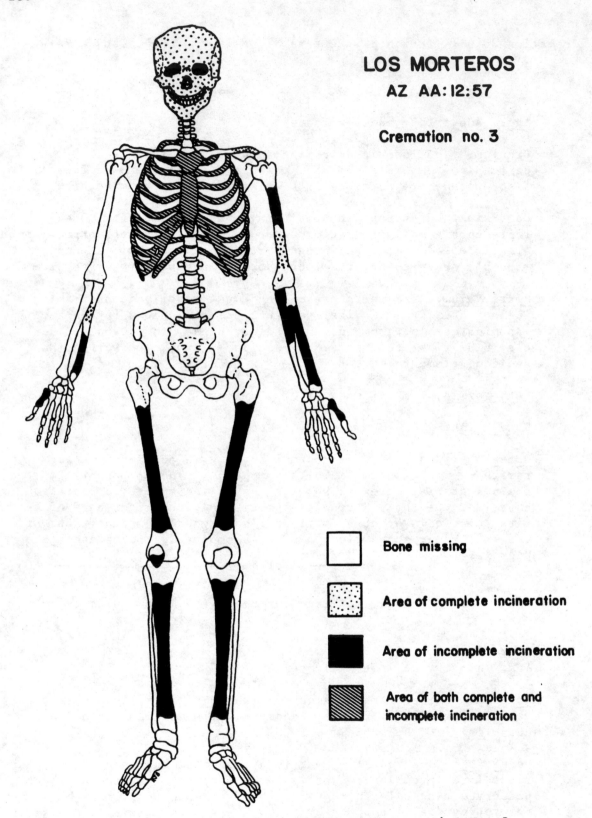

LOS MORTEROS
AZ AA:12:57

Cremation no. 3

Bone missing

Area of complete incineration

Area of incomplete incineration

Area of both complete and incomplete incineration

Figure K.1. Differential burning of Cremation No. 3.

Postcranium: The identifiable fragments present include miscellaneous vertebrae, both humerii and ulnae, ribs, right scapula, left femur, patella (side unknown), and various elements of the hands and feet.

Pathologies: No pathologies can be observed.

Bone Weight: 472.0 gm

Cremation No. 5: Mound 4, Tanque Verde Phase, in Tanque Verde jar with Cover Sherds

Sex: Male

Age: Adult (age indeterminate)

Cranium: Present are fragments of the parietals, temporals, left maxilla, mandible, frontal, occipital, and sphenoid.

Dentition: Antemortem tooth loss is exhibited in three lower sockets. The teeth involved are both central incisors and the left canine.

Postcranium: Those fragments present include humerii, radii, ribs, and a left capitate.

Pathologies: No overt bony pathologies are present.

Bone Weight: 264.0 gm

Table K.1 is a summary of some of the basic osteological findings derived from the examination of this material.

Miscellaneous Cremated Human Bone

Thirteen miscellaneous deposits of cremated human bone were also recovered from Los Morteros. This multifarious debris is composed of 89 fragments with a combined weight of 98.35 gm. Found were 57 miscellaneous shaft fragments, 15 indeterminate fragments and 17 cranial fragments. No pathologies or anomalies were observed in this osseous material.

Table K.1

AGE, SEX, AND BONE WEIGHT OF THE CREMATION DEPOSITS FROM LOS MORTEROS

Cremation No.	Sex	Age	Weight (in grams)
1*	unknown	adult	499.5
	unknown	immature	
2	unknown	adult	37.0
3	male	adult	625.0
4	female?	adult	472.0
5	male?	adult	264.0

*"multi-individual" cremation

Discussion and Conclusions

A substantial portion of the human cremated remains recovered from Los Morteros are contorted and warped, with "checking" and "transverse splitting" also occurring. The presence of these attributes indicates a "green bone" cremation or burning "in the flesh" (Baby 1954, Binford 1972b). Most of the bony debris is gray to white in color (see below for exceptions) indicating thorough burning of the skeleton. However, according to Herrmann (1976, 1977), complete incineration of the bony organic contents has occurred only in the lighter colored fragments. Nevertheless, it is evident from these remains that the crematory fires at Los Morteros were capable of reaching temperatures as high as 700 to 800 degrees centigrade (Herrman 1977: 101). Haury (1976: 171) and Wells (1960: 36) have reported that such temperatures are possible in open air pyres. It should be noted that the condition of the body (Wells 1960: 35) as well as prolonged exposure on the pyre may also have contributed to the complete incineration of the bone.

Two of the cremation deposits (No. 1 and No. 3) from AZ AA:12:57 exhibit differential burning, indicating less thorough incineration of the skeleton. In the case of Cremation No. 1, the parietal bones of the cranium display areas of incomplete consumption with charring and some carbonization. Another fragment from the same anatomical region appears unburned and shows no sign of being affected by the crematory fire. The remainder of the cremation is completely incinerated.

Various elements of the postcranial system of Cremation No. 3, a primary cremation, show charring and carbonization while other bony parts are completely incinerated (Baby 1954). A diagram illustrating the differential burning present in this interment can be found in Figure K.1. Bass (1979) and Shipman (1978) have both described primary cremations that show similar patterns of incineration.

The reason for the differential burning is difficult to discern. It could be the result of either a small funeral pyre or one that, for some reason, did not burn for a sufficient period of time. Another explanation is that the charred or "smoked" fragments represent those bones that fell out of or away from the fire during the cremation process.

Another feature of the Los Morteros cremations is severe fragmentation of the bones. Several cultural practices, including maneuvering the corpse with a pole to aid the cremation process (see Spier 1933: 303), or the use of water to cool the bone for easier handling, may have contributed to the break-up of the osseous material. Another possible cause of the fragmented state of this material is the practice of deliberate or intentional breakage in order to place the bones into funerary urns. Prolonged exposure to high intensity fires may be partially responsible for the fragmented state of Cremations 2, 4, and 5. A combination of any of these factors may be the cause of the fragmented condition of the Los Morteros cremations.

All of the Los Morteros cremations are well below 1,750 gm, the expected bone weight of a cremated adult male (Binford 1972a). This, along with the fact that the bone inventories are very incomplete, demonstrates that all of the deposits contain only the partial remains of individuals. This is particularly interesting with respect to Cremation No. 3, a primary cremation. One would expect the osseous remains from such a cremation to approach the expected weight described by Binford (1972a). It is evident that various bony elements from Cremation No. 3 have been interred or discarded elsewhere, and that this feature is probably a crematory pit rather than a primary cremation (see Reinhard and Fink 1982).

There are two plausible explanations for the low bone weights and incomplete inventories exhibited by the Los Morteros cremations: (1) partition burial, that is, the interment of the cremated remains of a single cremation episode in more than one location, and (2) poor gleaning of the crematoria. Support for the first explanation can be found in the archaeological and osteological evidence reported by Wasley and Johnson (1965: 6,88), Antieau (1981: 91-100), Long (1981), and McGuire (1977: 66-70) as well as the incompleteness of Cremation No. 3 from Los Morteros. Additional evidence for partition burial may be derived from Spier's (1933: 303) ethnographic documentation of the funeral customs of the Yuman tribes. However, Bradley (1980: 46-47) has questioned this description.

Evidence for the poor gleaning hypothesis, on the other hand, may be derived from excavation reports concerning Hohokam crematoria. Both Gladwin and others (1965: 95-96) and Haury (1976: 166-70) found layers of ash and bone covering the crematory floors at Snaketown; the same was true of the crematoria uncovered by Wasley and Johnson (1965) and by McGuire (1977). While a combination of both activities may be considered the principal cause for the incompleteness of the Los Morteros cremations, postmortem deterioration and archaeological recovery techniques may also be partly responsible. Continued research concerning the incompleteness of Hohokam cremation burials will hopefully identify additional factors as well as alternative hypotheses that can be tested archaeologically.

Summary

Archaeological investigations at Los Morteros uncovered four cremation deposits, one primary cremation and 13 miscellaneous parcels of calcined bone. The five formal interments may represent as many as six individuals, including one adult male, one probable adult male, one probable adult female, two adults (sex unknown), and one immature individual. The Los Morteros cremated remains, including those recovered from the primary cremation, were very incomplete. No pathologies or anomalies were observed.

SHELL FROM LOS MORTEROS

Sharon F. Urban

Since an initial check of the shell from Los Morteros (AZ
AA:12:57) in early 1980, two subsequent analyses have been conducted.
This report ties together all three analyses, and provides a basic
description of the shell material recovered, rather than a comprehensive
study. In January 1980, I performed the first study, which consisted of
material from test trenching activities. In 1982-1983, Felipe Jacome
studied the entire collection after excavations had been completed.
Finally, Arthur Vokes (1985) utilized the material from Feature 30 (a
pit house) as a class project. Using this earlier data a current
summary of the Los Morteros shell assemblage (consisting of 335 pieces
of shell) has been generated.

Species

Represented in the Los Morteros collection are fresh water,
land, and marine species. The freshwater and marine species are
artifactual, while the land species are environmental.

The fresh water species is Anodonta californiensis Lea, which
reportedly could be found in the Santa Cruz River as recently as 1880
(Bequaert and Miller 1973:221). The species was no doubt well
established during prehistoric times. A. californiensis Lea, an edible
clam, requires a free-flowing fresh-water stream and a host fish to
begin its life cycle. Shells of A. californiensis Lea were often turned
into items of personal adornment by the Hohokam.

The marine species recovered include:

Argopecten circularis Sowerby
Columbella sp. Lamarck
Conus sp. Linne
Docinea ponderosa Gray
Glycymeris sp. Dacosta
Haliotis sp. Linnaeus
Laevicardium elatum Sowerby
Nerita funiculata Menke
Olivella dama Wood
Nassarius sp. Dumeril
Pecten sp. Mueller
Pecten vogdesi Arnold
Turritella leucostoma Valenciennes

286

The three species of land snails found at the site are <u>Catinella</u> sp. Say, <u>Helisoma tenue</u> Durker, and <u>Succinea</u> sp. Say. Of these, <u>H. tenue</u> is by far the most common (Bequaert and Miller 1973: 208), followed by <u>Succinea</u> and then <u>Catinella</u>. This final snail is rare and not widespread in Arizona (Bequaert and Miller 1973: 157).

Artifact Types

The artifact categories listed are those defined by Jacome and are somewhat different from the typological system that I generally use (Gladwin and others 1965: 137; Urban 1986: 157). The basic categories used by Jacome are:

    I. Raw material
   II. Worked material
  III. Ornaments
       A. Beads
          1. Disc
          2. Whole Shell
       B. Bracelets
          1. Blanks
          2. Fragments
          3. Whole
       C. Pendants
          1. Blanks
          2. Cut and Ground
          3. Whole Shell
       D. Rings
          1. Narrow Band
          2. Wide Band

Raw Material is just that, whole or fragmentary pieces that show no workmanship (Fig. L.1). Included in this category are the environmental land snail specimens. The Worked Material category includes whole pieces or fragments that show some sign of alteration by man, but cannot be placed (to any degree of certainty) into an ornament category. These pieces show one or more areas of workmanship such as a cut or ground edge (surface), an incised line or groove, a drill hole (or portion thereof), or evidence of etching (Fig L.2.). The final major category is Ornaments. <u>Beads</u> (Figs. L.3 and L.4) are as listed. <u>Bracelets</u> (Fig. L.5) require a few added notes. In this case bracelets were not divided into types (I, II, or III based on band width) as defined by Haury (1976: 313-315). Bracelets with drilled beak perforations are generally classified as pendants, because a bracelet does not require a drill hole, but a pendant does. Jacome classified some <u>Laevicardium</u> sp. specimens (Fig. L.4e) as bracelets. The shell on this species is generally considered much too thin to hold up through use wear as a bracelet. To retain the integrity of Jacome's analysis, however, I have left the <u>Laevicardium</u> specimens in the bracelet

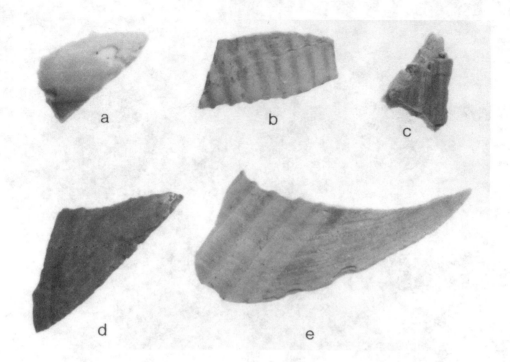

Figure L.1. Shell Artifacts: raw material: a, IN 188, from 600 E1100
(50) surface; b, IN 462, from Feature 6; c, IN 706, from N 1850 E 950
(50), surface; d, IN 1211, from Mound 2; e, IN 474, from Trench 77
(IN=inventory number). All specimens depicted are Laevicardium elatum.
The length of e is 55 mm.

category. Pendants (Fig. L.2) are straightforward in their
categorization. Rings (Figs. L.2m and L.5k-o) are divided into narrow
and wide bands. The narrow band (usually 2 to 4 mm) is made exclusively
from Glycymeris sp. shell, while the wide band (8 to 10 mm) is from
Conus sp. shell.

Sources

All of the marine species represented in the Los Morteros
collection occur in the Gulf of California, and Laevicardium is also
found on the Pacific Coast. Most of the species are from shallow water
(tidal to 9m [30 ft]) but a few are from moderately-deep water (20 to 60
m [80 to 200 ft] (Keen 1984; Morris 1966). The deeper water species
include Haliotis, Laevicardium, and Turritella. The shallow-water
species are more apt to appear on shore and can be collected by
beachcombing. The deeper water species do appear on shore after large
storms, but to obtain them on a regular basis, one would have to dive
for them.

288

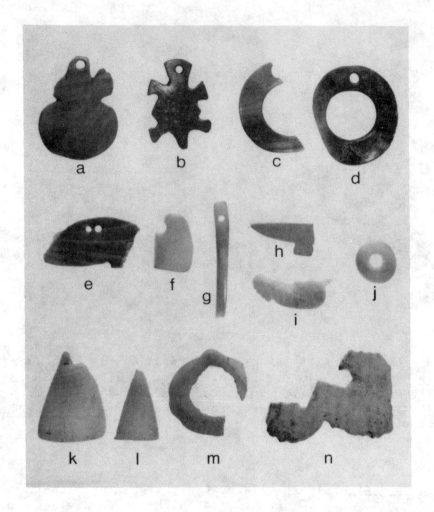

Figure L.2. Cut and shaped shell artifacts: a, Laevicardium elatum, IN 4056, from N1510 E1020 trench; b, Haliotis cracherodii, IN 2069, from Feature 30; c, Haliotis cracherodii, IN 3040, from Feature 30; d, Haliotis cracherodii, IN 3040, from Feature 30; e, Pectin vogdesi, IN 6476, from Feature 30; f, Conus sp., IN 5493, from Feature 39; g, Glycymeris sp., IN 4874, from N 1530 E 1020 trench; h, Laevicardium elatum, IN 6752, from Mound 5; i, Glycymeris sp., IN 6752, from Mound 5; j, Conus sp., IN 6691, from Mound 5; k, Conus sp., IN 6593, from Feature 62; l, Conus sp., IN 6594, from Feature 62; m, Glycymeris sp., IN 4844, from N1510 E 1020 trench; n, Laevicardium elatum, IN 1712, from Feature 20 (IN=inventory number). The length of g is 30 mm.

Manufacturing

The sample of 335 specimens is not large enough to determine precisely the presence of manufacturing of shell artifacts at this site. With the presence of the worked pieces and blanks, plus raw material, it is possible that some working or reworking of shell took place. Large quantities of shell were not recovered, so it is unlikely that a full-scale manufacturing center was present.

Some of the worked pieces found no doubt represent broken pieces of finished artifacts, and so do not necessarily represent manufacturing in progress. On the other hand, broken pieces (of finished artifacts) can be reworked into "new" artifacts.

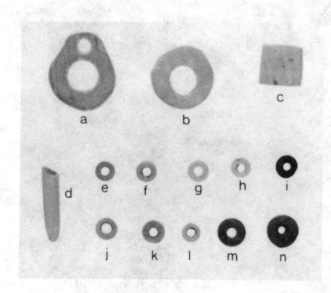

Figure L.3. Shell Ornaments: pendants and disc beads: a, IN 6786, from N1240 E820(10) surface; b, IN 7047, from N1130 W830(10) surface; c, IN 977, from Mound 1, 5W; d, IN 5169, from N1520 E 1020 trench; e, IN 2094, from Feature 39; f, IN 6599, from Feature 62; g, IN 6599, from Feature 62; h, IN 6599, from Feature 62; i, IN 4874 from N1530 E 1020 trench; j, IN 3213, from Feature 39; k, IN 4841, from N1510 E1020 trench; l, IN 6600, from Feature 62; m, IN 6599, from Feature 62; n, IN 4358, from Feature 137, trincheras. (IN=inventory number). a, b, c, and m are Laevicardium elatum, d is Glycymeris sp., and the rest are indeterminate. The diameter of b is 11 mm.

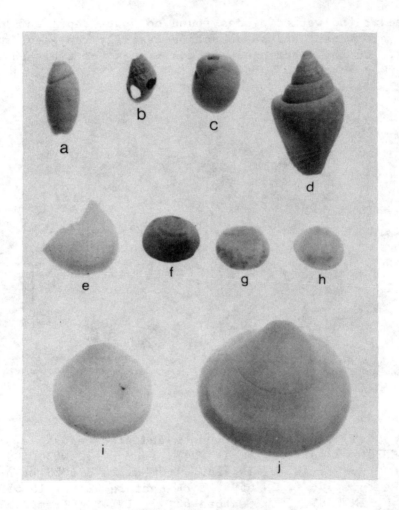

Figure L.4. Whole shells: a, Olivella dama, IN 1089 from Mound 1; b, Nassarius sp., IN 4070, from Feature 30; c, Nerite sp., IN 4103, from Feature 39; d, Columbella sp., IN 6928, from N1240 E870 (10) surface); e, IN 6596 from Feature 62; f, IN 6596, from Feature 62; g, IN 1213, from Mound 4; h, IN 6752, from Mound 5; i, IN 6596, from Feature 62; j, IN 6599, from Feature 62. (IN=inventory number). e through j are Glycymeris sp. The diameter of j is 30 mm.

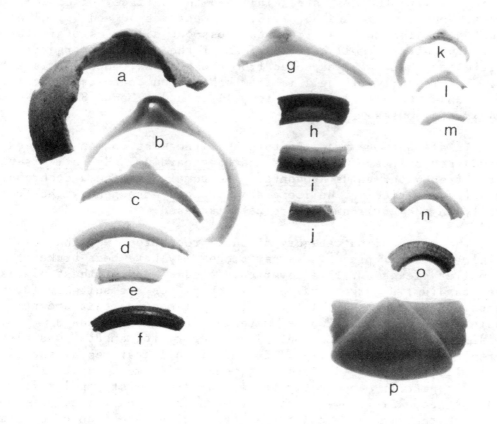

Figure L.5. Shell Artifacts: rings and bracelets: <u>a</u>, IN 849, from Trench 84; <u>b</u>, IN 6497, from Feature 30; <u>c</u>, IN 462, N1500 E 900, Trench 40; <u>d</u>, IN 1213, from Mound 4; <u>e</u>, IN 6596, from Feature 62; <u>f</u>, IN 845, from Feature 15; <u>g</u>, IN 4413, from Feature 30; <u>h</u>, IN 188, from N 600 E 1100 (50) surface; <u>i</u>, IN 188, from N 600 E 1100 (50) surface; <u>j</u>, IN 188, from N 600 E 1100 (50) surface; <u>k</u>, IN 706, from N 1850 E 950 (50) surface; <u>l</u>, IN 676, from Trench 47; <u>m</u>, IN 624, from Feature 32; <u>n</u>, IN 1146, from Mound 3; <u>o</u>, IN 3213, from Feature 39; <u>p</u>, IN 6997, from Feature 64 (IN=inventory number). All specimens depicted are <u>Glycymeris</u> sp. The length of <u>p</u> is 44 mm.

Analysis

Table L.1 shows shell species and Table L.2 shows artifact types by provenience from the site. Since I did not examine all the shell, a detailed analysis is not presented. Several comments can, however, be made with regard to the shell collection.

The contexts in which the shell is found are noteworthy. The proveniences with the most shell included the surface collection, test trenches, Mounds 1, 5A and 5B, 7, 8, and Features 30 and 39. The surface collection and test trenches cross-cut all types of features found at the site as well as most areas of the site, so larger quantities of shell were expected from these areas. Mound 1 is a trash mound. The majority of shell is from habitation contexts: there is a pithouse under Mounds 5A and 5B, as well as under Mound 8, and Features 30 and 39 are houses.

In all but one case (Feature 39), the most common species recovered per unit are Glycymeris and Laevicardium. Haliotis is next, then the freshwater genus Anodonta. The remaining genera occur but not in quantity. Catinella, Helisoma and Succinea, the genera that occur naturally in the environment, are not discussed.

The most common category of shell recovered, was that of "raw material," with 172 pieces. Larger pieces may have been broken to work into smaller pieces and were never completed. Many of these pieces are of Laevicardium, a large bivalve of which pieces are suitable for making pendants. Some pieces are lateral or distal margins that are not suitable for ornaments. "Worked material" (16 pieces) has a surprisingly low representation. The category "ornaments" was also a well-represented artifact type. In fact in all features at the site where shell was recovered, each contained one or more (up to 18) bracelet fragments. Apparently bracelets were a most popular item. The second most popular ornament was that of narrow band (finger) rings (22). Both the bracelets and these narrow rings are made of Glycymeris shell. The next most common ornament is that of whole shell beads (15) which are primarily juvenile forms of Glycymeris. The final category worth noting is that of cut or ground pendants (8), which are constructed on Haliotis and Laevicardium.

Discussion

A few comments can be made about several items recovered. Among the bracelet fragments are a few that are carved. Carved bracelets are not unique, but were probably considered special. Carving began in the Cañada del Oro phase and was at its height during the Rincon phase. The large Laevicardium shells with cut-out centers were popular during the Rincon Phase. One pictured in Gladwin and others (1965: Plate CXVIII)

Table L.1

SHELL SPECIES

Provenience	\<Marine\> Argopecten	Columbella	Conus	Docinea	Glycymeris	Haliotis	Laevicardium	Nerita	Olivella	Nassarius	Pecten	Pecten vogdesi	Turritella	Indeterminate Snail	\<Other\> Anodonta-Freshwater	\<Land\> Catinella	Helisoma	Succinea	Indeterminate	Totals
Surface Collection	3	1		1	17		42	1				1		1						67
Test Trenches	1				14		14					1								30
Mound 1		1			18		19				1	1		2				1		43
Mound 2					1		1								1					3
Mound 3					3	1	7						1	1						13
Mound 4					2															2
Mound 5A and B (Feature 51)					23		10								3	1	1	1	4	43
Mound 6					3		5													8
Mound 7 (Features 53-57)			1		9		11		1											22
Mound 8 (Feature 50)			1		7	1	10		1									2	1	23
Mound 27 (Features 52 and 60					1		2													3
Feature 30					16	4	21		1			1						6		49
Feature 39			1		6		1		1	1								9	2	21
Feature 44					3		4													7
Linda Vista Trincheras															1					1
TOTALS	4	2	3	1	123	6	147	1	4	1	1	4	1	4	5	1	1	19	7	335

Note: see Chapter 5 for feature descriptions.

Table L.2

SHELL ARTIFACT TYPES

	Beads		Bracelets			Pendants			Rings				
Provenience	Disc	Whole Shell	Blanks	Fragments	Whole	Blanks	Cut Ground	Whole Shell	Narrow Band	Wide Band	Worked Shell	Whole Shell	Totals
Surface Collection		1		14					2		4	46	67
Test Trenches		1	1	10			1		2		1	14	30
Mound 1	1	4		14		2			4		2	16	43
Mound 2				1							1	1	3
Mound 3				3					1			9	13
Mound 4		1		1									2
Mnd 5A & B (Feature 51)		1		18	2		1		3		2	16	43
Mound 6			3								1	4	8
Mound 7 (F. 53-57)		1		3					5	1		12	22
Mound 8 (Feature 50)		2		4			2		1	1		13	23
Mound 27 (Features 52 and 60)				1								2	3
Feature 30		1		14			4	1	2		3	24	49
Feature 39	1	3		3					2		2	10	21
Feature 44				3								4	7
Linda Vista Trincheras												1	1
TOTALS	2	15	1	92	2	2	8	1	22	2	16	172	335

looks like a bracelet, but the shell is nearly paper thin around the opening and it is quite heavy at the beak and lateral edges. It would have been a most awkward shell to wear as a bracelet (Haury 1976: 316). Other such examples have been reported, but they are not usually reported to be bracelets.

Eight acid-etched pieces of Laevicardium are included in the Los Morteros collection. Etched shell pieces were recovered during both Snaketown excavations (Gladwin and others 1965: 148-151; Haury 1976: 318-319). Such artifacts are not common, and the pieces from Los Morteros represent a high incidence of etching; especially since these fragments are from a variety of proveniences. In Anthony Pomeroy's (1959) study of etched shell, he reported on a total of 15 specimens (whole and fragmentary) from all of southern Arizona. Seven specimens came from the Tucson area, six of these were from the Hodges site (AZ AA:12:18), although in Isabel Kelly's (1978: 120) report, she mentions only one specimen as being etched. There is also one specimen from the Tucson Mountains near the town of Rillito. This is very near Los Morteros. This last specimen (Arizona State Museum Catalog Number 6550) is etched and painted, a very striking artifact (Urban 1966: 140-149).

With these etched specimens all coming from the northwest portion of the Tucson Basin, perhaps this area, more specifically Los Morteros, was a shell etching center. This is further substantiated by the recent work at Los Morteros by the Institute for American Research. William Doelle has indicated that at least one more piece has been found in a controlled context, and perhaps a few other pieces from miscellaneous proveniences.

Twenty-eight burned specimens were recovered. These are scattered over the entire site, but nearly every provenience had at least one or two such pieces. It is suspected that these were "chance" burnings (a piece was tossed into fire, or a load of ash was dumped on the shell) rather than deliberate (cremation offering) burning. Burned shell scattered around the site in this way is not significant.

Incising (Fig. L.6a and b) is another variable that was specifically noted in Jacome's analysis. Six pieces of shell (one piece each from the surface, test trenches, and Mound 1; and three pieces from Mound 7) reportedly were incised. Glycymeris and Laevicardium were each represented by three pieces. Incising of the Laevicardium pieces is understandable as it is a good way to delineate appendages such as those of zoomorphic pendants. One piece was incised on the interior. Of the Glycymeris specimens, these are a bit more unusual in that incising appears on what may be finished artifacts--one finger ring and two bracelets. Two items not specifically noted in Jacome's notes, but which appear in Figure L.6c-d, are incised (and carved) Glycymeris frogs. Also considered to be incised are the "V-"shaped grooves that are used for suspension on the Conus tinklers (Fig. L.2k-1).

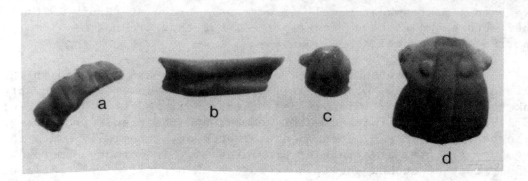

Figure L.6. Carved and incised shell artifacts: a, IN 1100, from Mound
1; b, IN 6498, from Feature 30; c, IN 977, from Mound 1; d, IN 6596,
from Feature 62 (IN=inventory number). All specimens depicted are
Glycymeris sp. The height of d is 19 mm.

Conclusions

The shell assemblage from Los Morteros is a good, representative
sample of shell artifacts from a large Hohokam site. The species
represented and artifact types fit with what is expected to be present
at such a site. The only thing lacking at this site is a greater
quantity of material.

Most of the artifact types and species are those found at other
sites in southern Arizona. Cut and ground style pendants are well-
represented, as are bracelets of the Type I and II categories (Haury
1976: 313-315). Beads of either the whole shell variety or of the
manufactured types are also certainly in evidence. The only artifact
type that would be expected to appear in much larger quantities would be
the whole shell bead of Olivella dama. Not finding it at this site in
greater quantity is surprising. As mentioned, earlier, the amount of
etched shell is outstanding.

The shell specimens from the site indicate a late Rillito (A.D.
850 to 900) to early Tanque Verde (A.D. 1200 to 1250) phase date for the
site. The early specimens include the intricately cut and ground
pendants, disc beads, and smaller-sized (Types I and II) bracelets. The
Tanque Verde phase indicators include the tinklers of Conus and the
larger (band) bracelets (Fig. L.5a and f). Carved rings and bracelets,
the geometrically shaped pendants, whole shell beads, and the etched
pieces can be placed in the Rincon phase (A.D. 900 to 1200). Shell
species and artifact types are by no means true indicators of period of
occupation at a site, but they can help substantiate dates derived from
other means.

Shell from the testing at Los Morteros and from the more recent work by the Institute for American Research barely shows the extent of the shell assemblage at this site. All too often, comprehensive excavations of these large sites are not possible and therefore the full range of shell—both species and artifact types—may not be known. Thus, shell researchers must content themselves with a small taste of what may be present at the site.

Appendix M

ARCHAEOMAGNETIC SAMPLE RESULTS

Table M.1

ARCHAEOMAGNETIC RESULTS

Sample Number	Field No.	Demag Level	Specimens Taken	Used	Intensity	I	D	Alpha-95	k	PLAT	PLONG	Dm	Dp
LM001	F.32	H200	10	10	1.13E+00	57.86	345.54	1.2	1363.23	76.72	190.77	1.82	1.34
LM002	F.8	H150	10	10	8.48E-01	55.82	349.56	1.2	1807.11	80.50	186.98	1.74	1.24
LM003	F.30	H200	9	9	3.37E-05	55.57	353.04	3.0	299.72	83.12	194.13	4.26	3.04
LM004	F.39	H300	16	15	2.20E-05	56.59	355.66	2.8	188.64	84.00	213.78	4.04	2.92
LM005	F.39	H300	9	7	2.73E-05	56.05	349.56	5.0	149.47	80.40	188.23	7.12	5.12
LM006	F.137	H200	9	9	2.97E-04	58.25	339.01	3.8	184.79	71.77	186.11	5.61	4.15
LM007	F.109	H300	6	5	2.20E-04	57.79	342.92	3.7	423.67	74.83	187.49	5.47	4.02
LM008	F.50	H050	10	10	1.88E-05	56.88	352.24	20.0	6.80	81.83	200.07	29.04	21.09
LM009	F.50	H050	10	9	9.70E-05	58.98	349.95	2.7	368.68	79.02	204.24	4.01	2.99
LM010	F.50	H050	9	8	1.30E-04	60.93	350.01	3.2	291.82	77.52	212.38	4.97	3.80
LM011	F.50	H025	8	8	2.02E-03	57.03	350.17	3.6	243.11	80.37	195.06	5.18	3.77
LM012	F.50	H050	8	7	4.50E-05	59.51	355.49	6.6	85.82	81.22	225.92	9.84	7.39
LM013	F.51	H025	8	8	5.01E-04	55.96	345.19	2.9	371.03	77.22	181.98	4.13	2.97
LM014	F.52	H050	8	8	1.75E-03	60.08	348.32	1.9	832.07	77.27	205.12	2.91	2.20
LM015	F.52	H100	8	8	1.32E-03	58.55	348.36	1.5	1399.67	78.30	198.61	2.20	1.63
LM016	F.60	H025	8	6	3.50E-03	56.74	352.49	1.6	1815.32	82.08	200.06	2.28	1.65
LM017	F.60	H100	8	8	1.09E-04	59.35	349.11	1.8	900.71	78.26	201.84	2.77	2.08

Demag level = level of demagnetization of the sample, given in oersteds; Intensity = the mean magnetization (J), given in gauss; I = mean archaeomagnetic inclination; D = mean archaeomagnetic declination; Alpha-95 = radius of the 95 percent circle of confidence about the mean direction; k = precision parameter; PLAT = virtual geomagnetic pole latitude; PLONG = virtual geomagnetic pole longitude; Dm = semimajor axis of the 95 percent oval of confidence about the pole position; Dp = semiminor axis of the 95 percent oval of confidence about the pole position.

Table M.2

DATING INTERPRETATIONS

Sample		Alpha-95	SWVGP 95%	SWVGP 63%	SWVGP B.F.
LM001	@	1.2	1030-1090,1060-1170	1040-1090,1060-1150	1070-1120
LM002	&	1.2	970-1070,1100-1150,1120-1280	1140-1240	1160-1210
LM003		3.0	890-1070,1140-1390	950-1070,1240-1330, 1300-1350	970-1070
LM004	*	2.8	870-1070,1220-1450	940-1070,1300-1410	1310-1360
LM005	*	5.0	940-1090,1060-1380	1090-1340	1160-1210
LM006		3.8	1040-1110	1050-1100	1050-1100
LM007		3.7	1000-1160	1040-1110	1050-1100
LM008	*	20.0	700-1450	700-1450	1250-1310
LM009		2.7	1000-1090,1060-1080	1000-1080	1030-1080
LM010		3.2	1000-1090,1070-1150	1000-1080	1000-1070
LM011	$	3.6	950-1090,1060-1350	1100-1150,1120-1330	1200-1250
LM012	*	6.6	870-1090,1060-1450	1240-1450	1300-1350
LM013		2.9	1000-1190	-------	1100-1150
LM014	+	1.9	1000-1090,1060-1150	1000-1080	1000-1070
LM015	+	1.5	1000-1090,1060-1220,1200-1250	1030-1080,1080-1160	1100-1150
LM016	+	1.6	950-1070,1150-1360	1190-1240,1220-1340	1250-1300
LM017	+	1.8	1000-1090,1060-1170	1000-1080	1030-1080

Key for feature type (listed after sample number): (no symbol) = hearth, * = floor, + = horno, @ = crematory, & = burned pit, $ = wall.

NOTE: All archaeomagnetic samples were analyzed and dated through the Paleomagnetism Laboratory, Department of Geosciences, University of Arizona. All date ranges are A.D. and are derived from the Southwestern VGP Curve (SWVGP) developed by Sternberg (1982) and are given for two standard deviations (95% confidence), one standard deviation (63% confidence), and for the interval on the curve statistically showing the best fit (B.F.).

Appendix N

RADIOCARBON SAMPLE RESULTS

Table N.1

RADIOCARBON DATING RESULTS

Los Morteros Feature Number	Lab Number	Sample Number	Years B.P.	δ¹³C (⁰/oo)
F. 8 (IN854)	A-2299		2670 ± 200	-25.9
F.32 (IN545)	A-2300		750 ± 50	-16.3
LVT F.137 (IN4385)	A-2746		600 ± 80	-24.9
F.51	2772	6272 B	700 ± 80	-24.3
F.52	2773	6223 B	1090 ± 80	-22.4
F.51	2774	6267 B	710 ± 90	-24.8
F.51	2775	6268 B	890 ± 90	-25.4
F.51	2776	6269	730 ± 110	-12.1
F.51	2777	6270 B	910 ± 90	-25.6

NOTE: All radiocarbon samples were analyzed by the Radiocarbon Laboratory, Department of Geosciences, University of Arizona, and results are reported in a conventional manner, based on 5,568 half-life years before 1950, normalized to δ¹³C = -25.0⁰/oo.

a. counted for 4,000 minutes; 2,000 is normal.

b. counted for 5,000 minutes; 2,000 is normal.

Appendix O

PHOTOGRAPHS OF LOS MORTEROS ARTIFACTS

Figure 0.1 Rincon Red-on-brown jar with Gila shoulder from Feature 30.
Height of vessel is 30 cm.

Figure 0.2 Rincon Red-on-brown jar from Feature 30.
Height of vessel is 33 cm.

Figure 0.3   Plain ware jar from Feature 30.
Height of vessel is 28 cm.

Figure 0.4   Rincon Red-on-brown bowl from Feature 30.
Diameter of vessel is 19 cm.

Figure O.5   Sacaton Red-on-buff bowl from Feature 30.

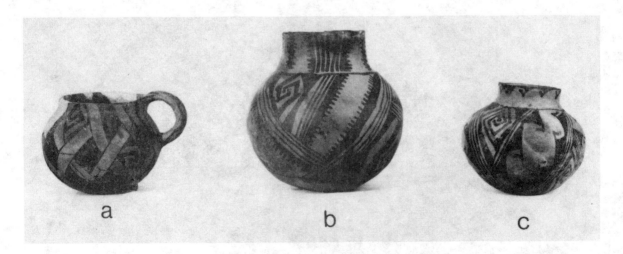

Figure O.6   Tanque Verde Red-on-brown cremation vessels: a, IN 534, from wall of Trench 47; b, IN 1264, from profile wall of Mound 4; c, IN 5489, from Mound 7, cremation cache vessel No. 3, no cover sherd or vessel.   Height of b is 18 cm.

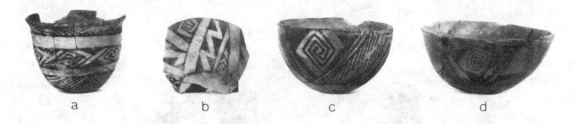

Figure 0.7 Tanque Verde phase cremation vessels: a, IN 5486, from Mound 7, cremation cache vessel No. 4, Tanque Verde Red-on-brown, was cover bowl for vessel No. 5 (IN 5490, Fig. 0.8a); b, IN 534, from Trench 47, was cover sherd for IN 534 (Fig. 0.6a); c, IN 5488, from Mound 7, cremation cache vessel No. 2, Tanque Verde Black-on-brown, it was the cover bowl for vessel No. 7 (IN 5492), a nonmicaceous plain ware jar that was not complete; d, IN 5487, from Mound 7, cremation cache vessel No. 6, Tanque Verde Red-on-brown, it was upside down, but not covering another vessel. Diameter of c is 15 cm.

Figure 0.8 Plain ware cremation vessels: a, IN 5490, from Mound 7, cremation cache vessel No. 5, nonmicaceous plain ware; it was covered by Vessel No. 4 (IN 5486, Fig. 0.7a); b, IN 5491, from Mound 7, cremation cache vessel No. 1, nonmicaceous plain ware; it did not have a cover sherd; c, IN 1263, from profile wall Mound 2. Height of b is 15 cm.

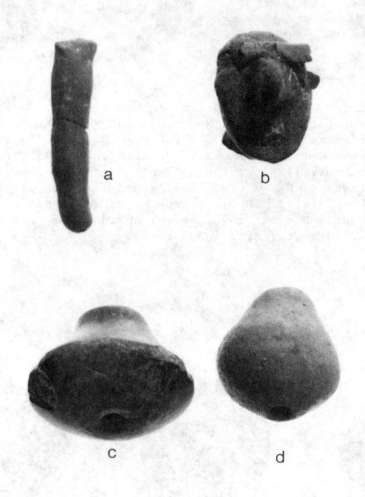

Figure 0.9 Miscellaneous ceramic artifacts: a, IN 1009, from Mound 1, figurine arm or leg; b, IN 1179, from Feature 39, figurine head; c, IN 2893, from Feature 39, spindle whorl; d, IN 1228, from Mound 1, spindle whorl. Length of a is 42 mm.

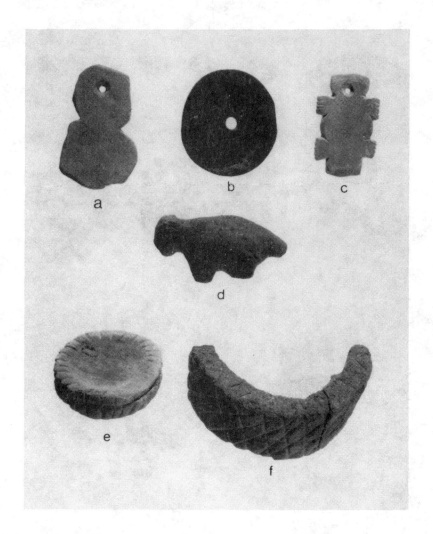

Figure 0.10   Miscellaneous artifacts: a, IN 885, from surface, siltstone pendant; b, IN 847, from Feature 32, burned stone disc; c, no number assigned, from Feature 39, schist pendant; d, IN 3430, from Mound 1, ceramic animal; e, IN 4805, from surface, stone palette/censer possibly made of tuff; f, IN 4074 and IN 4411 from Feature 30, ceramic censer.   Length of c is 42 mm.

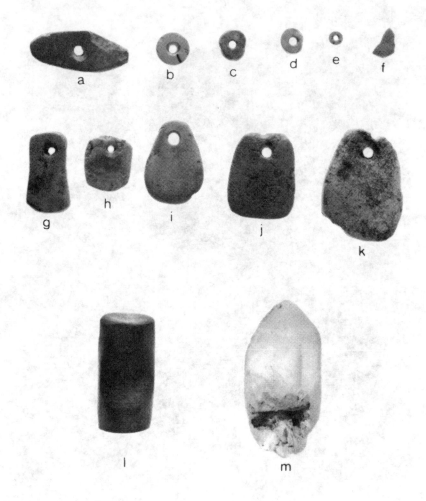

Figure O.11 Turquoise, argillite, and quartz artifacts: <u>a</u>, IN 7355, from Feature 39, siltstone; <u>b</u>, IN 6599, from Feature 62, turquoise; <u>c</u>, IN 458, from Trench 40, turquoise; <u>d</u>, IN 1161, from Mound 2, turquoise; <u>e</u>, IN 5171, from surface, turquoise; <u>f</u>, IN 6598, from Feature 62, turquoise; <u>g</u>, IN 6888, from Mound 5, turquoise; <u>h</u>, IN 5171, from surface, turquoise; <u>i</u>, IN 6999, from Feature 64, turquoise; <u>j</u>, IN 6465, from surface, turquoise; <u>k</u>, IN 4643, from Feature 39, turquoise; <u>l</u>, IN 4744, from Feature 109, trincheras, argillite; <u>m</u>, IN 2887, from Feature 39, quartz. Length of <u>l</u> is 20 mm.

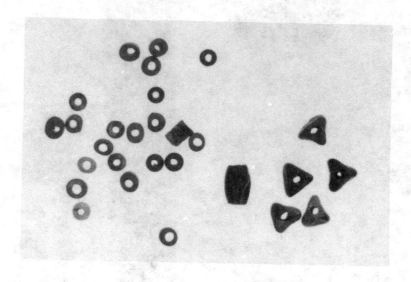

Figure 0.12 Beads from cremation, Feature 32: IN 622, all are burned
and material cannot be determined; but they could be shell, stone, or
clay. Diameter of beads averages 2 mm.

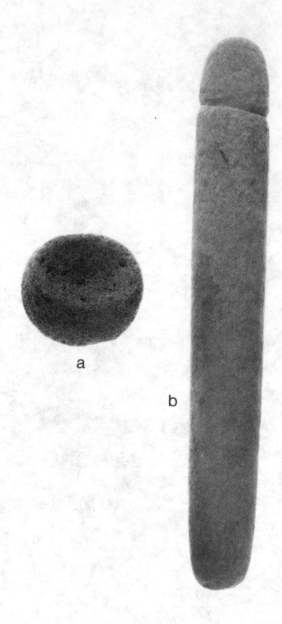

Figure 0.13 Stone mortar (IN 3351) and pestle (IN 3350); both are from "plaza" on top of trincheras hill and are made of basalt or rhyolite. Length of <u>b</u> is 29 cm.

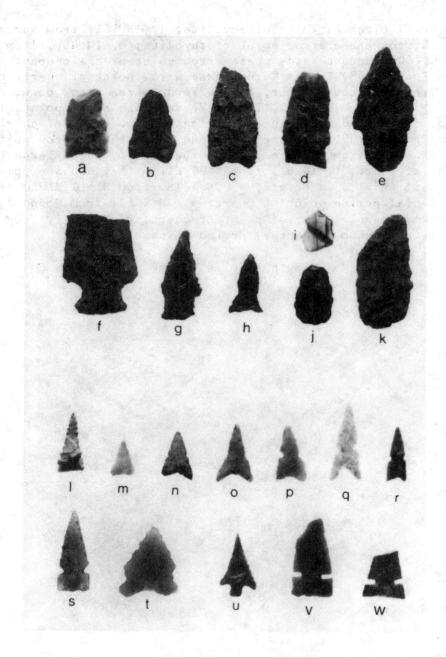

Figure O.14. Projectile points and bifacial knife: (identifications made by Bruce Huckell, Arizona State Museum): a, IN 406, from surface N1550 E900 (50), Cortaro Point (late Archaic) of chert; b, IN 1050, from Mound 1, Cortaro Point (late Archaic) of rhyolite; c, IN 124, from surface N1500 E950 (5), Cortaro Point (late Archaic) of rhyolite; d, IN 1290, from Mound 3, Archaic? point of chert; e, IN 865, from surface N1681 E1050, Early Archaic point, of basalt, compare Lake Mohave points; f, IN 4106, from Feature 39, San Pedro point, of rhyolite; g, IN 1064, from Mound 1, time period unknown, of rhyolite; h, IN 884, from surface N1500 E1050 (50), time period unknown, of rhyolite; i, IN 893, from Mound 1, time period unknown, of obsidian; j, IN 933, from surface N1309 E1000, time period unknown, of obsidian; k, IN 4499, from Feature

109 trincheras, bifacial knife of rhyolite; <u>l</u>, IN 162, from surface N650 E1100 (5), Rincon phase arrow point of rhyolite; <u>m</u>, IN 861, from surface N1450 E1050 (50), Tanque Verde phase arrow point of chalcedony; <u>n</u>, IN 4821, from Feature 48, Tanque Verde phase arrow point of chert; <u>o</u>, IN 335, from Trench 92 house floor, Tanque Verde phase arrow point of chert; <u>p</u>, IN 978, from Mound 1, Tanque Verde phase arrow point of chert; <u>q</u>, IN 1093, from Mound 1, Tanque Verde phase arrow point of chert; <u>r</u>, IN 4498, from Feature 109, trincheras, Tanque Verde phase arrow point of chert; <u>s</u>, IN 6570, from Feature 30 disturbed area, Tanque Verde phase arrow point of chert; <u>t</u>, IN 61, from N500 E1150 (5), Archaic point of chert, compare Chiricahua points; <u>u</u>, IN 4838, from N1510 E1020 trench, Hohokam Colonial period point of chert; <u>v</u>, IN 2663, from Mound 2, Gila Basin Hohokam, Sedentary period point of chert; <u>w</u>, IN 1701, from Feature 39, Gila Basin Hohokam, Sedentary period point of chert.

Length of <u>e</u> is 45 mm.

Appendix P

CHEMICAL ANALYSIS OF PIGMENTS ON SHERDS
FROM LOS MORTEROS

Susan L. Brantley

The chemical analysis was directed toward recording measurable amounts of manganese (Mn) from pigments on pottery sherds collected from Los Morteros. Manganese is a common pigment used prehistorically in the Southwest; its use results in a blackish-brown color in an oxidizing atmosphere. Manganese occurs in black nodules and also in the dark clays around the edges of ponds, streams, and marshy lands.

The purpose of the testing at analysis was to establish whether a Mn-oxide compound was used to produce differential coloring. The testing confirmed that a Mn-oxide compound was used to produce black pigments.

The two groups tested were Tanque Verde Red-on-brown and Tanque Verde black paint sherds. In order to insure that paint differences were not the result of differential firing, the samples selected had thick, even coats of paint and a dark orange ceramic background, which is evidence of exposure to only an oxidizing atmosphere.

The testing procedure was to use an atomic absorption machine to show percentages of manganese absorbed in each sample. With this data and supplementary calculations a calibration curve (linear regression) was constructed.

The sherds were collected from 14 different proveniences located on O'Daniel's northern fields at the site of Los Morteros (Table P.1). No sherds from the southern fields were selected for analysis.

Atomic absorption spectroscopy is a technique based upon the ability of atoms in the vapor state to absorb radiation at certain well defined characteristic wavelengths. Its major use is in analysis for trace-metal determinations. The sample generally is dissolved and aspirated into a flame to produce the atomic state. At ordinary flame temperatures the fraction of atoms that are in excited electronic states is very much less than the fraction that are unexcited. The absorption of radiant energy by electronic transitions from ground to excited state is an absolute measure of the number of atoms in the flame and hence the concentration of the element in a sample. Use of the hollow-cathode lamp (emission beam) discharges the element in question, providing the necessary sharp and intense line for maximum selectivity and sensitivity. The machine measures how much light the material absorbed at a particular wavelength and the absorption signal is transduced to

Table P.1

SHERDS SELECTED FOR ANALYSIS
TANQUE VERDE RED-ON-BROWN AND BLACK PAINT

Red Paint	Black Paint
FN 62 - two sherds	FN 62
FN 442	FN 442
FN 863	FN 438 - two sherds (same vessel)
FN 913	FN 912 - two sherds
FN 001 - (AZ:AA:12:57)	FN 946
FN 002 - Bill Deaver's	FN 945 - special fugitive brown pigment
	FN 442 - possible control sherd, is slightly misfired, paint appears black

readout. The intensity of absorption by a substance at any given wavelength is directly proportional to its concentration.

In its usual configuration, an atomic absorption spectrometer consists of four basic components: (1) a light source emitting the spectrum of the desired analyte element; (2) a sample atomization cell such as a flame or graphite tube furnace; (3) a monochromator to isolate the desired source emission line; and (4) a detector readout system to allow measurement of the change in source line intensity by sample atom absorption.

The light source is usually a hollow cathode discharge lamp, prepared with the desired element. Radiation from the source passes through the atomization cell, where it is absorbed by the same atoms as the source produced when the sample is introduced. Calibration is achieved with standard solutions containing known concentrations of the element being determined.

Bouguer-Lambert-Beer Law

By using the machine, the intensity of the light transmitted through an absorbing substance may be compared with the light intensity when no such substance is in the light beam. Two fundamental laws govern the intensity of the light transmitted by an absorbing material. The first law, called the Bouguer-Lambert Law, is given in equation (1):

$$(1) \qquad \log(I_o/I) = Kb$$

Here I_o is the intensity of the light beam with no sample present and I is the intensity of the light beam after passing through the sample. K is a constant, depending on the sample and wavelength of the light and b is the thickness of the absorbing material.

The second law, called Beer's Law, is shown by equation (2):

$$(2) \qquad \log(I_o/I) = K^1 c$$

Here I_o and I are as above, K^1 is a constant depending on the sample and wavelength of the light, and c is the concentration of absorbing material in the sample. Usually these two laws are combined in the form of equation (3):

$$(3) \qquad \log(I_o/I) = abc$$

I_o, I, b, and c are as previously described and a is a constant called the absorptivity or extinction coefficient. Two other terms are commonly used; these are transmittance (T) and absorbance (A) as defined by equations (4) and (5):

$$(4) \qquad T = I/I_o$$

$$(5) \qquad A = \log(1/T) = \log(I_o/I) = abc$$

The absorbance, (A), is directly proportional to the length of the light path through the sample and to the concentration of the absorbing material.

The Bouguer-Lambert-Beer law is strictly obeyed only when radiation of a single wavelength or frequency is used. In most quantitative analytical work, a calibration or standard curve is prepared by measuring the absorption of known amounts of the absorbing material at the wavelength at which it strongly absorbs. The absorbance of the sample is read directly from the measuring circuit of the machine. Calibration curves are usually linear.

320

Experimental Procedure

Initially, the pigments were scraped from the sherds with a sharp blade, and each sample was analytically weighed and noted. In order to break down the silica seal and make a clean sample, the scrapings were chemically broken down by using a Teflan balm. Each sample was placed in a balm with a three part acid mixture of 600 ml HF, 600 ml HNO_3, and 200 ml HCL, then heated at 100°C for two hours. After heating, they were allowed to cool and 6 ml of saturated H_3BO_3 added, in order to knock out the HF and save the glassware. Then, 1200 ml of NH_4OH was added in order to neutralize the remaining acid mixture. Finally, this solution was diluted to 25 ml with distilled water.

In order to compare concentrations of Mn in these samples, a reference (this is, a standard) was established. Standards were made up from a solution of 1,000 ppm reference standard solution put out by Fisher Scientific Company, using manganese nitrate in distilled water (Table P.2). The standard Mn solutions had a concentration range of 0.5 to 20.00 parts per million.

The Jarrell Ash Atomic Absorption machine was used with an Air - C_2H_2 flame. Settings for the Jarrel Ash Atomic Absorption Machine were: lamp current of 20 mA; gas pressures, air at 60 psi, C_2H_2 at 10 psi; resonance line of 2798A for Mn; recorder voltage of 1 mV; recorder speed of 4 cm/min; and damping of O.

Sample Calculations

In this example the data from the 5.00 ppm standard is used.

Because the recorder was set with its limits at 0.95 units for 0 percent absorption and 5.00 units for 100 percent, the 0-100 percent absorption scale spanned 90 recorder units.

For the 5.00 ppm standard, there was a 24 recorder unit absorption, leaving a 66 unit amount to be transmitted. Therefore:

Transmittance = T/To

= $\frac{66 \text{ recorder units Transmitted}}{90 \text{ units total}}$

= 0.7333

Table P.2

DATA TABLES FOR TRANSMITTANCE AND ABSORBANCE

Standard Manganese Solutions

Concentration (ppm)	Recorder Units Absorbed	Recorder Units Transmitted	Transmittance	Absorbance
0.5	2	88	0.9778	0.0098
1.0	5.5	84.5	0.9389	0.0273
2.0	8.5	81.5	0.9056	0.0431
5.0	24.0	66	0.7333	0.1347
10.0	51.0	39	0.4333	0.3632
15.0	63.0	27	0.3000	0.5229
20.0	72.0	18	0.2000	0.6990

Sample No.	Recorder Units Absorbed	Recorder Units Transmitted	Transmittance	Absorbance	Sample Weight (mg)	Absorbance Weight
Odd Colored Samples						
M-442[a]	26.5	63.5	0.7056	0.1515	87	0.0017
442[b]	7.5	82.5	0.9167	0.0378	70	0.0005
Black Samples						
62	20	70	0.7778	0.1091	43	0.0025
438	15	75	0.8333	0.0792	62	0.0013
442	19.5	70.5	0.7833	0.1061	76	0.0014
912	15.5	74.5	0.8278	0.0821	58	0.0014
945sp	14	76	0.8444	0.0734	50	0.0015
946	1	89	0.9889	0.0049	63	0.0001
Red Samples						
001	0.5	89.5	0.9944	0.0024	71	3.408E-05
002	0.75	89.25	0.9917	0.0036	80	4.543E-05
62	1.0	89	0.9889	0.0049	65	7.465E-05
62*	1.0	89	0.9889	0.0049	40	1.213E-04
863	0.2	89.8	0.9978	0.0010	18	5.368E-05
913	0.5	89.5	0.9944	0.0024	64	3.780E-05

a. Brown/brown color.
b. Red/brown color.

By Beer's Law:

$$\text{Absorbance} = -\log[T/To]$$

$$= -\log[0.7333] = 0.1347$$

In the case of the samples, this absorbance value was then divided by the weight of the paint sample, in order to compensate for different amounts of paint in each sample.

The plot was made using only the data from the standards up to 5.00 ppm, since all of the samples fell into this range.

The data from these paints was used in a least squares fit equation (linear regression) to get the equation:

$$y = 0.02751x - 0.0047$$

This line was then plotted on the graph (Figs. P.1 - P.5).

The concentrations for the sample were then read off this plot, or in this case the plot was only used to check to see if the data was linear and followed Beer's Law. The results for the concentration of Mn in the sample was found by using the above equation (standard addition could have been tried).

Example of Least Squares Fit Equation

An example of a least squares fit is given below. The data from the sample of Black # 62 is used. The regression line is:

$$y = 0.02751x - 0.0047$$

Therefore:
$$x = \frac{0.004727 + y}{0.02751}$$

where x = concentration of Mn per 1 mg of sample
      y = absorbance of sample per 1 mg of sample

For Black #62

$$\frac{\text{Absorbance}}{\text{Weight}} = 0.0025$$

Therefore:

$$\frac{\text{concentration of Mn}}{\text{mg sample}} = \frac{0.004727 + (0.0025)}{0.02751} = 0.2628$$

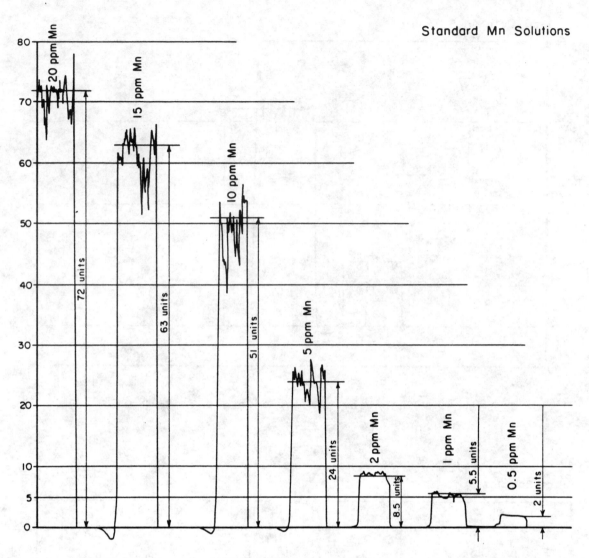

Figure P.1. Absorbance of standard manganese solutions.

324

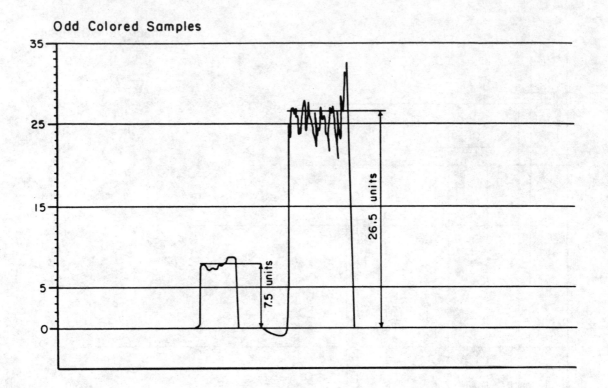

Figure P.2. Absorbance of odd-colored samples.

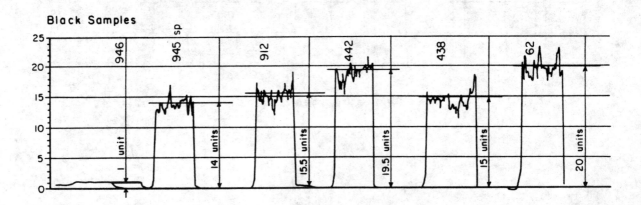

Figure P.3. Absorbance of black samples.

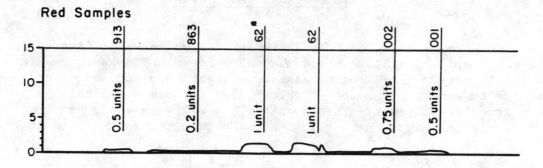

Figure P.4. Absorbance of red samples.

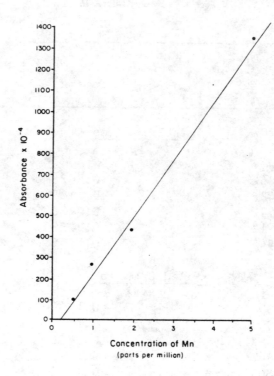

Figure P.5. Plot of concentration of manganese versus absorbance.

326

Summary and Discussion

The results show that the black paint samples have three to four parts per million manganese and the red paint samples have less than one-half parts per million manganese, a percentage too small for the machine to accurately detect (Table P.3). This is a reliable demonstration of the hypothesis that black pigments would produce measurable amounts of Mn, while the red pigment would not produce Mn.

Table P.3

RESULTS OF PIGMENT ANALYSIS

Sample No.	Concentration of Mn (ppm/mg)
Black Samples	
62	0.2628
438	0.2129
442	0.2228
912	0.2228
945	0.1755
Red Samples	
001	0.1731
002	0.1735
62	0.1746
62*	0.1763
863	0.1738
913	0.1733
Odd Colored Samples	
M-442	0.2337
442	0.1901

Note: Each of the values for concentration is in units of ppm Mn per mg. M-442 correlates with the black sample results. 442 seems to correlate with the red samples.

Two further refinements to the testing could be done to insure even greater accuracy. First, in these tests the standard Mn solutions were 0.5 ppm Mn to 20.00 ppm Mn. If the standard Mn solutions were more concentrated, that is, greater ppm Mn, the results would have been more precise. Second, a background subtraction test using the unpainted pottery could have been included. The background analysis could then have been subtracted from the paint tests, thereby showing what elements were solely in the paint.

At present, the study of prehistoric pottery consists of mainly a visual examination. I believe that these tests demonstrate that atomic absorption spectroscopy is a valuable addition to ceramic studies. Although this test was confined to detecting traces of Mn, atomic absorption spectroscopy can be broadened to allow a multi-element analysis of the sherds. This may help to establish localities and the developmental phases of paint-type orientations. In collaboration with other testing methods, this would provide a dependable basis for comparison.

Acknowledgments

This analysis was accomplished with the cooperation of the Department of Chemistry, University of Arizona, with the assistance of Steve Brown and Mike Riggleman.

Appendix Q

HOHOKAM PROJECTILE POINTS
AND THEIR LOCALITIES OF MANUFACTURE
IN THE TUCSON BASIN

Felipe Carlos Jacome

Hohokam projectile points come in a wide variety of shapes and sizes. The points recovered from Hohokam sites tend to be well made, which suggests craft specialization among Hohokam stoneworkers (Crabtree 1973: 10-12). This specialization resulted in the production of enormous quantities of points. Haury (1976: 296) states, "The great effort in fabricating hundreds of long points must have resulted in accumulation of debitage of no small matter." This tremendous production of points can be seen in collections from such sites as Las Colinas (Huckell 1981: 172-178), Hodges Ruin (Kelly 1978: 89-91), and the Painted Rocks sites (Wasley and Johnson 1965: 30, 100, 105). The largest point collection recovered from a single Hohokam site to date is from Snaketown (Haury 1976: 296). This collection has been used to develop a point sequence that is tied to changes in Hohokam ceramics. The bulk of this massive collection was recovered from cremation offerings and caches. This phenomenon is observed at other sites and it seems to indicate that well made points were valued as offertory items that were accorded special treatment. This special treatment often assures that the archaeologist will recover quantities of points in relatively well dated contexts. Relatively few points are recovered from other contexts such as habitation areas, irrigation features or trash deposits. These considerations tend to support the notion that points are being used for (1) mortuary and ritual offerings or (2) hunting, warfare and other activities that would cause the points to be discarded in a wide pattern of distribution (both on and off the sites).

At sites where points were produced, an abundance of lithic debitage and debris at specific loci of point production would be expected, yet as Haury (1976: 296) notes, "paradoxically, no concentrations of wastage were encountered anywhere in our diggings (at Snaketown), and there was only nominal recovery of small, pressure-chipped flakes in the residue when fine screens were employed" (1976: 296). The lack of debitage has prompted the development and implementation of an experimental program designed to locate these elusive flakes, which are the direct evidence for small tool and projectile point manufacture.

Crabtree has successfully replicated a number of Hohokam points by means of controlled pressure flaking (Crabtree 1973: 31-33). By examining the results of Crabtree's experiments in replication, and attempting my own replications, I find my results to confirm his. Hohokam points were finished by the employment of retouch techniques such as abrasion and pressure flaking. It is the small retouch flakes produced by these techniques that are the subject of this study. This type of micro-artifactual evidence has never been systematically examined or reported from excavations at Hohokam site. Though various authors clearly recognize that retouch techniques were employed by the Hohokam, no one has actually described and discussed the tiny debitage that is typically produced by these techniques (Doyel 1974: 56, Huckell 1981). These small retouch flakes fall into a size range of roughly 0.8 cm to 0.15 cm. Considering this small size range, it is no wonder that the flakes are not recovered, as they will pass through all but the finest screens. Most screens used by archaeologists in the Southwest tend to be either quarter- or eighth-inch mesh. Thus we cannot expect to recover the many small pieces of debitage, even if we were to make a particular effort to recover them. This brings us to our next problem, which is to answer a simple question: If we know that the Hohokam were producing projectile points in quantity, why are we not finding their manufacturing loci?

To answer a question such as this, one must consider a rather large number of variables that characterize both the nature of the data and the techniques of investigation employed. Haury laments the lack of points found during the 1964-1965 seasons at Snaketown and notes that this is to be expected in major clearing operations of prehistoric subsurface habitation and irrigation features. Because the largest percentages of Hohokam points recovered at Snaketown were found in caches or cremations, it seems likely that the Hohokam were moving most points from the place of production to other areas. This confirms notions derived from other archaeological examples, in which various tool types have been removed from the loci of their production (Collins 1975: 56, Jelinek 1967: 110-111).

The next aspect to be considered is that the points recovered tend to come from large, Hohokam habitation sites, and relatively few have been encountered at small sites or between sites. It is recognized that Hohokam sites may be typed by their relative sizes, and by the differential activities that are associated with them. With the great increase in contract archaeology, more archaeological work has been done in the Hohokam region, and to date proportionally more points have been found at large sites such as Los Morteros and Hodges in the Tucson Basin, and Snaketown, Las Colinas, and Los Muertos in the Gila Basin. To date, no sites have been reported that demonstrate a primary orientation toward point manufacture. Though quarries are known in the Hohokam area, they have never been investigated in a systematic way. For now we cannot rule out the possibility that point manufacture occurred at specialized sites or at quarries. A final consideration should be mentioned: projectile point manufacturing localities have never been identified within individual sites. This may result from the sample bias imposed by the comparatively small excavated areas that are known from very large Hohokam sites, or it may be that we simply have not yet managed to place a test pit in the middle of a small-tool workshop.

Natural processes also may be hiding the evidence of point manufacture. Many Hohokam sites are located in floodplain zones (often alluvial terraces), and they are therefore frequently flooded during the summer rainy season. This factor makes for a great deal of rather rigorous sheetwash that may well act to scour sites and remove small artifacts such as retouch flakes. This kind of transformation process could well be to blame for the type of incomplete debitage collections that are frequently reported in the literature. We have examples of cobble reduction and decortification localities from a number of sites, but no reported retouch debris (Cameron 1977: 154-155). Perhaps we can blame the lack of retouch flakes on sheetwash, though it is difficult to believe that all the retouch debris from a given knapping locus could have been completely washed away.

Beyond the previously discussed problems resulting from the lack of fine screening during excavation, we should briefly examine the problems associated with both artifact recognition and reporting. The recognition of retouch flakes comes from having dealt with them repeatedly, and from having precise definitions of what is meant by retouch debitage, and debris. The small size of these objects tends to inhibit one's developing a good working familiarity with retouch flakes, unless a good deal of time is devoted to examining fairly large samples of various product groups produced by retouch (Sullivan 1980: 101-107). One can hardly hope to work with highly proficient field crews who are capable of identifying each and every artifact that comes their way. This kind of high-level, technical expertise is simply not available to the average investigator.

The next problem is in the reporting of flaked lithic remains from Hohokam sites. Many authors have reported on Hohokam flaked stone assemblages and the single factor that unites all these treatments is the rather general descriptions and discussions that they employ (Cameron 1977: 139-155, Huckell 1981: 194-197, and Kelly 1978: 89-91). This unfortunate circumstance can be blamed partly on the very nature of the nondescript, Hohokam lithic items, but the reporting of any flaked stone assemblages should include precise descriptions of all the materials encountered to allow for comparison with materials from other areas. In this way, one can draw sharp comparisons from one site to another and see any patterns that may exist.

A second problem in reporting is that too often the typologies employed are empirical ones that are grounded primarily on what the investigator believes rather than on accurate assessments based on observations of the materials. Typologies based on clearly defined hierarchical taxonomies that are capable of accounting for all examples of a particular phenomena seem to be best suited to account for data such as Hohokam lithic material (Sullivan 1980: 100-101). Lithic descriptions should aid us in the determination of the specific behavioral processes that produced the assemblage we find (Binford and Quimby 1972; Osborne 1965, Rozen 1979). In this way, we can account for prehistoric cultural behavior and reveal the patterns of production, use and disposal that are associated with these behaviors.

Since the primary goal of this study is to demonstrate that the evidence for Hohokam point production does exist at specific Hohokam sites, us consider some known loci of flake production and the evidence from the sampling at Los Morteros. Localities of primary, or secondary cobble reduction are known from a number of Hohokam sites. Perhaps the best discussion of this is Bayham's analysis of lithics from sites in the Florence area (Bayham 1976: 154-163). Bayham discusses a discreet locus of primarily reduction encountered at a site, as well as the natural formation processes that may be inferred by the spatial distribution of the artifacts. Other discussions of this kind include Cameron's analysis (1977: 139-155). From the Baca Float sites of the middle Santa Cruz River Valley. Bayham's and Cameron's descriptions provide us with the notions of what flake-tool production areas are like in terms of artifact types encountered, but in both cases the flakes encountered are large and clearly produced in the reduction of cobbles. No evidence for the production of retouch flakes is provided, so it is implied that these materials do not occur at the sites discussed. Probably the situation at both places is a reflection of the lack of recovery of retouch flakes at these sites.

At Los Morteros, a suggestion made by Professor Longacre of the University of Arizona was adopted and a large number of 42 gram samples of soil from trash deposits were recovered from a variety of loci at the site. These samples were then screened through 0.2-cm-mesh screen in the field, and then the matrix was screen-washed through 0.1-cm mesh to remove the silt present in the samples. The remaining material consisted primarily of coarse, river-washed, subangular gravel. The samples were then dried and examined with a 10-power hand lens to see if any retouch flakes could be found. Of the first batch of 20 samples examined, 7 contained minute retouch flakes that were likely produced during reduction of blanks (or preforms) in the manufacture of small artifacts, such as projectile points (see Table Q.1). As the site is located on a river floodplain, it seems quite likely that the materials we recovered may represent sheetwashed trash that was moved to the localities sampled after the site's occupation. The flakes recovered were then classified according to Sullivan's taxonomic hierarchy (1980: 101-107).

Secondary evidence for the production of small tools, such as projectile points, was recovered by this process. Further samples have been recovered from other locations at Los Morteros, and from flotation samples removed from sites under investigation by the Arizona State Museum's Salt-Gila Project. Due to time constraints, I was unable to examine any more of the over 80 samples already recovered from Los Morteros, and so the inspection figures presented in Table Q.1 represent only a small portion of the total sample recovered. Among the tool types that characterize the Hohokam stone industry, only projectile oints and small flake tools require that retouch techniques be applied during their production (Huckell 1981: 198). So, by implication we have found localities in which direct evidence of this "retouch stage" of production has been recovered.

Table Q.1

MICROFLAKE DATA FROM TEST SAMPLES RECOVERED FROM LOS MORTEROS

Context	Retouch Flakes and Debris	Material
Mound 5A overburden	2 complete, noncortical flakes	Chert
Unit 8, Level 1	1 broken, noncortical flake	Chert
(Above Feat. 51, Pit house)	1 broken, noncortical flake	Chert
(trash fill)	2 noncortical debris	Chert
Feature 30 (Pit house)	1 complete, noncortical flake	Obsidian
backdirt from excavation	1 broken, noncortical flake	Jasper
	2 complete, noncortical flakes	Jasper
Mound 27 overburden	1 noncortical debris	Andesite
backhoe backdirt	1 broken, noncortical flake	Jasper
Canal fill	1 complete, noncortical flake	Chalcedony
backdirt from excavation	2 complete, cortical flakes	Basalt
	1 broken, cortical flake	Quartzite
	1 cortical debris	Rhyolite
Mound 8 overburden	1 noncortical debris	Basalt
backhoe backdirt	1 broken, cortical flake	Quartzite
(trash fill)		
Mound 6 overburden	1 complete, noncortical flake	Chert
backhoe backdirt,	1 complete, noncortical flake	Quartzite
North-South trench	1 noncortical debris	Chert
(trash fill)	1 noncortical debris	Chalcedony
	1 broken, noncortical flake	Chert
Mound 6 overburden	2 complete, noncortical flakes	Obsidian
backhoe backdirt,	1 noncortical debris	Quartzite
East-West trench		
(trash fill)		

The results of this study can be summarized as follows. First, the Hohokam produced finished, chipped, small stone tools on site at Los Morteros, and least some of the flakes and debris recovered represent retouch debitage produced during the manufacture of small tools, such as

334

projectile points. Second, so-called quarry sites seem to be localities
where cobbles were reduced into blanks and preforms. Third, the high
incidence of noncortical flakes and debris from Los Morteros indicates
that some of the materials recovered derived were from the reduction of
previously prepared blanks. Fourth, direct evidence of retouch
technology is difficult to find, due to a number of different factors
that include both natural and possibly cultural formation processes, and
the lack of investigation into Hohokam lithic industry. Fifth, this
study confirms Huckell's hypothesis that Hohokam projectile points were
the result of "unpatterned pressure work on small flakes" (Huckell 1981:
172). Sixth, it is suggested that retouch materials may be encountered
in a variety of loci that include trash fill in cultural features as
well as canals and agricultural features.

It seems quite likely that if these field methods were applied
to samples recovered from a large number of different kinds of Hohokam
sites, we might be able to see a regional pattern of projectile point
and small-tool production at habitation sites. This sampling strategy
should concentrate on trash deposits at a range of sites from several
different areas in order to examine regional variability in Hohokam
small tool production. Efforts should be made to ensure standard sample
sizes and standardized recovery from a specific range of on site,
activity areas. Now that we have an indication that retouch materials
can be found at Hohokam sites, the emphasis must shift to one of
explaining the variation in the assemblages of this material, and the
specific agents (natural or cultural) involved in the formation of those
assemblages. By doing this, we can be much more particular in our
approach and can identify the debitage and debris associated with each
stage of small-tool manufacture.

Acknowledgments

My thanks to Dr. William Longacre, Thomas Somermier, Greg L. Bowen,
Laurie Reiser, and Adah Leah Wolf for their help in formulating this
study.

REFERENCES

Antieau, John M.
 1981   The Palo Verde Archaeological Investigations, Hohokam
          Settlement at the Confluence: Excavations Along the Palo
          Verde Pipeline. Museum of Northern Arizona Research Paper
          20. Flagstaff.

Arnold, Lee W.
 1940   An Ecological Study of the Vertebrate Animals of the
          Mesquite Forest. MS, master's thesis, Department of
          Biology, University of Arizona, Tucson.

Arrhenius, Olaf
 1963   Investigation of Soil from Old Indian Sites. Ethnos 2-4:
          122-136.

Audubon, John W.
 1906   Audubon's Western Journal: 1849-1850. Glorieta, New
          Mexico: Rio Grande Press.

Baby, Raymond S.
 1954   Hopewell Cremation Practices. Ohio Historical Society
          Papers in Archaeology 1: 1-7.

Baker, Charles M.
 1975   Experimentation with Soil Phosphate Analysis. In "Arkansas
          Eastman Archeological Project," edited by C. M. Baker.
          Arkansas Archeological Survey, Research Report 6: 67-82.

Bass, Charles
 1979   Analysis of Cremation 1 from AZ Y:8:1. (Component 2). In
          "The Coronet Real Project: Archaeological Investigations on
          the Luke Range, Southwest Arizona," by Bruce Huckell.
          Arizona State Museum Archaeological Series 129: 167-168.
          Tucson: University of Arizona.

Bass, William M.
 1971   Human Osteology: A Laboratory and Field Manual of the Human
          Skeleton. Columbia: Missouri Archaeological Society.

Bayham, Frank E.
 1976   Lithics. In "Desert Resources and Hohokam Subsistence: The
          Conoco Florence Project," by William Doelle. Arizona State
          Museum Archaeological Series 103: 195-218. Tucson:
          University of Arizona.

Beckwith, Kim E.
 1984   Dairy Site Ceramics, Preliminary Report. MS, Archaeology
          Division, Arizona State Museum, University of Arizona,
          Tucson.

336

Beckwith, Kim E.
    1987   Decorated Ceramics. In "The Archaeology of the San Xavier
            Bridge Site (AZ BB:13:14) Tucson Basin, Southern Arizona,"
            edited by John C. Ravesloot. Arizona State Museum
            Archaeological Series 171: 205-238. Tucson: University of
            Arizona.

Bequaert, Joseph C. and Walter B. Miller
    1973   The Mollusks of the Arid Southwest. Tucson: University of
            Arizona Press.

Binford, Lewis R.
    1972a   Analysis of a Cremation Burial from the Riverside Cemetery,
            Menominee County, Michigan. In An Archaeological
            Perspective, edited by Lewis R. Binford, pp. 383-389. New
            York: Seminar Press.

    1972b   An Analysis of Cremations from Three Michigan sites. In An
            Archaeological Perspective, edited by Lewis R. Binford, pp.
            378-382. New York: Seminar Press.

Binford, Lewis R., and George J. Quimby
    1972   Indian Sites and Chipped Stone Materials in the Northern
            Lake Michigan Area. In An Archaeological Perspective,
            edited by Lewis R. Binford, pp. 346-372. New York: Seminar
            Press.

Birkby, Walter H.
    1973   Discontinuous Morphological Traits of the Skull as
            Population Markers in the Prehistoric Southwest. MS,
            doctoral dissertation, Department of Anthropology,
            University of Arizona, Tucson.

Blake, William P.
    1910   Sketch of Pima County, Its Mining Districts, Minerals,
            Climate, Agriculture, and Other Resources. Tucson.

Bradley, Bruce A.
    1980   Excavations at Arizona BB:13:74, Santa Cruz Industrial Park,
            Tucson, Arizona. CASA Papers 1. Oracle: Complete
            Archaeological Service Associates.

Brand, Donald P.
    1935   The Distribution of Pottery in Northwest Mexico. American
            Anthropologist 37(2): 287-305.

Brothwell, Don
    1963   Digging Up Bones. London: British Museum.

Cameron, Cathy
    1977   Chipped Stone Assemblages from the Baca Float Sites. In
            "Excavations in the Middle Santa Cruz River Valley,

Southeastern Arizona," by David E. Doyel. Arizona State Museum Contributions to Highway Salvage Archaeology in Arizona 44: 139-155. Tucson: University of Arizona.

Castetter, Edward F., and Willis H. Bell
    1942   Pima and Papago Indian Agriculture. Albuquerque: University of New Mexico Press.

Castetter, Edward F., and Ruth M. Underhill
    1935   The Ethnobiology of the Papago Indians. Ethnobiological Studies in the American Southwest II, University of New Mexico Biological Series 4(3). Albuquerque: University of New Mexico.

Cockrum, E. Lendell
    1960   The Recent Mammals of Arizona: Their Taxonomy and Distribution. Tucson: University of Arizona Press.

    1964   The Recent Mammals of Arizona, Part V. In The Vertebrates of Arizona, edited by Charles H. Lowe, pp. 249-259. Tucson: University of Arizona Press.

Collins, Michael B.
    1975   Lithic Technology as a Means of Processual Inference. In Lithic Technology, Making and Using Stone Tools, edited by Earl Swanson. Chicago: Aldine Press.

Colton, Harold S.
    1953   Potsherds: An Introduction to the Study of Prehistoric Southwestern Ceramics and Their Use in Historic Reconstruction. Museum of Northern Arizona Bulletin 25. Flagstaff: The Northern Arizona Society of Science and Art.

Colton, Harold S., and Lyndon L. Hargrave
    1935   Naming Pottery Types, and Rules of Priority. Science 82(2133): 462-463.

    1937   Handbook of Northern Arizona Pottery Wares. Museum of Northern Arizona Bulletin 11. Flagstaff: The Northern Arizona Society of Science and Art.

Crabtree, Don E.
    1972   An Introduction to Flintworking. Idaho State University Museum Occasional Papers 28. Pocatello: Idaho State University.

    1973   Experiments in Replicating Hohokam Points. Tebiwa 116(1): 10-46.

Cruxent, J.M.
    1962   Phosphorous Content of the Texas Street "Hearths." American Antiquity 28:9 0-91.

338

Dahlberg, Albert
    1963   Analysis of the American Indian Dentition. In <u>Dental
            Anthropology</u>, edited by D. R. Brothwell, pp. 149-177.
            Oxford: Pergamon Press.

Danson, Edward B.
    1957   Pottery Type Descriptions. In "Excavations, 1940, at
            University Indian Ruin," by Julian D. Hayden. <u>Southwestern
            Monuments Association Technical Series</u> 5: 219-231. Globe,
            Arizona: Gila Pueblo.

Deaver, William L.
    1982   Some Notes on Tucson Basin Pottery: Color Scheme Variations
            During the Rincon and Tanque Verde Phases. Paper presented
            at Tucson Basin Archaeology Conference, University of
            Arizona, Tucson.

    1984   Pottery. In "Hohokam Habitation Sites in the Northern Santa
            Rita Mountains," by Alan Ferg, Kenneth C. Rozen, William L.
            Deaver, Martyn D. Tagg, David A. Phillips, Jr., and David A.
            Gregory. <u>Arizona State Museum Archaeological Series</u> 147(2):
            237-420. Tucson: University of Arizona.

    1988   Ceramics. In "Hohokam Archaeology Along Phase B of the
            Tucson Aqueduct, Central Arizona Project," Volume 2:
            Excavations at Fastimes (AZ AA:12:384), A Rillito Phase Site
            in the Avra Valley," edited by Jon S. Czaplicki and John C.
            Ravesloot. <u>Arizona State Museum Archaeological Series</u>
            178(2): 139-174. Tucson: University of Arizona.

    1989a   Ceramics. In "Hohokam Archaeology Along the Phase B of the
            Tucson Aqueduct, Central Arizona Project, Volume 4:
            Excavations at Water World (AZ AA:16:94), A Rillito Phase
            Ballcourt Village in the Avra Valley," edited by Jon S.
            Czaplicki and John C. Ravesloot. <u>Arizona State Museum
            Archaeological Series</u> 178(3): 153-192. Tucson: University
            of Arizona.

    1989b   Ceramics. In Part 1 of "Hohokam Archaeology Along the Phase
            B of the Tucson Aqueduct, Central Arizona Project, Volume 4:
            Small Sites and Specialized Reports," edited by Jon S.
            Czaplicki and John C. Ravesloot. <u>Arizona State Museum
            Archaeological Series</u> 178(4): 51-62. Tucson: University of
            Arizona.

    1989c   Ceramics. In Part 2 of "Hohokam Archaeology Along the Phase
            B of the Tucson Aqueduct, Central Arizona Project, Volume 3:
            Small Sites and Specialized Reports," edited by Jon S.
            Czaplicki and John C. Ravesloot. <u>Arizona State Museum
            Archaeological Series</u> 178(4): 167-170. Tucson: University
            of Arizona.

Deaver, William L., and Martyn D. Tagg
    1984   Further Archaeological Investigations at the Observatory
            Site (AZ BB:9:101), a Middle-Late Rincon Site in the Tucson
            Basin. MS, Cultural Resource Management Division, Arizona
            State Museum, University of Arizona, Tucson.

Dietz, E. F.
    1957   Phosphorous Accumulation in Soil of an Indian Habitation
            Site. _American Antiquity_ 22: 405-409.

DiPeso, Charles C.
    1951   The Babocomari Village Site on the Babocomari River,
            Southeastern Arizona. _The Amerind Foundation_ 5. Dragoon,
            Arizona: The Amerind Foundation.

    1956   The Upper Pima of San Cayetano del Tumacacori: An
            Archaeohistorical Reconstruction of the Ootam of the Pimeria
            Alta. _The Amerind Foundation_ 7. Dragoon, Arizona: The
            Amerind Foundation.

Doelle, William H.
    1985   Excavations at the Valencia Site: A Preclassic Hohokam
            Village in the Southern Tucson Basin. _Institute for_
            American Research Anthropological Papers 3. Tucson:
            Institute for American Research.

    1988   Preclassic Community Patterns in the Tucson Basin. In
            "Recent Research on Tucson Basin Prehistory: Proceedings of
            the Second Tucson Basin Conference," edited by William H.
            Doelle and Paul R. Fish. _Institute for American Research_
            Anthropological Papers 10: 277-312. Tucson: Institute for
            American Research.

Doelle, William H., and Paul R. Fish
    1986   Recent Research on Tucson Basin Prehistory: Proceedings of
            the Second Tucson Basin Conference. _Institute for American_
            Research Anthropological Papers 10. Tucson: Institute for
            American Research.

Doelle, William H., and Henry D. Wallace
    1986   Hohokam Settlement Patterns in the San **Xavier** Project Area,
            Southern Tucson Basin. _Institute for American Research_
            Technical Report 84-6. Tucson: Institute for American
            Research.

Downum, Christian E.
    1986   The Occupational Use of Hillspace in the Tucson Basin:
            Evidence from Linda Vista Hill. _The Kiva_ 51: 219-232.

Doyel, David E.

1974   Excavations at The Escalante Ruin Group, Southern Arizona.
         Arizona State Museum Archaeological Series 37. Tucson:
         University of Arizona.

1977   Excavations in the Middle Santa Cruz River Valley,
         Southeastern Arizona. Arizona State Museum Contribution
         to Highway Salvage Archaeology in Arizona 44. Tucson:
         University of Arizona.

1984   From Foraging to Farming: An Overview of the Preclassic in
         the Tucson Basin. The Kiva 49(3-4): 147-166.

1988   Rio Rico Polychrome Pottery: Ceramic Interaction along the
         Southern Borderlands. In "Recent Research on Tucson Basin
         Prehistory: Proceedings of the Second Tucson Basin
         Conference," edited by William H. Doelle and Paul R. Fish.
         Institute for American Research Anthropological Papers 10:
         349-372. Tucson: Institute for American Research.

Eidt, Robert C.

1973   A Rapid Chemical Field Test for Archaeological Site
         Surveying. American Antiquity 38: 206-210.

1977   Detection and Examination of Anthrosols by Phosphate
         Analysis. Science 197(11): 1327-1333.

Ervin, Richard G.

1982   Archaeological Monitoring and Salvage Excavations at AZ
         BB:9:101, a Late Rincon Site in Tucson, Arizona. MS,
         Cultural Resource Management Division, Arizona State Museum,
         University of Arizona, Tucson.

Ferg, Allen

1984   Discussion. In "Hohokam Habitation Sites in the Northern
         Santa Rita Mountains," by Alan Ferg, Kenneth C. Rozen,
         William L. Deaver, Martyn D. Tagg, David A. Phillips, Jr.,
         and David A. Gregory. Arizona State Museum Archaeological
         Series 147(2): 725-822. Tucson: University of Arizona.

Fewkes, Jesse Walter

1909   Prehistoric Ruins of the Gila Valley. Smithsonian
         Miscellaneous Collections 52(4). Washington: Government
         Printing Office.

Fish, Paul R., Suzanne K. Fish, and John H. Madsen

1985   Spatial, Functional, and Social Differentiation in a Tucson
         Basin Classic Community. In Organization of Classic Period
         Hohokam Society Symposium, organized by Jerry Howard and
         Owen Lindauer. Paper presented at the 50th Annual Meeting
         of the Society for American Archaeology, Denver.

Fish, Paul R., Suzanne K. Fish, John H. Madsen, Charles Miksicek, Christine Szuter, and John Field
    1987   A Longterm Pioneer Adaptation in the Northern Tucson Basin. Paper presented at 52nd Annual Meeting of the Society for American Archaeology, New Orleans, Louisiana.

Fish, Suzanne K., Paul R. Fish, and Christian L. Downum
    1984   Hohokam Terraces and Agricultural Production in the Tucson Basin, Arizona. In "Prehistoric Agricultural Strategies in the Southwest," edited by Suzanne K. Fish, and Paul R. Fish <u>Anthropological Research Paper</u> 33: 55-71. Tempe: Arizona State University.

Fish, Suzanne K., Paul R. Fish, and John H. Madsen
    1985   A Preliminary Analysis of Hohokam Settlement and Agriculture in the Northern Tucson Basin. In "Proceedings of the 1983 Hohokam Symposium, Part I," edited by A. E. Dittert, Jr., and D.E. Dove. <u>Occasional Paper</u> 2: 75-100. Phoenix: Arizona Archaeological Society.

    1989   Classic Period Hohokam Community Integration in the Tucson Basin. In <u>Sociopolitical Structure of Prehistoric Southwestern Societies</u>, edited by Kent Lightfoot and Steadman Upham. Westview Press, Denver.

Fish, Suzanne K., Paul R. Fish, Charles Miksicek, and John Madsen
    1985   Prehistoric Agave Cultivation in Southern Arizona. <u>Desert Plants</u> 7(2): 107-112.

Fogg, Graham E.
    1978   A Ground Water Modeling Study in the Tucson Basin. MS, master's thesis, Department of Hydrology, University of Arizona, Tucson.

Franklin, Hayward H.
    1980   Excavations at Second Canyon Ruin, San Pedro Valley, Arizona. <u>Arizona State Museum Contribution to Highway Salvage Archaeology in Arizona</u> 60. Tucson: University of Arizona.

Fraps, Clara Lee
    1935   Tanque Verde Ruins. <u>The Kiva</u> 1: 1-4.

Frick, Paul Sumner
    1954   An Archaeological Survey in the Central Santa Cruz Valley, Southern Arizona. MS, master's thesis, Department of Anthropology, University of Arizona, Tucson.

Gabel, Norman E.
    1931   Martinez Hill Ruins, An Example of Prehistoric Culture of the Middle Gila. MS, master's thesis, Department of Anthropology, University of Arizona, Tucson.

Gelderman, Frederick W.
    1972   Soil Survey of the Tucson-Avra Valley Area, Arizona. USDA
            Soil Conservation Service. Washington: Government Printing
            Office.

Gifford, James C.
    1960   The Type-Variety Method of Ceramic Classification as an
            Indicator of Cultural Phenomena. American Antiquity 25(3):
            341-347.
    1976   Prehistoric Pottery Analysis and the Ceramics of Barton
            Ramie in the Belize Valley. Memoirs of the Peabody Museum
            of Archaeology and Ethnology 18. Cambridge: Peabody Museum.

Gilbert, B. Miles
    1973   Mammalian Osteo-Archaeology: North America, edited by David
            R. Evans. Special publications, Missouri Archaeological
            Society. Columbia: University of Missouri.

Gladwin, Harold S.
    1965   Conclusions. In Excavations at Snaketown: Material Culture,
            by Harold S. Gladwin, Emil W. Haury,
            E. B. Sayles, and Nora Gladwin, pp. 247-269. Tucson:
            University of Arizona Press. Originally published 1937,
            Medallion Papers 25: 247-269. Globe, Arizona: Gila Pueblo.

Gladwin, Harold S., Emil W. Haury, E. B. Sayles, and Nora Gladwin
    1965   Excavations at Snaketown: Material Culture. Tucson:
            University of Arizona Press. Originally published 1937,
            Medallion Papers 25. Globe, Arizona: Gila Pueblo.

Gladwin, Winifred, and Harold S. Gladwin
    1929   The Red-on-buff Culture of the Papaguería. Medallion Papers
            4. Globe, Arizona: Gila Pueblo.

    1930   A Method for the Designation of Southwestern Pottery Types.
            Medallion Papers 7. Globe, Arizona: Gila Pueblo.

Grebinger, Paul F., and David P. Adams
    1974   Hard Times? Classic Period Hohokam Cultural Development,
            Tucson Basin, Arizona. World Archaeology 6(1): 226-241.

Greene, Jerry L., and Thomas W. Mathews
    1976   Faunal Study of Unworked Mammalian Bones. In The Hohokam,
            Desert Farmers and Craftsmen: Excavations at Snaketown,
            1964-1965, by Emil Haury, pp. 367-373. Tucson: University
            of Arizona Press.

Greenleaf, J. Cameron
    1975   Excavations at Punta de Agua in the Santa Cruz Basin,
            Southeastern Arizona. Anthropological Papers of the
            University of Arizona 26. Tucson: University of Arizona
            Press.

Gregonis, Linda M.
1977   Summary of Excavations at AZ BB:9:14, Fort Lowell County
        Park, September 1976 to May 1977. MS, Arizona State Museum
        Library, University of Arizona, Tucson.

1982   Preliminary Report on the Hardy Site at Fort Lowell, Tucson.
        Paper presented at Tucson Basin Archaeology Conference,
        University of Arizona, Tucson.

Gundlach, H.
1961   Tupfelmethode auf phosphat, angewandt in praehistoricher
        forschung (als feldmethode). Mikrochimica Acta 5: 735-737.

Hall, E. Raymond, and Keith R. Kelson
1959   The Mammals of North America, Volumes I and II. New York:
        Ronald Press.

Hassan, Fekri
1978   Demographic Archaeology. Advances in Archaeological Method
        and Theory (1), edited by Michael B. Schiffer, pp 49-105.
        New York: Academic Press.

Haury, Emil W.
1950   The Stratigraphy and Archaeology of Ventana Cave. Tucson:
        University of Arizona Press.

1976   The Hohokam, Desert Farmers and Craftsmen: Excavations at
        Snaketown, 1964-1965. Tucson: University of Arizona Press.

Hawley, Florence M.
1929   Prehistoric Pottery Pigments in the Southwest, American
        Anthropologist 31(4): 731-754.

1930   Prehistoric Pottery and Culture Relations in the Middle
        Gila. American Anthropologist 32(3): 522-536.

Hayden, Julian D.
1957   Excavations, 1940, at University Indian Ruin. Southwestern
        Monuments Association Technical Series 5. Globe, Arizona:
        Gila Pueblo.

Heidke, James
1986a   Plainware Ceramics. In "Archaeological Investigations at
        the Tanque Verde Wash Site: A Middle Rincon Settlement in
        the Eastern Tucson Basin," by Mark D. Elson. Institute for
        American Research Anthropological Papers 7: 181-232.
        Tucson: Institute for American Research.

1986b   Plainware Ceramics. In "Archaeological Investigations at
        the West Branch Site: Early and Middle Rincon Occupation in
        the Southern Tucson Basin," by Frederick W. Huntington.
        Institute for American Research Anthropological Papers 5:
        165-196. Tucson: Institute for American Research.

Heidke, James
1988   Ceramic Production and Exchange: Evidence from Rincon Phase
         Contexts. In "Recent Research on Tucson Basin Prehistory:
         Proceedings of the Second Tucson Basin Conference," edited
         by William H. Doelle and Paul R. Fish. Institute for
         American Research Anthropological Papers 10: 387-410.
         Tucson: Institute for American Research.

Herrmann, Bernd
1976   Neuere Ergebnisse Zur Beurteilung Menschlicher Brandknochen.
         Zeitschrift fur Rechtsmedizin 77: 191-200.

1977   On Histological Investigations of Cremated Human Remains.
         Journal of Human Evolution 6: 101-03.

Huckell, Bruce B.
1978   Test Excavations at AZ BB:9:58, the Vista del Rio Site.
         Arizona State Museum Archaeological Series 124. Tucson:
         University of Arizona.

1981   The Las Colinas Flaked Stone Assemblage. In "The 1968
         Excavations at Mound 8, Las Colinas Ruins Group, Phoenix,
         Arizona," edited by Laurens C. Hammack and Alan P. Sullivan.
         Arizona State Museum Archaeological Series 154: 171-200.
         Tucson: Arizona State Museum, University of Arizona.

Huckell, Bruce B., Martyn D. Tagg, and Lisa W. Huckell
1987   The Corona de Tucson Project: Prehistoric Use of a Bajada
         Environment. Arizona State Museum Archaeological Series
         174. Tucson: University of Arizona.

Huntington, Ellsworth
1913   The Fluctuating Climate of North America. Smithsonian
         Institution Annual Report 1912, pp. 383-412. Washington.

Huntington, Frederick
1982   Archaeological Data Recovery at AZ BB:9:72 (ASM), the Band
         Quarters, Kitchen, and Corral Wall at Fort Lowell, and
         AZ BB:9:54 (ASM), a Rincon phase habitation site, Craycroft
         Road, Tucson, Arizona. Arizona State Museum Archaeological
         Series 163. Tucson: University of Arizona.

Jelinek, Arthur J.
1967   A Prehistoric Sequence in the Middle Pecos Valley, New
         Mexico. Anthropological Papers 31. Ann Arbor: Museum of
         Anthropology, University of Michigan.

Keen, A. Myra
1984   Sea Shells of Tropical West America. Second Edition.
         Stanford University Press.

Kelly, Isabel T.
   1978   The Hodges Ruin, A Hohokam Community in the Tucson Basin,
            edited by Gayle H. Hartmann. _Anthropological Papers of the
            University of Arizona_ 30. Tucson: University of Arizona
            Press.

Kidder, Alfred V.
   1932   The Artifacts of Pecos. _Papers of the Southwestern
            Expedition_ 6. New Haven: Yale University Press.

Krogman, W.M.
   1962   _The Human Skeleton in Forensic Medicine._ Springfield,
            Illinois: Charles C. Thomas.

Leopold, A. Starker
   1972   _Wildlife of Mexico._ Berkeley: University of California
            Press.

Long, Jeffery C.
   1981   Cremated Human Remains from the Cashion Site. In "The Palo
            Verde Archaeological Investigations, Hohokam Settlement at
            the Confluence: Excavations Along the Palo Verde Pipeline,"
            by John M. Antieau. _Museum of Northern Arizona Research
            Paper_ 20: 116-121. Flagstaff.

Lowe, Charles H.
   1964   _Arizona's Natural Environment: Landscape and Habitats._
            Tucson: University of Arizona Press.

   1978   _The Vertebrates of Arizona._ Tucson: University of Arizona
            Press.

Masse, W. Bruce
   1982   Hohokam Ceramic Art: Regionalism and the Imprint of Societal
            Change. In "Southwestern Ceramics: A Comparative Review,"
            edited by Albert H. Schroeder. _The Arizona Archaeologist_
            15. Phoenix: Arizona Archaeological Society.

McGuire, Randall H.
   1977   The Copper Canyon-McGuireville Project: Archaeological
            Investigations in the Middle Verde Valley, Arizona. _Arizona
            State Museum Contributions to Highway Salvage Archaeology in
            Arizona_ 45. Tucson: University of Arizona.

Monson, Gale, and Allan R. Phillips
   1964   _A Checklist of Birds of Arizona._ Tucson: University of
            Arizona Press.

Morris, Percy A.
   1966   _A Field Guide to Shells of the Pacific Coast and Hawaii._
            Second Edition. Boston: Houghton Mifflin Company.

Nie, N. H. and others
1975   SPSS: Statistical Package for the Social Sciences. New
        York: McGraw-Hill.

Olsen, Sandra L.
1977   Faunal Analysis of Four Sites. In "Excavations in the
        Middle Santa Cruz Valley, Southeastern Arizona," by David E.
        Doyel and others. Arizona State Museum Contributions to
        Highway Salvage Archaeology in Arizona 44: 178-181. Tucson:
        University of Arizona.

1979   A Study of Bone Artifacts from Grasshopper Pueblo,
        AZ P:14:1. The Kiva 44: 341-373.

Osborne, Douglas
1965   Chipping Remains as an Indication of Cultural Change at
        Wetherill Mesa. In "Contributions of the Wetherill
        Archaeological Project," assembled by Douglas Osborne.
        Memoirs of the Society for American Archaeology 19: 30-44.

Overstreet, D.
1974   A Rapid Chemical Field Test for Archaeological Site
        Surveying: An Application and Evaluation. The Wisconsin
        Archaeologist 55: 262-276.

Pomeroy, J. Anthony
1959   Hohokam Etched Shell. The Kiva 24:12-21.

Ravesloot, John C., Jon S. Czaplicki, and Ronald Gardner
1989   Interpretation and Chronology. In Part 1 of "Hohokam
        Archaeology Along the Phase B of the Tucson Aqueduct,
        Central Arizona Project, Volume 3: Small Sites and
        Specialized Reports," edited by Jon S. Czaplicki and John C.
        Ravesloot. Arizona State Museum Archaeological Series
        178(4): 127-136. Tucson: University of Arizona.

Reinhard, Karl J.
1982   The Cortaro Phase in the Tucson Basin: A Reevaluation.
        Paper presented at the 1982 Tucson Basin Archaeology
        Conference, University of Arizona, Tucson. MS, Arizona
        State Museum Library, University of Arizona, Tucson.

Reinhard, Karl J., and T. Michael Fink
1982   The Multi-individual Cremation Phenomenon of the Santa Cruz
        Drainage. The Kiva 47: 151-161.

Robbins, C., B. Brunn, and H. Zim
1966   A Guide to Field Identification. New York: Golden Press.

Roscoe, John T.
1975   Fundamental Research Statistics for the Behavioral Sciences.
        New York: Holt, Rinehart, and Winston.

Rozen, Kenneth
1979   Lithic Analysis and Interpretation. In "The AEPCO Project",
        by Deborah A. Westfall, Kenneth Rozen, and Howard Davidson.
        Arizona State Museum Archaeological Series 117: 209-322.
        Tucson: University of Arizona.

Sauer, Carl O., and Donald Brand
1931   Prehistoric Settlements of Sonora with Special Reference to
        the Cerros de Trincheras. University of California
        Publications in Geography 5(3). Berkeley: University of
        California Press.

Saul, Frank P.
1972   The Human Skeletal Remains of Altar de Sacrificios.
        Cambridge, Massachusetts: Peabody Museum.

Scantling, Frederick H.
1940   Excavations at the Jackrabbit Ruin, Papago Indian
        Reservation, Arizona. MS, master's thesis, Department of
        Anthropology, University of Arizona, Tucson.

Shepard, Anna O.
1956   Ceramics for the Archaeologist. Carnegie Institution of
        Washington Publication 609. Washington: Government
        Printing Office.

Shipman, Jeff H.
1978   Human Skeletal Remains from AZ Z:11:5. In The Quijotoa
        Valley Project, by Jane E. Rosenthal, Douglas R. Brown, Marc
        Severson, and John B. Clonts. Tucson: Western
        Archeological and Conservation Center, National Park
        Service.

Shirk, Elizabeth C.
1979   Intra-site Phosphate Analysis: A Test Case at Cold Springs.
        Laboratory of Archaeology Series 20. Athens: University of
        Georgia.

Simpson, Kay, and Susan J. Wells
1983   Archaeological Survey in the Eastern Tucson Basin: Saguaro
        National Monument, Rincon Mountain Unit, Cactus Forest Area.
        Western Archeological and Conservation Center Publications
        in Anthropology 22. Tucson: National Park Service.

1984   Archaeological Survey in the Eastern Tucson Basin: Saguaro
        National Monument, Rincon Mountain Unit, Tanque Verde ridge,
        Rincon Creek, Mica Mountain Areas. Western Archeological
        and Conservation Center Publications in Anthropology 22(3).
        Tucson: National Park Service.

Sjoberg, Alf
    1976   Phosphate Analysis of Anthropic soils. <u>Journal of Field Archaeology</u> 3: 447-454.

Slawson, Laurie
    1988   The Classic Period Continental Site, AZ EE:1:32. In "Recent Research on Tucson Basin Prehistory: Proceedings of the Second Tucson Basin Conference," edited by William H. Doelle and Paul R. Fish. <u>Institute for American Research Anthropological Papers</u> 10: 135-144. Tucson: Institute for American Research.

Solecki, R.S.
    1951   Notes on Soil Analysis and Archaeology. <u>American Antiquity</u> 16: 254-256.

Sparling, John
    1974   Analysis of Faunal Remains from the Escalante Ruin Group. In Excavations of the Escalante Ruin Group, Southern Arizona, by David E. Doyel. <u>Arizona State Museum Archaeological Series</u> 37: 215-252. Tucson: Arizona State Museum, University of Arizona.

Spier, Leslie
    1933   <u>Yuman Tribes of the Gila River</u>. Chicago: University of Chicago Press.

Stebbins, Robert C.
    1954   <u>Amphibians and Reptiles of Western North America</u>. New York: McGraw-Hill Book Company.

Stein, Pat H.
    1982   Historical Resources of the Northern Tucson Basin. MS, Arizona State Museum Library, University of Arizona, Tucson.

Steinbock, R.T.
    1976   <u>Paleopathological Diagnosis and Interpretation</u>. Springfield, Illinois: Charles C. Thomas.

Sternberg, Robert S.
    1982   <u>Archaeomagnetic Secular Variation of Direction and Paleointensity in the American Southwest</u>. Doctoral dissertation, Department of Geosciences, University of Arizona, Tucson. Ann Arbor: University Microfilms.

Stewart, T. Dale
    1979   <u>Essentials of Forensic Anthropology</u>. Springfield, Illinois: Charles C. Thomas.

Sullivan, Alan P.
1980   Prehistoric Settlement Variability in the Grasshopper Area,
          East Central Arizona. MS, doctoral dissertation, Department
          of Anthropology, University of Arizona, Tucson.

Urban, Sharon F.
1966   Etched and Painted Shell, Catalog Number 6550. Arizona
          State Museum Student Papers in Museology, Paper No. 30, pp.
          140-149. MS Arizona State Museum Library, University of
          Arizona, Tucson.

1986   Shell Analysis. In "The Coronado Project Archaeological
          Investigations: Studies Along the Coal Haul Railroad
          Corridor," compiled by Sara T. Stebbins, Dana Hartman, and
          Steven G. Dosh. Museum of Northern Arizona Research Paper
          32, Coronado Series 8: 153-185. Flagstaff.

Vokes, Arthur W.
1985   Shell Exchange and the Economic Structure of the Tucson
          Basin in the Rincon Phase. Student Paper for Anthropology
          640X, Department of Anthropology, University of Arizona.
          MS, Arizona State Museum Library, University of Arizona,
          Tucson.

Walker, Ernest P.
1975   Mammals of the World, 3rd edition, Vols. 1 and 2.
          Baltimore: John Hopkins University Press.

Wallace, Henry D.
1985a   Decorated Ceramics. In "Excavations at the Valencia Site:
          A Preclassic Hohokam Village in the Southern Tucson Basin,"
          by William H. Doelle. Institute for American Research
          Anthropological Papers 3: 81-135. Tucson: Institute for
          American Research.
Wallace, Henry D.
1985b   The Late Rincon Phase in the Tucson Basin. In "Proceedings
          of the 1983 Hohokam Symposium," edited by Alfred E. Dittert,
          Jr. and Donald E. Dove. Arizona Archaeological Society
          Occasional Paper 2: 531-544. Phoenix: Arizona
          Archaeological Society.

1986a   Decorated Ceramics. In "Archaeological Investigations at
          the Tanque Verde Wash Site: A Middle Rincon Settlement in
          the Eastern Tucson Basin," by Mark D. Elson. Institute for
          American Research Anthropological Papers 7: 125-180.
          Tucson: Institute for American Research.

1986b   Decorated Ceramics. In "Archaeological Investigations at
          the West Branch Site: Early and Middle Rincon Occupation in
          the Southern Tucson Basin," by Frederick W. Huntington.
          Institute for American Research Anthropological Papers 5:
          127-164. Tucson: Institute for American Research.

Wallace, Henry D.
1986c   Rincon Phase Decorated Ceramics in the Tucson Basin: A
         Focus on the West Branch Site. Institute for American
         Research Anthropological Papers 1. Tucson: Institute for
         American Research.

1988   Ceramic Boundaries and Interregional Interaction: New
         Perspectives on the Tucson Basin Hohokam. In "Recent
         Research on Tucson Basin Prehistory: Proceedings of the
         Second Tucson Basin Conference," edited by William H. Doelle
         and Paul R. Fish. Institute for American Research
         Anthropological Papers 10: 313-348. Tucson: Institute for
         American Research.

Wallace, Henry D., and Douglas B. Craig
1988   A Reconsideration of the Tucson Basin Hohokam Chronology.
         In "Recent Research on Tucson Basin Prehistory: Proceedings
         of the Second Tucson Basin Conference," edited by William H.
         Doelle and Paul R. Fish. Institute for American Research
         Anthropological Papers 10: 9-30. Tucson: Institute for
         American Research.

Wallace, Henry D., and James Heidke
1986   Ceramic Production and Exchange. In "Archaeological
         Investigations at the Tanque Verde Wash Site: A Middle
         Rincon Settlement in the Eastern Tucson Basin," by Mark D.
         Elson. Institute for American Research Anthropological
         Papers 7: 231-270. Tucson: Institute for American
         Research.

Wallace, Henry D., and James P. Holmlund
1983   Mortars and Cupules. The Kiva 48: 143-182.

1984   The Classic Period in the Tucson Basin. The Kiva 49: 167-
         194.

Wasley, William W., and Alfred E. Johnson
1965   Salvage Archaeology in Painted Rock Reservoir, Western
         Arizona. Anthropological Papers of the University of
         Arizona 9. Tucson: University of Arizona.

Wells, Calvin
1960   A Study of Cremation. Antiquity 34(133): 29-37.

Wheat, Joe Ben, James C. Gifford, and William W. Wasley
1958   Ceramic Variety, Type Cluster, amd Ceramic System in
         Southwestern Pottery Analysis. American Antiquity 24(1):
         34-47.

351

White, Richard S.
    1978   Archaeological Fauna From the Quijotoa Valley, Arizona. In
              The Quijotoa Valley Project, by Jane E. Rosenthal, Douglas
              R. Brown, Marc Severson, and John B. Clonts, pp. 224-254.
              Tucson: Western Archeological and Conservation Center,
              National Park Service.

Whittlesey, Stephanie M.
    1986   The Ceramic Assemblage. In "The 1985 Excavations at the
              Hodges Site, Pima County, Arizona," edited by Robert W.
              Layhe. Arizona State Museum Archaeological Series 170: 61-
              126. Tucson: University of Arizona.

    1987a   A Stylistic Study of Tanque Verde Red-on-Brown. In "The
              Archaeology of the San Xavier Bridge Site (AZ BB:13:14),
              Tucson Basin, Southern Arizona," edited by John C.
              Ravesloot. Arizona State Museum Archaeological Series 171:
              117-148. Tucson: University of Arizona.

    1987b   Problems of Ceramic Production and Exchange. In "The
              Archaeology of the San Xavier Bridge Site (AZ BB:13:14),
              Tucson Basin, Southern Arizona," edited by John C.
              Ravesloot. Arizona State Museum Archaeological Series 171:
              99-116. Tucson: University of Arizona.

    1988   Variability in Tanque Verde Red-on-brown. In "Recent
              Research on Tucson Basin Prehistory: Proceedings of the
              Second Tucson Basin Conference," edited by William H. Doelle
              and Paul R. Fish. Institute for American Research
              Anthropological Papers 10: 373-386. Tucson: Institute for
              American Research.

Wilcox, David R., Thomas R. McGuire, and Charles Sternberg
    1981   Snaketown Revisited: A Partial Cultural Resource Survey,
              Analysis of Site Structure and an Ethnohistoric Study of the
              Proposed Hohokam-Pima National Monument. Arizona State
              Museum Archaeological Series 155. Tucson: University of
              Arizona.

Withers, Arnold M.
    1941   Excavations at Valshni Village, Papago Indian Reservation.
              MS, master's thesis, Department of Anthropology, University
              of Arizona, Tucson.

Woods, William I.
    1975   The Analysis of Abandoned Settlements by a New Phosphate
              Field Test Method. The Chesopiean 13(1-2): 1-45.

Zahniser, Jack L.
    1965   Some Late Prehistoric Villages Southeast of Tucson, Arizona.
              MS, doctoral dissertation, Department of Anthropology,
              University of Arizona, Tucson.

352

Zahniser, Jack L.
    1966   Late Prehistoric Villages Southeast of Tucson, Arizona, and
            the Archaeology of the Tanque Verde phase. The Kiva 31:
            103-204.

    1970   The Archaeological Resources of the Saguaro National
            Monument. The Kiva 35: 105-121.